# Racial Feelings

In the series ASIAN AMERICAN HISTORY AND CULTURE
edited by David Palumbo-Liu, K. Scott Wong,
Linda Trinh Võ and Cathy Schlund-Vials.
Founding editor, Sucheng Chan; editor emeritus, Michael Omi

Also in this series:

(A list of additional titles in this series appears at the back of this book.)

# RACIAL FEELINGS

## ASIAN AMERICA IN A CAPITALIST CULTURE OF EMOTION

JEFFREY SANTA ANA

TEMPLE UNIVERSITY PRESS
*Philadelphia • Rome • Tokyo*

Temple University Press
Philadelphia, Pennsylvania 19122
www.temple.edu/tempress

Published 2015

LIBRARY OF CONGRESS CATALOGING-IN-PUBLICATION DATA

Santa Ana, Jeffrey, 1965–
    Racial Feelings : Asian America in a capitalist culture of emotion /
Jeffrey Santa Ana.
        pages cm. — (Asian American History and Culture)
    Includes bibliographical references and index.
    ISBN 978-1-4399-1192-1 (hardback : alk. paper)
    ISBN 978-1-4399-1193-8 (paperback : alk. paper)
    ISBN 978-1-4399-1194-5 (e-book)
        1. American literature—Asian American authors—History and criticism. 2. Asian
Americans in literature. 3. Capitalism and literature. 4. Asian Americans—Ethnic
identity. 5. Asian Americans in popular culture. 6. Asian Americans in motion pictures.
7. Literature and society—United States—History. I. Title.
PS153.A84S36 2015
810.9'895—dc23

                                                                    2014044061

∞ The paper used in this publication meets the requirements of the American
National Standard for Information Sciences—Permanence of Paper for Printed
Library Materials, ANSI Z39.48–1992

Printed in the United States of America

2  4  6  8  9  7  5  3  1

THE
AMERICAN
LITERATURES
INITIATIVE

A book in the American Literatures Initiative (ALI), a collaborative
publishing project of NYU Press, Fordham University Press, Rutgers
University Press, Temple University Press, and the University of Virginia
Press. The Initiative is supported by The Andrew W. Mellon Foundation.
For more information, please visit www.americanliteratures.org.

# CONTENTS

# Acknowledgments

I am indebted to friends and colleagues for the help they gave as I was writing this book. In particular, Sau-ling C. Wong was my inspiration for a career in Asian American studies. While I was in graduate school at UC Berkeley, I benefited greatly from her professional guidance as well as her pioneering work in the discipline. Her important theory of necessity and extravagance in Asian American literature was the source for many ideas developed in this book. I am also grateful to Maxine Hong Kingston and Susan Schweik at Berkeley for stirring in me the idea that I could achieve the life of a teacher-scholar. I owe them inestimable thanks for their faith in me and my work.

I profoundly appreciate Greg A. Mullins, who was my companion from this book's beginnings when I was in graduate school to my first years as an assistant professor at Mount Holyoke College and Dartmouth College. Greg's intelligence, sensitivity, and indeed ethical commitments define what it means to be a model scholar and a human being. Henry Abelove and Dorothy Wang also motivated my scholarly development in addition to this book's progress from its incipience. They, too, are models of brilliance and generosity. I am most fortunate to have them as mentors and friends.

My gratitude goes further to Ivy Schweitzer, my colleague in English, and Jean J. Kim, my colleague in Asian American studies, when I was at Dartmouth College. Jean's collaboration with me on numerous projects had a positive impact on my work. Also important to this book's progress has been the reading group of Asian Americanists in New York

City who read drafts of chapters. The astute input of Wen Jin, Elda Tsou, James Kim, and Thuy Linh Tu shaped parts of the book. I am thankful for their guidance and expertise.

A semester of research leave and a grant from the dean of the College of Arts and Sciences at Stony Brook University provided essential time and funding to write and bring the book to fruition. I am much obliged to colleagues and coworkers in the English Department who buoyed me during these past years, especially Margaret Hanley, Eugene Hammond, Andrew Newman, Helen Choi, Lizabeth Rehn, Susan Scheckel, Peter Manning, Douglas Pfeiffer, Ayesha Ramachandran, Stephen Spector, Dorothy Mason, Celia Marshik, Eric Haralson, E. Ann Kaplan, Adrienne Munich, Kenneth Lindblom, and Patricia Dunn. At Stony Brook I have been fortunate to have received intellectual camaraderie and support from the following colleagues: Lisa Diedrich, Victoria Hesford, Iona Man-Cheong, E. K. Tan, Robert Harvey, Shirley Lim, and Janet Clarke. I am grateful for the assistance I received from Naomi Edwards, my graduate research assistant in English. Naomi's skillful attention to detail and accuracy were a big help with the book's citation style and formatting.

An especially warm and heartfelt thanks go to Nerissa Balce, my colleague in Asian American Studies at Stony Brook, and her partner, the brilliant poet Fidelito Cortes. Nerissa and Lito are my home in Long Island away from my home in Brooklyn. From California to New England to New York, they have been a family of friends to me, for which I will always be grateful. Salamat sa aking mga minamahal na kaibigan!

I am indebted to Min Hyoung Song, who gave me invaluable advice when I was completing the book's proposal. I owe it to him for helping me substantially with the submission process. I also owe sincere thanks to colleagues in American studies and Asian American studies for the good-hearted support they have given me: Allan Isaac, Martin F. Manalansan, David Eng, Monica Chiu, Cathy Schlund-Vials, Sharon Delmendo, Kale Fajardo, Larin McLaughlin, Vijay Prashad, Eleanor Ty, and Lisa Lowe. While writing this book I received encouragement from my friendships with Edilberto Soriano, Jacqueline Chu, Jean Chu, Leah Gilbert, Anita-Cristina Calcaterra, Steve Wolf, Tim Howell, Leslie Heller, Domenick Danza, Keith Sjoholm, Richard Binkhoff, Alan Crouch, Niles Dolbeare, Robert Driscoll, Benjamin Kohen, Todd McKee, Isaias Sarmiento, Richard Chu, Beth Glennie, and Lisa Jean Cohen.

I am grateful to David Palumbo-Liu, whose work enlightened me to see the importance of history in the nexus between emotions and capitalism in Asian American racialization. I am thankful to him, moreover, for referring me to Temple University Press to consider my book for publication in its Asian American History and Culture series. Janet Francendese is a model senior editor. Her sustained commitment to my project from the start of its publication at the press was an indispensable source of assurance. I am grateful for her and her colleagues' professionalism, and I very much appreciate their continuing dedication to publishing in Asian American studies. I also give thanks to the anonymous reviewers at Temple University Press who read my book manuscript with obvious care and dedication. Their astute comments and suggestions aided me to shape the book into its final form. Additionally, as part of the American Literatures Initiative, this book benefits from the generous funding of the Andrew W. Mellon Foundation.

I am fortunate to have Paul Rovinelli in my life. He is a true partner to me in every sense of the word. His abiding love has seen me through the completion of my project, and for this I am forever grateful to him. Special thanks are due to my parents, Benjamin and Susan Santa Ana, and to my sister, Elizabeth, who have believed in me for many years. I dedicate this book to Paul and to my family with love.

# Introduction: Asian America and Racial Feelings

*I need an Oriental, he said, because this thing, this Feng Shui, is the province of an Oriental. And I've looked. I've looked and haven't found anyone who can go as low as you've gone. . . . He made this sound like a compliment. You and me, he said. You and me are the right team. With your face and my plans . . .*

        —HAN ONG, *FIXER CHAO*

William Paulinha in Han Ong's *Fixer Chao* is a destitute Filipino gay immigrant in 1990s Manhattan, wandering the streets and feeling resentful of the city's new wealth. Because he cannot find stable employment in a ruthlessly competitive job market, he resorts to prostituting himself to overweight white businessmen in a toilet at the Port Authority Bus Terminal. Drowning his sorrows at a seedy Times Square bar one evening, William meets Shem C., a failed Jewish American writer incensed by his expulsion from New York's literati. Shem recruits William in his revenge plot against the high society that has spurned him. Under Shem's manipulations, William transforms into Master Chao, a revered practitioner of Feng Shui, a Chinese art of harmonizing the human environment that promises its believers a good life with the comforts of wealth, security, and well-being. With his decidedly Asian face, William can easily be perceived as an "Oriental," Shem explains, and can perform as Master Chao, who enters the homes of Manhattan's upper crust to deceive and scam them for money. Such is the route that William's resentment and Shem's indignation take in *Fixer Chao*. They manage their anger by channeling it into their vengeful scheme to exploit the elite's perception of the Asian as an agent of prosperity and happiness.

The anger expressed in *Fixer Chao* is directed against the objectification and containment within capitalism of persons of Asian descent by a racializing perception that arises from capitalism's emotional production of Orientalism and racial typecasting. Perception is by definition an affective process that transmutes a previously unintelligible vagueness into an identifiable and representable shape in the present. As a systematic chain of sensory actions whose outcome of signification and detection is influenced by human feeling, perception clearly has much to do with racialization. For both are processes that transform something hitherto unknown and indiscernible into a materialized *form* that becomes recognizable and commonly understood through the senses. For Asian Americans who have been historically materialized into beings that are racially different from European Americans, perception and the emotions that power it are central to the racialization process.[1] Scholars who have examined the formation of Asian Americans as a race group point out that perception is an essential sensory activity that determines racialization.[2] They've argued that emotionally influenced perception has generated a racial form for Asian Americans that represents them through economic tropes of Western capitalist modernity, defining them as agents of economic profit and loss in US liberal democracy.[3] Racialized as economic subjects through perception, then, Asian Americans bear *the* distinction of being one minority group that has been and continues to be construed, represented, and formed through the signs, values, and meanings of capitalist exchange relations.

Seeking to address that distinction, this book examines the emotions generated in US liberal capitalism, analyzing their discursive legibility in the perception of Asians as a racially different people and their function as *feelings* that give rise to Asian American cultural works. The feelings explored in the following chapters—happiness, optimism, comfort, anxiety, fear, ambivalence, and the emotions of remembering and forgetting Asian heritage and immigrant history that I call "feeling in historical memory" and "feeling ancestral"—can be understood as the emotional effects of liberal personhood and individualism. These affectively maintained ideals inform and shape the perception of Asian Americans as a racially different people—a racialized perception through and against which Asian Americans in their cultural works articulate affective elements in consciousness, memory, and criticism important to representing Asian America's collective history. This perception is premised on a mediation between Euro-American subjectivity and individualism through the relations of property ownership and personhood, a logic of proprietary relations traditionally manifested, delegated, and preserved for white male citizens in the US capitalist system.

The perception of Asians both as models of success and as threats to standards of living has been a primary factor in the formation of

Asian Americans as a race group. In the United States, the perception of Asians both as financial exemplars and as menaces has largely been influenced by sentiments for and against Asian immigration. A history of anti-Asian sentiment and positive reception for Asians in America has affected their being seen, interpreted, and identified by Americans as unassimilable aliens and as economic agents of achievement and opportunity.[4] Affectively charged perceptions of Asians have informed discourses that have shaped and determined US economic trade activity and policy, immigration exclusion acts, antimiscegenation laws, and discriminatory legislation, which have all constructed Asian Americans as a race group. Sentiments both for and against Asians are *racial feelings* that have influenced how Americans have sensed, experienced, and apprehended people of Asian descent through discursive practices that create and reinforce stereotypes.

Following Michael Omi and Howard Winant in their theory of racial formation, I want to emphasize that stereotypes of Asians as economic agents inform *and* express a racial ideology that has framed a "common identity" for Asian Americans (89). State-based racial projects and initiatives have reinscribed and transformed racial ideology that forms Asian Americans as a race group, and Asian Americans have redefined the meaning of *Asian American* in their own racial projects and movements that reshape racial ideology. In the US capitalist system, racial feelings affect perceptions of Asians as *racialized* economic subjects that the state reinforces and alters as racial ideology and that Asian Americans rearticulate as both accommodation and resistance in their political movements and cultural works. But why are these emotions that play such a critical role in the racialization of Asian Americans specific to economics? And why have they formed Asian Americans as a race group by representing them as agents of finance capital?

Critical analysts of capitalism have noted that this economic system uses, organizes, and generates human subjectivities to structure an emotional life that is consistent with preserving capitalist material interests and social relations. Karl Marx, for example, theorized capitalism as a system that engenders emotions, referring to his thesis that capitalist economics and the relations peculiar to upholding free enterprise are the foundation for all modern human institutions and organizations, including religion, which assembles beliefs, worldviews, and social norms into a culture of "spiritual production" (Marx and Engels, *On Literature* 140). As Marx's concept of capitalism as "spiritual production" implies, capitalist economics are about the private ownership of the means of production and the accumulation of profit through the management and creation of feelings to maintain the capitalist system. Capitalism's emotional production is, according to Marx, hostile to other "branches of spiritual production, for example, art and poetry," which express the humanist ideals that inspire genuine artists (141). In coining the term *spirit of capitalism* to distinguish the attitudes and temperaments that favor the rational pursuit of economic gain and that were based on a Protestant ethics to engage in trade and accumulate wealth, Max Weber argued that religious practice fostered capitalism, and, despite reversing Marx's thesis, his argument further demonstrates the production of emotions (i.e., "spirit") in capitalist economics. As the economist Albert O. Hirschman argued in his classic study of the drives and desires of self-interest that led to the rise of capitalism in eighteenth-century Europe, the pursuit of material interests through a market economy became understood as a social good in the Enlightenment era (63). Economic activities were seen to improve the self while channeling the unruly and destructive passions into "new ideological currents" that bolstered benign interests and developed positive feelings vital to sustaining civil order (63). For our current modern capitalist era, Eva Illouz has devised the term emotional capitalism to describe a contemporary social phenomenon in which emotions and economic practices mutually define and shape each other, producing a culture "in which affect is made an essential aspect of economic behavior and in which emotional life—especially that of the middle classes—follows the logic of economic relations and exchange" (5). Illouz's argument that a culture of emotional capitalism saturates today's popular media and determines economic discourses and activities is a compelling demonstration of the way modern capitalism structures human subjectivities and creates new feelings befitting a consumerist lifestyle predominating in liberal capitalist societies.

As these critiques of capitalism and the emotions suggest, capitalist economics has created an enduring culture of feeling that affects racialized perception. Nowhere is this more obvious than in the United States, where Asians have been construed as agents of wealth and property acquisition. They have also been seen as threats to liberal democracy when they attempt to transcend their position as subjects of finance capital for white entitlement and privilege. A capitalist culture of emotion influences the way Americans have understood themselves on the basis of their desires, drives, and interests. It also affects how they've identified other people different from themselves, particularly those who come from another country, speak a foreign language, have a different skin color and physiognomy, and thus appear racially dissimilar. To understand why the racialization of Asian Americans has been and continues to be specific to economics, it is important to note that capitalism structures human subjectivities and generates emotional values and cultures that influence perception. If, as Asian Americanist critics have argued, Americans have identified Asians through economic tropes as signs of globalization, this is because the capitalist production of racial feelings has been and continues to be central in reproducing discourses for norms, entitlements, and rights that uphold recognitions of personhood and citizenship in liberal democracy.[5] These affectively charged discourses structure and maintain perceptions of Asians in America as economic subjects, forming them as a race group that falls *outside* the norms and social values traditionally determined by Euro-Americans.[6] These norms and values have historically preserved and continue to sustain white entitlements to define subjectivity in liberal democratic capitalism. Two questions, then, guide this book: How do racial feelings in the historical and social contexts of US liberal democracy affect the perception of Asians both as economic exemplars and as threats? And how do Asian Americans in their own cultural works characterize, accommodate, and resist their discursive portrayal as economic subjects in a capitalist culture of emotion?

## Asian America in a Culture of Happiness

The pursuit of happiness in prosperity and upward mobility, which are common concepts of the American Dream, is fundamental to the ideals of liberal personhood and individualism. Conventionally, the pursuit of happiness means living the good life with its comforts of wealth and well-being. Capitalism produces aspirations for an everyday life that is normative in terms of one's desire to prosper in liberal democracy. To aspire to the American Dream is thus to desire the good life of material comfort and protection from hardship, loss, and precarity. In this sense, happiness can be thought of as a primary feeling in a liberal capitalist society that is compressed with the cultural meanings and social relationships of *belonging* as both a person and an individual. In America today, happiness may be understood to consist of an emotional culture of liberal personhood expressing the values and temperaments of individuals who take comfort in experiencing the achievements of success and belonging. But also this comfort means knowing that the work of others in capitalism's social relations, which maintain structural inequalities and differences, allows and protects the subjectivity—the happiness—of those who are privileged enough to live the good life promised in liberal democracy.

*Racial Feelings: Asian America in a Capitalist Culture of Emotion* explores various cultural forms—literature, graphic narratives, film, and advertising—to demonstrate affects such as comfort and unease in racialized perceptions that have constructed Asian Americans as a race group and have also given rise to their cultural works.[7] By investigating the media's imaging of happiness, optimism, anxiety, and fear in the depiction of Asians as figures of economic opportunity and threat, this book shows Asian America's importance in the making of a capitalist culture of emotions—a culture producing and maintaining the ideals of liberal personhood and individualism. As the phrase *a capitalist culture of emotions* implies, a particular set of affects in the US cultural imaginary has shaped and determined the racialized perception of Asians both as economic exemplars and as threats. Happiness, optimism, fear, and anxiety are the emotions that have structured sentiments for and against people of Asian descent in America. They are affects of liberal capitalism that construe and represent the Asian in a position of containment as a racialized subject of finance capital.

The Korean American writer Don Lee provides a compelling example of this containment. In a recent interview, Lee discusses an upsetting question he was once asked when promoting his novel *Country of Origin*. An interviewer, Lee explains, "asked me why I thought Koreans as an immigrant group seemed to do better economically in the U.S. than other groups. That was bizarre to me. I mean, *Country of Origin* wasn't even set in the U.S.; it takes place in Tokyo in 1980. How, then, did I become a socioeconomist specializing in U.S. immigration? I felt very *uncomfortable* being put in that position, being asked to speak as an expert on all things Asian American" ("Interview," italics added). Lee's discomfort here is striking for the way it situates him affectively *against* the interviewer, who clearly felt at ease placing Lee in the position of an economic subject, a racially stereotyped role of the Asian American as an agent of finance capital. That the interviewer expected Lee to be eminently knowledgeable in the financial matters of Korean immigrants exemplifies the perception of Asians as models of economic efficiency.

This perception is an affective typecasting of Asian Americans as subjects who signify the desired emotionality of liberal personhood, experienced in attaining the American Dream. By identifying Asians through an economic trope that generally depicts them as agents of finance capital, and by assuming Lee to rearticulate this trope by explaining it in the case of Korean immigrants, the interviewer's perception is couched in the American Orientalist rhetoric of Asians as figures of capitalist relations. Moreover, both assumption and perception here imply comfort on the part of the interviewer. In supposing Lee was a "socioeconomist specializing in U.S. immigration," the interviewer clearly felt at ease casting him "in a role," to borrow David Palumbo-Liu's words, "that has been worked out and placed into the realm of a *naturalized assumption*" ("Assumed Identities" 767).

The interviewer's comfort is also quite telling for what it implies about occupying a certain symbolic position to perceive Lee as an economic subject and publicly identify him as such. This discursive position of power to identify and render Lee a subject through language—through interpellation in which the Asian American comes into being as a racialized subject—constrains Lee within the realm of a naturalized assumption about how a person of Asian ancestry characterizes capital accumulation.[8] Through an Orientalist logic that discursively configures "race" for Asians through economic tropes, this position essentializes and contains the Asian as an agent of finance capital. In this manner, the interviewer's perception of Lee as an economic subject brings to mind one of the most salient points in Edward Said's argument that "Orientalism is—and does not simply represent—a considerable dimension of modern political-intellectual culture, and as such has less to do with the Orient than it does with 'our' world" (12). Following Said here, we might understand how desirable and seemingly positive affects such as happiness and comfort express one's given position in America's liberal capitalist society. To be comfortable, as Lee's interviewer is, in perceiving an Asian to typify and perform the assumed role of economic subject is to express one's inside position within the realms of representation, autonomy, and authority—a position acquired by embodying the white racial ideals of liberal personhood and individualism.

## Comfort and Containment in the Forms of Capital

Traditionally, to be in the comfortable position of having representation and inclusion in a liberal capitalist society signals the privilege of being able to acquire and move readily between various forms of capital, as Pierre Bourdieu maintains in his theory of capital ("Forms").[9] Bourdieu's concept of the forms of capital, which I can explain here broadly, expands the notion of economic capital, defined as one's command over sums of money or assets that are accumulated, exchanged, and put to productive use. Economic capital is different from other forms of capital that may not necessarily reflect a monetary or exchange-value but are in certain conditions convertible into economic capital. These other forms of capital are social, cultural, and symbolic. However, for the purposes of my argument, it is the cultural and symbolic forms of capital, in addition to economic capital, that are important.[10] Cultural capital is the knowledge, skills, education, and advantages that give an individual a higher status in society ("Forms" 47–50). Symbolic capital refers to the resources available to individuals who have acquired honor and prestige widely recognized by the public. As Mark Chiang explains in *The Cultural Capital of Asian American Studies*, Bourdieu's argument about how individuals convert and interplay or move readily between various forms of capital shows that "objective social relations are reproduced through the struggles of social agents who 'play the game' of capital accumulation" (26–27). The ability to convert and move effortlessly between the forms of capital means, furthermore, being able to achieve and acquire the public recognition of accumulating, possessing, and *producing* capital in its cultural and symbolic forms.

But what does such comfort acquired by playing between these forms mean for the Asian American writer and artist? To address this question, I turn to Sau-ling Wong in her classic book *Reading Asian American Literature: From Necessity to Extravagance*. In her reading of mobility themes in Asian American literature, Wong makes the important claim that "America is founded on myths of mobility. . . . Yet the idea that the *essence of America* consists in freedom, in both a physical and spiritual sense, has worked itself deep into the national imagination and continues to exert a potent hold on the American imagination. Since its birth as a political and social entity, it is safe to say, America has customarily defined its uniqueness in terms of the enhanced mobility it can offer: the opportunity to go where one wants, do what one wants, shape life anew" (118, italics added). At its heart, America is defined by a national ethos of freedom bequeathed to Americans who are able to employ this freedom to "shape life anew," define a sense of self, and achieve an individualism that attests to having and actualizing a free life in liberal democracy. Yet for early Asian immigrants in America, freedom was traditionally the distinction and preserve of Euro-Americans, who historically perceived Asians as implements for making and accumulating capital, as well as for contributing to their own comfort, security, and contentment, which largely make up the subjective experience of freedom. America has traditionally envisioned and maintained its "essence" of freedom by rendering natural the supposed great capacity of Asians for economic activity and development. The naturalizing of Asians as prototypical economic characters has been, as Colleen Lye meticulously demonstrates in *America's Asia*, the primary mode of configuring race for Asians in the US cultural imaginary. Today's perception of Asian Americans as agents of finance capital is a racialized discernment that emerges from America's historical "identification of the Asiatic as a sign of globalization" (9). America's cultural depictions of the Asiatic as a "racial form" of finance capital helps to explain the primarily economic themes of Asian American racial representation (11).

Whether Asians have worked as field hands, miners, food canners, domestic helpers, launderers, service staff, coolies, and indentured servants—positions that demonstrate the significance of early Asian migrant labor in enabling America's transition to industrial capitalism and growth as a global economy—or achieved as doctors, lawyers, bankers, engineers, and business managers—positions that designate model minority status for Asian Americans—the consequence of their performing their putative capacity for hard work and economic efficiency has been their signification in the American mind as implements to make and accumulate money. This signification has effectively ascribed to Asians an economic nature that Americans have construed paradoxically as both exemplary and threatening. This ascription has proceeded, moreover, through racialized perceptions that *contain* Asian Americans within the economic form of capital, disenabling their movement into the cultural and symbolic forms that traditionally have fashioned the idea that America's essence consists in freedom.

Containment within finance capital by racialized perception, as is the case for Don Lee in being "put in that position" by his interviewer, *immobilizes* the Asian American artist, provoking his sense of feeling contained when he expresses discomfort, frustration, and ambivalence. The inability to convert finance capital into cultural and symbolic forms denies the comfort acquired in being able to move between and claim representation within these various forms of capital. This is especially the case in our present era of capitalist globalization, whereby the Asian perceived as an exemplar of liberal multiculturalism embodies the economic form of capital that serves the interests of a global market economy, as well as the transnational capitalist class maintaining this economy.[11] To be sure, the Asian perceived as a multicultural exemplar of the global economy is defined and circumscribed by transnational capital. Yet this restriction enables the accumulation of economic capital for America's wealthy elite and allows them to convert it into the political and symbolic forms, thereby facilitating movement between these forms. For example, American corporations use the media to represent people of Asian descent as figures of *optimism* in liberal multiculturalism for the global economy. This media representation is a racial commercialization of optimism, a feature of commodity happiness, to market corporate consumerism's global services and products. In depicting Asians as figures of optimism for economic processes of globalization, corporations transmute the Asian into a happy object of liberal multiculturalism. Although this racial commercialization of the Asian enables optimism for the global economy and thus capital for America's upper class, it denies critical subjectivity and agency to the Asian American, who is regarded as a mere commodity.

Further elaboration of this book's argument requires some historical context of how people of Asian ancestry have emerged as economic agents in the American imagination. From the nineteenth to the mid-twentieth century, Asians in America were highly visible in advertising, journalism, and the media as racial aliens who both epitomized and endangered the American Dream of freedom, individualism, and the pursuit of happiness. At this time, Americans perceived Asians as indispensable for enabling their nation's shift from mercantile to industrial capitalism, but they also identified the Asiatic as an ominous figure of capital's unbridled movement in consequence of America's imperialist expansion into the Asia-Pacific. The increasing presence of Asian immigrants in the United States connoted America's irreversible entrance and advancement into capitalist modernity. Asians were indispensable to the concentration of wealth for US capitalists who hired Asian laborers to work in factories, mines, and railroad construction. For these businessmen, the Asian laborer possessed, to borrow Lye's phrase, an "unusual capacity" for work efficiency and economic development (*America's Asia* 15). But for white working-class men, Asian laborers were threats to their wages and standards of living, perils to their settled way of life and their own pursuit of happiness through individualism.

## Individualism's Concept of Happiness

That the media and popular culture have historically depicted Asians both as models and as destroyers of the proverbial American Dream evinces that dream as an ideological vision suffused with the affects of modern capitalist societies. The desire for the good life's happiness and comfort that registers the American Dream as a passion-filled fantasy—an emotional culture dynamically influencing day-to-day relations of people with others and with themselves—is, moreover, a normative aspiration that Americans traditionally have wanted to fulfill in the achievements of personhood and individualism.

Capitalism's economics are fundamental to discursive practices that uphold and protect freedom, individualism, and social equality as the defining features of life in liberal democracy. The most significant document in America's founding as a sovereign nation, the Declaration of Independence, characterizes freedom, individualism, and equality in terms of an emotional life that follows the logic of capitalist relations and exchange. Famous for his Poor Richard's maxims on how careful time management and practicality can allow Americans to become wealthy, Benjamin Franklin, along with the Declaration's four other drafters, penned what is the most celebrated sentence in this document:[12] "We hold these truths to be self-evident, that all men are created equal, that they are endowed by their Creator with certain unalienable Rights, that among these are life, liberty, and the pursuit of happiness." According to Franklin and the fifty-five other signers of the Declaration, the happiness generated and sustained by economic activity is an entitlement of every American. The US capitalist system as the heart and protectorate of liberal democratic government is premised on the production and preservation of happiness attained through material acquisition.

The Declaration's "pursuit of happiness" is covertly linked to the ownership and protection of private property framed by the liberal political theory of possessive individualism. Material possession as the basis for individual rights, freedoms, and self-definition in the United States derives from the language of personhood and autonomy in John Locke's labor theory of self-ownership as individual property rights. Locke's famous statement that "every Man hath a Property in his Person" (*Two Treatises* 287) defines the self as an individual who is able to own; the first thing he owns is himself as well as the materials of "the Earth" he can acquire through "the Labour of his Body, and the Work of his Hands" (287). A man achieves personhood and becomes an individual by possessing himself through all objects in nature that he labors to acquire and convert into his own property. As C. B. MacPherson argued in his classic reading of possessive individualism, Locke's theory of the self-possessing individual through property ownership has defined liberal democratic society as a series of relations among proprietors. In America's emergence as a liberal democracy, these proprietary relations that maintain the self-possessing individual are the basis of the modern liberal-capitalist state, whose function is not only to protect the property rights of individuals but also to preserve the social relations that allow a subjectivity of possessive individualism to flourish. Adopted by the Declaration of Independence and instituted through narratives of citizenship under liberal democracy, Locke's definition of personhood, which he logically extends as the right to "life, liberty, and property" (*Second Treatise* 19), is a proprietary and materialistic right reconfigured as an *affective* right for every man legally recognized as a citizen of the state. The ability to own produces the self-possessing individual's subjectivity and defines it as an affective possession to be protected by the state as a right of citizenship. In the United States, self-possession and its social relations of acquisitive happiness are the premise of not only property rights but also "citizenship rights, as well as the very notion of the liberal individual" (Greeson 919).

It is through capitalism, then, that a person becomes a self-possessing individual by owning both material property and a subjectivity acquired from proprietorship. The state as a liberal democratic polity, which protects the rights of ownership for all legally recognized citizens, exists for the express purpose of capitalism and its complex social network, including the subjectivity—the desires, interests, and drives—of owning property as an affective possession that both maintains and is generated by relations among proprietors. According to Grace Hong, property ownership and the rights of "propertied subjects" became the only justification for the formation of the US nation-state (10). The state is founded upon free market conceptions of property ownership and individual entitlements that are agreeable among citizens through a hypothetical social contract—a contractarian liberalism that defines the rights, duties, and government responsibilities that are to be pursued, fulfilled, and defended as the law for maintaining a liberal capitalist order. Insofar as capitalism is the reason for the liberal democratic state's existence, and liberalism is hegemonic through a conceptual Lockean contract that requires the propertied citizen's contentment to assure the preservation of liberal democracy, American citizenship is premised on the ability to own private property and have such property's protection under the law. This legally codified and contractarian national ethos of liberal individualism delineates, moreover, the citizen's subjectivity as his happiness through material acquisition. In this regard, the language of rights and duties in liberalism is a social contract for individualism whose objective is emotional: to protect and preserve the citizen's acquisitive happiness as his rightful possession. Hence, the "pursuit of happiness" in individualism, which is the primary affective achievement and demonstration of citizenship in liberal democracy, not only determines the subjectivity of personhood but renders it the exclusive right of citizenship.

Citizenship in the United States, however, has from the beginning been restricted on the basis of race. American citizenship is defined by a liberalism that has, as Charles Mills puts it, "historically been predominately a racial liberalism" (1381), in which liberal capitalist "conceptions of personhood and resulting schedules of rights, duties, and government responsibilities have all been racialized. And the contract, correspondingly, has really been a racial one, an agreement among white contractors to subordinate and exploit nonwhite noncontractors for white benefit" (1381). Mills forcefully shows how the contractarian liberalism that frames the dominant political outlook of modern America and preconditions the discursive practices of US liberal democracy is premised on the limitation of personhood and citizenship rights to white Americans. Traditionally, the propertied subject that is the self-possessing individual whose proprietary subjectivity underwrites a narrative of citizenship under US liberal democracy is white and male. Liberal political theory, as it has been devised and implemented by white men to define personhood and delineate the liberal individual, has articulated citizenship as the domain of white men and has reserved it as their right. The mechanisms of American social and political institutions are founded on European cultural traditions, Western civilizing constructs, and Anglo notions of ethnic superiority and centrism—all of which underpin the workings of the US state and the law to uphold a white status quo, maintain white privilege, and racially codify normative subjectivity as white.

Yet liberalism as it has been realized in the contract form in America is an abstraction from the European experience of modernity. It is a conceptual device for implementing life in a consensual democracy of citizens who are abstract subjects of the state and are assumed to be moral equals without the social particulars of race and racial difference. Liberalism as an abstraction in the metaphorical contract form for the American citizen renders that citizen and his subjectivity implicitly white, male, and normative on the basis of the *forgetting* and *denial* of historical atrocities against nonwhite people: European colonialism, imperialism, white settlement, slavery, apartheid, Native American genocide, indentured labor, immigration exclusion acts, and antimiscegenation laws that have all shaped America's modern society. As the US citizen is an idealized abstraction from forces of racism and oppression that have, in large part, historically assumed this citizen to be normative on the basis of his whiteness and male gender, his subjectivity is also an abstraction from Euro-American experiences of modernity.

It can be further claimed, to extend the argument that both personhood and citizenship are racially founded and constructed as white abstractions, that the citizen's happiness through material acquisition is also racial. It is racial feeling. Happiness in its racial liberalism context as the affective possession of the white propertied self fundamentally structures the attitudes and temperaments that Americans have about race and racial difference. The US state has sought to authorize and preserve the subjectivity of American personhood. In the effort to sanction the pursuit of happiness as one of the most basic entitlements and freedoms in liberal democracy, the state has through its courts of law and government institutions undertaken racial projects and initiatives such as exclusion acts, alien land laws, rules of naturalization, wartime relocation and internment of civilians, and legalized discrimination and segregation. These state-based racial projects and initiatives, which were upheld and implemented often on the basis of popular ideology and beliefs about Asians as aliens and Orientals, have maintained the acquisitive happiness that has traditionally structured white male subjectivity as self-possessing individualism.

## The Advent of Asiatic Racial Sentiments

If the pursuit of happiness is both a right and an abstraction of proprietary subjectivity, then how might such happiness as the racial feeling of white personhood structure the Asiatic racial sentiments that proliferated among Americans from the nineteenth to the early twentieth century? In particular, how is liberal individualism's happiness evident in nineteenth-century popular depictions of anti-Asian sentiment? Such happiness, I contend, not only conditioned the racial hostilities that led to violence and legalized discrimination against Asian immigrants in nineteenth-century America but also created a culture of anxiety and fear that directly affects perceptions of the Asiatic as the sign of globalization today.

One goal of *Racial Feelings* is to show the way US media and popular culture represent Asians as emotionally charged figures of globalization. Another is to explore how the contentment, security, and comfort that are the desired emotionality of US liberal personhood are articulated *over against* Asians. If Asians in the United States are "hypervisible, commodified, assimilated, and excessive" (So 9), it is largely because of their figuration as racialized subjects who embody the logics of economic exchange. Historically perceived by Euro-Americans as figures of capital accumulation and as commodities for labor abstraction, Asians are an objectified means through which US citizens have traditionally attained happiness. In *The Promise of Happiness*, Sara Ahmed characterizes the means through which one attempts to acquire happiness as the "happy object" (26). When one becomes desirous and possessive of a particular thing as a means of acquiring happiness, the thing transmutes into a happy object suffused with the possessor's desire to attain security, contentment, and comfort by using this object as a "container" (30–31). According to Ahmed, "Happiness by providing a container in which we can deposit our wants might also contain those wants" (31). Yet if the container does not deliver what the possessor wants, or if the possessor construes the container as a thing that impedes the means to happiness, then the container as a formerly happy object is perceived to contain loss and thus becomes an obstacle that deprives the possessor of happiness. Following Ahmed's theory of the happy object as a container for desire or loss, we can see how Asians are a means through which the propertied subject has traditionally pursued the happiness of liberal individualism. We might also see the historical signification and containment of Asians as economic subjects of happiness, optimism, anxiety, and fear. In this racial liberalism context of the individual's pursuit of happiness—a pursuit achieved by objectifying the Asian as a means or as an impediment to acquiring the desired emotionality of American personhood—the security, contentment, and comfort that are the affective possession of the propertied self are, I further contend, premised on Asiatic racial sentiments, on feelings for and against Asians.

Shaped by liberal capitalism's processes of production and circulation, American media and popular culture have been primary venues for the perpetuation of racial images that have generated a culture of Asiatic racial sentiments. Film, television, and the Internet are popular forms of visual media that US capitalism maintains as an economic and emotional system of reproduction. These media's representations of Asiatic racial sentiments underscores how a capitalist emotional culture affects the perception of Asians as a racially different people.

It is, then, important that today's capitalist emotional culture shaping and determining these sentiments is historically premised on

Euro-American aspirations for an independent way of life. Contemporary media depictions of the Asiatic as both an optimistic and ominous sign of globalization may be traced to an American emotional culture that, from the 1850s through the 1880s, expressed and maintained the white racial ideals of liberal individualism. In particular, recent media expressions of anti-Asian sentiment emerge from a proliferation of anti-Chinese racism and "yellow peril" fears in nineteenth-century popular culture. The Asiatic racial sentiments from this time affect visual media and popular culture in the twenty-first century, structuring an emotional culture that influences the racialization of Asian Americans and contains them within the form of economic capital.

In the mid-1850s in California, for example, widespread beliefs about Chinese immigrants as agents of economic collapse and social chaos were expressed in music and stories that popularized a nostalgic pastoral image of California for American audiences. Many white Californians, especially of the working class, construed the increasing growth of Chinese immigrant populations as a threat to their small producer economies and independent way of life. As Robert Lee has argued, racialized perceptions of the Chinese as coolies and yellow peril threats were expressed in a nostalgic popular culture that blamed the Chinese for the passing of California's "golden era" (*Orientals* 16–17).

The rise of industrial capitalism in the 1850s was not only the cause for anxieties among white Californians about the passing of their state's golden era. It was *the* basis for their nostalgic popular culture in which they mourned losing the freedom, independence, and autonomy that had once been imaginable to them in a premodern capitalist idyll. Their nostalgia in music and stories articulates this loss and does so in decidedly racial terms with the invocation of the Chinese as impediments to the political aims of the Free Soil and Free Labor movements in California (Robert Lee, *Orientals* 45). The Free Soil movement was a national political party that opposed the expansion of slavery into US western territories. It argued that free men on "free soil" constituted a morally and economically superior system to slavery. Free Soil Californians saw the arrival of Chinese immigrant workers and coolies (indentured laborers) to represent the Eastern Seaboard's disruptive capitalist system.[13] The Free Labor movement subscribed to the Jeffersonian-Jacksonian ideal of *Herrenvolk* democracy, the notion of an "egalitarian republic" that would achieve "happy unity" for white workingmen by acting in agreement with natural law (47).

White racial feeling was, I would argue, evident in Free Labor ideology. That a "happy unity" for white workingmen in California was to be achieved in accordance with natural law under a Lockean contract of personhood and individualism underscores how such happiness was contingent upon defining the racial and cultural otherness of Chinese immigrants. By defining the Chinese as racial others, Free Laborers could restrict their movement's sense of freedom to whites only in the racial liberalism context. In doing so, they could racialize meanings of proprietary subjectivity and the pursuit of happiness as experiences reserved for white workingmen. "Chinese labor was not Free Labor in the republican sense," Lee points out, "because it had been decided that the Chinese were not capable of transcending their status as wage labor to become independent producers (notwithstanding the widespread existence of Chinese laundry operators, shopkeepers, masons, carpenters, tailors, etc.), and therefore participants in civic life" (*Orientals* 59). If, according to Free Labor ideology, the Chinese were not able to transcend their lowly position as wage laborers to become independent producers and, therefore, participants in civic life, then they were not capable of becoming propertied subjects, which was necessary for being self-possessing individuals, as well as acquiring the happiness of such individualism.

A culture of nostalgia for a lost white California was also evident in popular songs that were premised on anxieties about the transition to industrial capitalism. In his analysis of the lyrics to "California As It Was and Is," a popular song by the gold rush–era songwriter Old Put (the pseudonym of John A. Stone), Lee explains how this song's nostalgia for California's small producer economy is premised on Free Soil ideology. "California imagined [by Put] as a small producer economy, free of slavery, free of cash nexus, and free of the Chinese, 'when the Yuba used to Pay, with nothing but a pan and pick, five hundred dollars in a day,' represented the nostalgic heart of Free Soil California" (19). That Free Soil Californians characterized the Chinese as agents of economic decline for free white workingmen, as evoked in Put's song, shows how anxiety and the culture of nostalgia generated by such anxiety influenced their perception of the Chinese as impediments to happiness. In the context of racial liberalism, the happiness of liberal individualism structured the "nostalgic heart" of Free Soil California. For white workingmen who were nostalgic for a sense of autonomy imaginable before the rise of industrial capitalism, the Chinese were collectively a "racial thing" that inhibited the pursuit of happiness. Following Ahmed, we can see how Chinese immigrants became a "container" of Euro-American disappointment and loss—perceived by white Californians to contain the ghostly presence of their departed dreams of freedom, and all that this freedom had promised in terms of acquiring independence, individualism, and acquisitive happiness. Figuratively containing lost white freedom as embodiments of this loss, the early Chinese immigrants in California were "racial others" through which Euro-Americans defined themselves as *white* Californians, believing they were living a way of life that was pastoral and unique from the rest of modernizing America. Further, Euro-Americans in California thought they led an idyllic lifestyle that needed to be memorialized, if not protected, because of the irrevocable changes wrought by America's ambitions to modernize through industrialization.

By blaming the Chinese and thus racially othering them, white Californians were able to interplay psychologically with capitalism's profound transformations of their way of life. In this sense, an account of racial melancholia would suggest how the nostalgic cultural productions of white Californians expressed their psychical negotiation with industrial capitalism. Through nostalgia they managed their racialized grief for a lost way of life on which the basis of a white racial ideal for Californians was built.

If the nostalgia of white Californians here evidences a melancholic racial form of Euro-American identity in the nineteenth century, then so does happiness. If it can be understood that their nostalgia for a lost idyllic lifestyle was their yearning for the individual's happiness in the context of racial liberalism, then such happiness would indicate how white Californians sought to protect and memorialize their white identity melancholically. In *Orientals*, Lee gives a particularly striking example of this racially melancholic happiness. He quotes a broadside printed by the *Marin Journal* in March of 1876. This broadside, Lee explains, "summed up several charges that had been leveled against the Chinese presence in California 'on behalf of the workingmen of the state and their families'" (61). Of particular interest are the broadside's last two sentences: "That [the Chinese] are driving the white population from the state, reducing laboring men to despair, laboring women to prostitution, and boys and girls to hoodlums and convicts. That the health, wealth, prosperity and *happiness of our State* demand their expulsion from our shores" (qtd. in Lee, *Orientals* 62). As indicated in the broadside's demand that the Chinese be expelled "from our [white] shores," the anticoolie movement in California sought to protect and memorialize the happiness of white personhood. The movement represented a racial form of white identity that operated melancholically. Its ideals of prosperity, freedom, and individualism were to be secured by racially interpellating the Chinese as impediments to the pursuit of happiness. And Chinese expulsion clearly meant their containment as racialized subjects and their exclusion from the realms of political and symbolic forms of capital, because these realms were the preserve of Euro-Americans.

## Yellow Peril Fear: A Culture of Anxiety in Twentieth-Century America

Today's association of Asian Americans with an Asian "tiger economy" exemplifies how in America the Asian has always been a popular figure for capital accumulation. Conjoined and complementary to the Asian as an embodiment of economic optimism is the other side of an Orientalist antinomy: the Asiatic as an ominous sign of America's anxieties about social change from the financial restructurings and intensification of commodity relations under globalization. This contradiction of Asians as incarnations of fiscal accrual and as figurations of economic menace is traceable to white racial fears of a yellow peril in the early twentieth century, emerging from the advent of Asiatic racial sentiments. As a term to describe the fear of Asiatic invasion, however, *yellow peril* originates in Europe during the late nineteenth century at the height of European colonial empires in Asia, Africa, the Middle East, and the Americas.[14] In their attempt to define Western civilization against an Asian continent that was simultaneously alluring and threatening to them, Europeans conceived of a yellow peril to create the geopolitical awareness of themselves as a racially distinct people and culture, whose dominance as an empire was to be maintained through the extraction of Asia's resources and the labor exploitation of its people. Europe's proprietary and mercenary relations with Asia, in the effort to expand their imperial and colonial domains in the Orient, required preserving European cultural identity by rendering Asians as both an inferior people and a threat. The geographical immensity of Asia and its diverse populations and cultures, while irresistible for territorial acquisition and resource extraction, were in the European imagination a great source of fear for the possibility that Asians would desire Europe and want to invade it, thereby overtaking Europeans and racially polluting their civilization.

At the turn of the twentieth century, Americans adopted the notion of yellow perilism through the practice of exchanging cultures of anti-Asian sentiment with Europeans. This transnational exchange of Orientalist emotional cultures allowed the United States to develop and transmit throughout the Pacific, Americas, and the Caribbean its own geopolitical status as an imperial world power that was distinct from Europe's status accruing from colonial regimes in India, Africa, Asia, and the Middle East. As Gary Okihiro explains, Europeans sent popular images and paintings of Asians to Americans that depicted the "irrational fear of Oriental conquest, with its racist and sex-fantasy overtones" (*Margins* 119). Americans, in return, disseminated throughout Europe their own popular narratives of encountering indigenous people— "imagined Indians or Asiatic offshoots" (120)—whose inhabitance of the New World had to be contained and overcome in order to make possible the communal success of the Puritan way. With the removal of indigenous people whom European settlers deemed inferior, the conversion of the New World into a Euro-American civilization would begin and extend westward into Asia-Pacific regions through Manifest Destiny. However, America's transformation from republic to world power through the imperial expansion of its frontiers into Asia created anxieties among Euro-American workers that US trade activity and imperialism in the East would instill in Asians the desire to migrate to America en masse. These Euro-American fears about Asiatic hordes flooding the West Coast, overtaking whites in population, and outcompeting them for resources and jobs were an emotional corollary to xenophobic anxieties about US imperialist relations in the Orient.

Here we may infer and theorize a racial politics of anxiety intrinsic to the historical development of anti-Asian sentiment in the contexts of US imperialism, the pursuit of business, and commercial enterprise in the East. If anxiety is, according to Sara Ahmed (*Cultural Politics* 65–66), a feeling one has when moving *toward* an imperceptible or incorporeal danger, then we can understand that American anxieties about Manifest Destiny and westward imperialist expansion turned into fears of Asiatic threat: an identifiable embodiment of the other, the alien, and the foreign that portends to infiltrate domestic borders in consequence of economic interests and colonial incursions abroad. If fear is caused by the *approach* of a perceptible object or being (66), then it may be understood how popular representations of threatening Orientals were based on Euro-American workers' anxieties, which popular culture turned into yellow peril fears. The anxieties of working-class whites that US imperialism and capitalist enterprise in the Asia-Pacific would lead to economic hardship and social disorder at home thus became the fear of Oriental conquest. Through this circuit of affects in which anxieties were channeled and transformed into fear, Euro-Americans perceived Asians overseas as invasive Orientals in America. Popular culture exploited and circulated these anxieties to construct a fearsome Oriental coming to the United States in consequence of America's approaching, entering, and accessing the Asia-Pacific to pursue business interests and to make clear its intentions of becoming a colonial empire.[15] Hence the capitalist-based routes and dimensions of affects in the perception of Asians as a racially different people: America's production of Orientalist emotional cultures and racial feelings shaped and defined, in large part, an Asiatic racial form.

When large numbers of Asians did arrive in the US West from the late 1800s to the 1920s, yellow peril fears found their way through popular culture into perceptions of Asians as threats to white producer economies and working-class identity. Anxieties about white "racial suicide" because of invasive and competitive Asian migrant workers were pronounced in debates over nationality, naturalization, and family in which the Oriental was consolidated as the yellow peril. Through the media and popular culture especially, yellow peril fears were represented to articulate the struggle over defining American nationality in the emotionally charged racial terms of Asiatic threat. Popular culture in this historical context shaped and determined an emotional culture of anti-Asian racism through which Euro-Americans sought to preserve the "whiteness" of America's body politic, while the United States expanded its national terrain as an empire and pursued business and geopolitical interests overseas. Popular culture's representation and construction of yellow perilism as a pervasive anti-Asian sentiment thus defined Euro-American identity within both national and international settings at the turn of the twentieth century, when United States imperialism in the Asia-Pacific was in full swing.

## Articulating a Critical Structure of Feeling in Asian America

*Racial Feelings* is a project at once political and critical: political insofar as it presents a series of studies in the politics of emotions and race in America's liberal capitalist society, and critical because it shows how Asian American cultural works accommodate as well as resist the racialized perception of Asians as economic subjects. By articulating negative emotions of alienation, anger, ambivalence, and shame in their works, Asian Americans register the historical signification and containment of Asians in America as economic subjects. In this sense, this project's title phrase *racial feelings* highlights an implicit critical objective in these works: to lay bare the way Asians have been perceived in America as an objectified means either to acquire or to impede affects of contentment, comfort, and security in liberal individualism, which has historically equated personhood and citizenship with the white racial ideals of being and belonging in America. Bringing into sharp relief America's perception of Asians as figures of happiness, optimism, fear, and anxiety in economic processes of globalization, these works depict a set of emotions and affects as a *structure of feeling* generally involved in the formation of Asian Americans as a race group. In referring to Raymond Williams's concept that characterizes the lived experience of the quality of life at a particular time and place, I contend that Asian American artists and writers depict "characteristic elements of impulse, restraint, and tone; specifically affective elements of consciousness and relationships" (*Marxism* 132).[16] Their affects of remembering, in addition to their negative emotions, are contradictions to the comfort of belonging in America, instigated by the attempt to live up to the ideals of liberal personhood and individualism. These artists and writers thus articulate their own structure of feeling—a set of affects particular to Asian American emotional life in modern capitalist society, which has "specific internal relations, at once interlocking and in tension" with the affects of belonging embedded in white racial ideals (Williams, *Marxism* 132). That the affectively charged vision of the American Dream has been and continues to be utterly central to Asian American cultural expressions shows that racial feelings both make up and give rise to a structure of feeling specific to Asian America. This vision not only generates and maintains the perception of Asians as model economic characters but also animates and directs the lived experiences of Asian Americans to *aspire toward* performing and embodying a racializing discourse of model minority success, and subsequently, accommodating their own containment within economic capital.

A structure of feeling, however, not only manifests how Asian Americans accommodate this model minority discourse—often employing it "with ingenuity, alacrity, and pride, from within" (Ninh 9)[17]—but also registers their *criticism* of containment within the economic form of capital. In this regard, when Asian American writings articulate negative emotions to assert the way Asians in the past and the present have been objectified and defined by the racialized form of economic capital, we may understand these emotions to constitute a *critical* structure of feeling. In expressing such emotions, these works situate the Asian American affectively against the perception of Asians as economic subjects, as shown in Don Lee's discomfort with a person who readily assumed him in the position of a model minority. Insofar as Asian American writers articulate a critical structure of feeling, they evaluate the racial formation of Asian America in a capitalist culture of emotion, assessing the racial feelings that make up this culture. Further, they critically disclose how Asian-ancestry people in America are put in the position of having to negotiate with their discursive representation as subjects of economic optimism and peril. Their critique demonstrates the significance of racial feelings not only in evaluating Asian America's racialization but also in diagnosing this process as a characteristic feature of emotional life in the totality of capitalism.

As Sau-ling Wong argued in conceptualizing the term *Asian American* (*Reading* 5), Asian Americans in their works mediate their experiences with living in America while reconciling with the country's history of anti-Asian exclusion and discriminatory practices. Consequently, being Asian American in these works is a negotiation with the *felt* process of racialization, carrying within it layers of history that are mediated by aspirational attachments to achieving a sense of home and belonging. These attachments, which entail an optimistic and intractable investment in the Euro-American ideal of personhood—and which provoke in Asian Americans melancholic feelings of self-reproach, divided loyalty, and ambivalence—suffuse the signifying term *Asian American* with affective import and meaning. In doing so, they show how Asian America in capitalism's production of racial feelings is a site of contestation for a host of geopolitical and cultural forces, rendered evident and construable through critical attention to emotions and affects. In this regard, Asian American writers reveal through the racial feelings that give rise to their works how capitalism is a totality of social relations that forms them as a race group. And their criticism, in turn, suggests how Asian America has been and continues to be a racial formation important to maintaining circuits of affects that shape and define the proprietary subjectivity constituting the good life—emotions in capitalism that reinforce the ideal of liberal individualism.

In rearticulating this critical mode, *Racial Feelings* proposes a critical theory of affects in relation to capitalism's economic and emotional system of reproduction, analyzing the operation of capitalism's emotional cultures in Asian American texts. By theorizing these operations, the book shows how Asian American narratives communicate and critique, to varying degrees, the emotions that power the perception of Asians as a racially different people. What Asian Americans portray in their writings is a critical awareness of how they've been perceived as objects of acquisitive happiness and subjects of economic decline. When William realizes, for instance, that Shem has used him for his own gain and bitterly proclaims at the end of *Fixer Chao*, "I'd been hurt. I'd been cast aside. Passed over (Shem's joke to me: I've been passed over so many times it's enough to make me twice Jewish)" (355), we understand that William's anger not only targets the capitalist forces of objectification that have racially exploited him but also critiques economic processes of globalization in which profit is made routinely for a wealthy elite by exploiting poor immigrants, racial minorities, and the socially marginalized.

A critical structure of feeling is accordingly discernable in Asian American writings such as Ong's novel—writings that articulate capitalism's affective contradictions as they arise in an emotional life that follows the logic of economic relations and exchange. These writings commonly share the imperative to narrativize the experiences of dislocation, displacement, and estrangement as a characteristic feature of this emotional life for Asian Americans.

## Asian American Works: Racial Allegories in a Capitalist Culture of Emotion

In his study of the Asian model minority stereotype, Victor Bascara contends that Asian Americans "know intimately the processes that have kept them at a distance from the promises of equality and equivalence under citizenship" (12). Asian Americans assert a cultural politics that is "characterized by a radical critique of the civilization that produced the Asian Americans who make that critique" (12). As an expression of this politics, Asian American works narrativize an awareness of the way Asians have been perceived as an objectified means to make and preserve the happiness of American personhood. In this critical manner, as well, they *allegorize* the affects in capitalism that construct an Asiatic racial form and accordingly show how the racial othering of Asians has maintained the experience of feeling American by belonging in America.

The widespread belief that Asians are models of prosperity and scholastic achievement is a perception that many contemporary Asian-ancestry Americans have embraced for themselves, using and exploiting this perception as racialized capital to formulate and affirm their own sense of belonging. In doing this, Asian Americans assert an understanding that the pursuit of happiness and economic relations shape the aspiration to belong. They know that belonging or failing to fit in has historically been a consequence of Euro-Americans' perceiving them as racially different. They realize that manifestations of anti-Asian fear—in yellow perilism, for example—and Orientalist expressions of economic optimism—in the model minority discourse of achievement and success—function through spheres of economic activity and affects that serve the needs of liberal capitalist societies. Their critique of these affects demonstrates that Asians have been important to producing the experiences and expressions of liberal personhood and individualism, the making of a capitalist culture of emotion in modern America.

*Racial Feelings* is premised on the argument that the nexus between economics and affects produces racial antinomies in which Asians are subjects of optimism and unease for capitalism's global expansion. The book insists that a critical theory of affects in conjunction with Asian American texts can show us why people of Asian descent in America continue to be racially objectified as both hopeful and fearsome signs of globalization. The first two chapters provide further context for the argument that the capitalist system from the nineteenth to the mid-twentieth century produced the emotions that racialize Asian Americans in a current era of neoliberalism.[18] By focusing on particular historical events—anti-Chinese racism under white supremacist culture, Chinese indentured servitude and coolie labor, the 1882 Chinese Exclusion Act and American Sinophobia, US colonial rule of the Philippines (1899–1946), the influx of Filipino migrant workers on the US Pacific Coast, and the Tydings-McDuffie Act of 1934 and anti-intermarriage legislation—these chapters read works that represent the first period of Asian migration and immigration to the United States (1850s–1950s). The three subsequent chapters dialectically pair Asian American texts and recent media depictions of Asians as agents of economic optimism and threat in Cold War politics, electoral campaign videos, and Hollywood films. Collectively, the chapters and the Conclusion analyze works by artists and writers of Asian descent that characterize, accommodate, and critique the racialized perception of Asians as economic subjects of happiness, optimism, anxiety, and fear.

I use the term *artists and writers of Asian descent* to mention that one of the authors, Shaun Tan, whose graphic narratives are the focus of the first chapter, is not an American. Tan is a mixed-race Asian Australian, the child of a Chinese Malaysian immigrant father and a European Australian mother. Although Tan is not American and his graphic narratives largely depict everyday life in Australia, his stories contain abstracted iconic images in the historical memory of US immigration.

By including abstracted images and symbols of US immigrant history in his art, Tan suggests that we interpret his work comparatively with the immigrant experience in America. In this manner, we can think of his art alongside Asian American narratives, such as Maxine Hong Kingston's *China Men*, which evokes and represents the historical memory of early Asian immigrants in America. We can understand Tan's art as registering problematic histories of anti-Asian exclusion and containment in the Western world, which an Asian American memory narrative such as *China Men* reconstructs, and, in that reconstructing, as recounting a specific history necessary to understanding Asian America as a racial formation.[19]

Both *China Men* and Tan's graphic narratives critically depict freedom and the pursuit of happiness in the contexts of individualism and property ownership, which are premised on a racial liberal contract in America from the nineteenth century. By implying this history in his drawings of emotions as landscapes, Tan illustrates the experience of living in a modern capitalist system that has become alienating because people in this system overlook their shared histories. This visual conceit in Tan's art provokes empathic affects of recognizing and remembering a history of Asian diaspora in the Western world. Hence this empathic *feeling in historical memory* enables Tan's readers to imagine placing this history in the setting and time frame of his international migration stories. Through his emotions as landscapes Tan thus provokes our awareness of Asian immigrant histories in other countries and continents of the Western world, such as Australia, Europe, and North America, as well as in an Asian American cultural work like *China Men*. Therefore, we can read Tan's stories alongside *China Men* to see how Kingston's narrative figuratively registers Asian American racialization in a global frame. Because Tan's art and Kingston's memoir provoke empathic feeling in the historical memory of Chinese migrant experience, chapter 1 contends that we read these works comparatively to rethink an early period of Asian American history in new critical contexts.

By their critique of freedom and happiness, Kingston and Tan allow us to draw important connections between capitalism's economic relations and the emotions that express the aspiration to belong in a liberal democracy. Asian American writers show how the Asian American subject must identify and negotiate with an Asiatic racial form from the nineteenth century that contradicts today's optimistic attachments to the American Dream. This emotional contradiction turns the aspiration to achieve equality and belonging into *anger* and *ambivalence*.

What anger and ambivalence critically register here is the containment of Asian Americans within the economic form of capital. Historically, this containment of the Asian has helped to shape and define a culture of happiness essential to the American Dream of self-made success and upward mobility.

Chapter 2 further investigates this containment by focusing on the anger of Carlos Bulosan, a Filipino migrant writer in the early to mid-twentieth century. Bulosan's anger critiques the beginnings of a paradoxical racial form for Filipinos who lived and worked as colonial subjects in America. While the Philippines was under US colonial rule, Americans perceived Filipinos as happily servile because of the exploitable labor they performed as household servants, farm hands, and cannery workers. But paradoxically, Americans also considered Filipino men to be sexually threatening because they viewed them through stereotypes of black males as hypersexual predators of white women. In his prose writings and his semiautobiographical *America Is in the Heart*, Bulosan depicts social processes by which Filipino bodies and subjectivities become objectified in exploited and alienated labor. He describes the regulation and objectification of the emotions as features of racial containment for Filipino laborers. By taking into account Bulosan's antagonism to alienation in the workplace, chapter 2 argues that we especially understand the relevance of Bulosan's oeuvre to critique racial oppression and injustice through his Marxian depiction of the Filipino worker's alienation in a process I call the *emotional labor of racialization*. Through his anger at work exploitation, Bulosan articulates a materialist analysis of the emotions that critiques racial containment and scrutinizes the emergence of a Filipino racial form. Moreover, through both expressing and describing his struggle to manage a vehement affect such as anger, Bulosan critiques the perception of Filipinos as objects of commodity happiness—as subjects of happiness for hire—in the eyes of white Americans who ascribed to the Filipino laborer the Chinese migrant's supposedly unusual capacity for highly exploitable work.

Chapter 3 also examines the alienation of Asian migrants in America, but it shows how this alienation causes ambivalence for diasporic Asians in the late twentieth century. Andrew X. Pham's memoir *Catfish and Mandala* and Ha Jin's novel *A Free Life* reveal the conflicting feelings of Asian migrants about belonging in America in the years both during and after the Cold War. In their narratives, Pham and Jin depict the aspiration of Asian migrants for normative American lives of comfort and protection from hardship, loss, and precarity. This aspiration is an affect of social belonging mobilized within late-capitalist culture: the American Dream thus emerges as a feeling in neoliberalism that would be produced through economic uplift and prosperity, and through historically contingent modes of consumption and wealth accumulation. Yet this aspiration is also about *feeling normal* as a fully assimilated private citizen, a neoliberal belonging in America without regard to race, ethnicity, and national origin. Feeling normal is, in other words, a racialized affect in neoliberalism that I call *postracial sensibility*. This affect emerged from Cold War liberalism's color-blind politics, which aimed to remedy America's "embarrassment" in the eyes of the world on account of domestic acts of racial discrimination and to create a modern society free of racism based on liberal capitalist ideals of individualism and private property ownership. The chapter argues that the ambivalent feelings of Asian migrants in Pham's and Jin's narratives critique America's national credo of freedom and the pursuit of happiness—an ethos of liberal individualism underpinning today's politics of color blindness and generating neoliberalism's postracial sensibility.

The next chapter further examines postracial sensibility in Asian American writings. Chapter 4 focuses on mixed-race fiction by Changrae Lee and Ruth Ozeki to show how Asian Americans in the late twentieth century try to accommodate postracial sensibility through their attachments to normative life in a color-blind new world order.[20] Although Asian Americans in Lee's *Native Speaker* and Ozeki's *My Year of Meats* attempt to accommodate postracial sensibility, this ultimately signals their containment within a racial form of neoliberalism. These novels depict a dialectical tension between color blindness in America's liberal capitalist society and literature's memory of immigrant history—a memory affirming identification with Asian heritage and genealogy. By exploring this tension in mixed-race literature, this chapter develops the concept of *feeling ancestral* to theorize Asian Americans' purposeful reviving of shame, suffering, and loss from their immigrant pasts, not to submit to their debilitating sway, but to draw on resources for elaborating the representation of racial hybridity that emerges from material conditions and historical forces of immigration and border crossing under globalization. If shame, suffering, and loss affectively constitute, in part, the debased self-consciousness of an Asian diasporic underclass, then the re-embracing of shame, suffering, and loss amid the neoliberal politics of color blindness returns Asian Americans not to some essential identity but to a sense of agency grounded in a complex history woven of colonial, gender, and class oppressions.

The final chapter focuses on a specific set of emotions in today's US capitalist system—happiness, optimism, anxiety, and fear—that encompass the perception of Asians both as economic exemplars and as threats in globalization. By exploring recent media depictions of Asians as agents of economic success and decline, chapter 5 shows how perceptions of the Asiatic as an Oriental figure of capital's transnational movement are shaped by emotions and affects. In its 2012 report "The Rise of Asian Americans," the Pew Research Center proclaimed Asian Americans to be the most "successful" race group in the United States. The chapter begins by analyzing the report's characterization of Asian Americans as subjects of happiness and optimism for assimilation into economic processes of globalization. But in contradiction to this report, the 2012 political election campaigns generated advertisements, particularly for Republican candidates, that were salient for featuring anti-Asian sentiment that expressed anxieties about Asia as an economic threat. Another contemporary media form that features anti-Asian sentiment is Hollywood cinema. In particular, *Crash* and *Contagion* are two recent blockbuster films that portray Asian immigrants in association with anxieties about globalization. I examine *Crash* and *Contagion* to show how they express worries about Asiatic border crossing and deterritorialization by typecasting Asians as exploited and exploiting subjects of capitalism—subjects onto whom fears about uncontrollable migration and the transgression of privatized space are projected under neoliberal globalization.

Placing the 2012 Pew Research Center Report, the campaign advertisements, and the two films in critical dialogue, I pair these media depictions of sentiments for and against Asians with recent Asian American texts. These texts both accommodate and resist the media's Asiatic racial sentiments that structure Asian American racialization in the twenty-first century. By reading Marx's idea of commodity fetishism in Karen Tei Yamashita's *Tropic of Orange*, Paolo Freire's concept of critical consciousness in *Fixer Chao*, and Bourdieu's theory of capital in Don Lee's *The Collective*, I argue that these texts narrate the Asian American subject's confrontation with racialized perceptions that contain people of Asian descent within economic capital.

*Racial Feelings* concludes by addressing America's ongoing perception of Asians as economic subjects, specifically as exemplars of upward mobility and assimilation into the emotional culture of the American Dream. The Conclusion turns to Jhumpa Lahiri's *The Namesake* to point out that this novel critiques America's culture of comfort, a culture into which Asian immigrants and their children attempt to assimilate as the realization of the American Dream. In Lahiri's novel, Gogol Ganguli is the American-born child of Bengali immigrants who experience cultural displacement while living in a Massachusetts suburb. Gogol grows up, graduates from college, and becomes a successful architect in New York City. But his feelings of alienation and ambivalence about belonging in America contradict his success and articulate his sense of divided identity. We can understand, then, that the comfort of belonging as Gogol experiences it is powerfully modeled by the white racial ideal of liberal individualism. Comfort in this sense is an affect that structures and animates Lahiri's novel. It is one of the racial feelings generated in liberal capitalism giving rise to all Asian American cultural works.

That these works depict capitalism's economic production, management, and exploitation of affects shows us what it feels like to undergo racialization. Through their languages of subjectivity, Asian Americans offer their own insights into how circuits of affect construct race. In the texts of *Racial Feelings*, we see the routes and dimensions of emotions that structure the perception of Asians as a racially different people. By their expression of affects that shape and define an Asiatic racial form, these texts affirm the significance of Asian America's racial formation in a capitalist culture of emotion. Articulating a critical structure of feeling, they disclose this formation's history and material conditions depicted, experienced, and shared throughout the transnational literature of Asian Americans. In this cross-cultural effort to engage in a critique of emotions and race, we thus begin our exploration of this literature, an investigation demonstrating how racialization is an affectively charged process in liberal capitalist societies.

# 1 /   Feeling in Historical Memory: Reimagining Kingston's *China Men* with Shaun Tan's Graphic Narratives

Shaun Tan is a Chinese Australian artist whose picture books depict experiences of migration, estrangement, and historical memory. In his best-known graphic narrative, *The Arrival*, Tan portrays the story of one man's passage to another country, illustrating the sense of displacement, bewilderment, and awe that migrants experience when arriving in a strange new land they yearn to call home. The story unfolds through black-and-white drawings whose sepia tones call up memories of immigrants in the Western world from bygone eras. It begins with a two-page grid of faces that bear a haunting resemblance to photographs taken of immigrants arriving in America from the late nineteenth to the mid-twentieth century (see Figure 1.1). In his "Artist's Note" at the end of the book, Tan explains this resemblance: "Several drawings of immigrant processing, passport pictures, and the 'arrival hall' are based on photographs taken at Ellis Island, New York, from 1892 to 1954." Hence it appears that America is the migrant man's destination. When he and hundreds of other passengers onboard a ship arrive in the harbor of the new country, we see what they see: a towering edifice approximating the Empire State Building and two soaring statues shaking hands in welcome, conjuring the Statue of Liberty (see Figure 1.2). Is this new country America? Is the city New York? *The Arrival* never names these places. They're entirely make-believe. We can only suppose that the migrant is landing in America sometime in the late nineteenth to the mid-twentieth century. We can only wonder whether the busy inspection station through which he is processed and photographed is Ellis Island (see Figure 1.3). And we can only imagine *The Arrival*'s time

FIGURE 1.1. Shaun Tan's *The Arrival* opens with faces that resemble photographs taken of immigrants at Ellis Island, New York, 1892–1954. Copyright © by Shaun Tan 2006. (Reprinted by permission of Shaun Tan)

FIGURE 1.2. Passengers onboard a ship arrive in a city that looks like New York in *The Arrival*. Copyright © by Shaun Tan 2006. (Reprinted by permission of Shaun Tan)

and place in these contexts of US immigrant history if we're able to recognize and recall this history.

That Tan has extracted iconic images in the historical memory of immigrants at Ellis Island to illustrate his own story about international migration raises a host of questions. What does he imply by beginning his book within the frame of US immigrant history? Since Tan is an Australian artist of Chinese descent, is he suggesting that we interpret his work comparatively with the Asian immigrant experience in America? How, if at all, are we to make sense of his book's visual abstraction of US immigrant history in relation to Asian American works that narrate a specific immigrant history? Is this abstraction to be understood in the context of everyday life in modern Western societies?

One of the best-known narratives to portray the Asian immigrant experience in America is Maxine Hong Kingston's *China Men*. In her book, Kinston weaves together memory, myth, and fact in a series of stories that chronicle the lives of three generations of Chinese men from the late nineteenth to the mid-twentieth century. The stories are told in a sequence that slides between first and third person, an indirect narrative in which time, place, and history are abstracted, fragmentary, and fantastic. In this

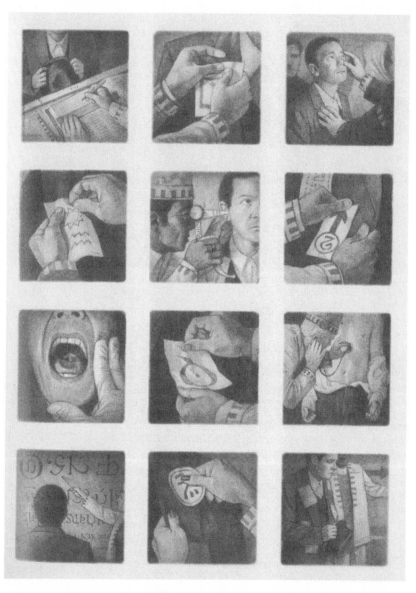

FIGURE 1.3. We can only wonder if *The Arrival*'s inspection station is Ellis Island. Copyright © by Shaun Tan 2006. (Reprinted by permission of Shaun Tan)

manner, *China Men* unfolds elliptically like Tan's narratives with their extraction of iconic images and symbols from US immigrant history. As in *The Arrival*, Kingston depicts in *China Men* a significant moment in America's history of immigration: the internment of Chinese migrants at the Angel Island Immigration Station in California. In "The Father from China," Kingston tells a fictive story about her father's immigration as a "paper son," a Chinese man who came to America by purchasing a forged birth certificate claiming him to be the son of a Chinese American citizen (Takaki 235–39). Upon his arrival in California, the man whom Kingston calls her "legal father" is detained at Angel Island. "In the middle of the night when he was the only man awake, the legal father took out his Four Valuable Things, and using spit and maybe tears to mix the ink, he wrote a poem on the wall, just a few words to observe his stay. He wrote about wanting freedom. He did not sign his name; he would find himself a new American name when he landed. If the US government found out his thoughts on freedom, it might not let him land" (56). By imagining her father at Angel Island, Kingston refers to Chinese immigrants who were unjustly interrogated and confined at the island's quarantine stations because Americans perceived them as aliens carrying diseases who sought entry into the United States illegally. Many of these men were artistically expressive. They carved poetry on the barracks walls to protest their captivity. Known as the Angel Island Poems, the carvings express the immigrants' alienation and exclusion from America. The legal father's assertion of "wanting freedom" by carving his own poem registers his awareness of being perceived as a racial other in *opposition* to America's national definition of freedom for white citizens. Kingston's imaginary remembrance of her father as an Angel Island detainee thus exemplifies why *China Men* is a canonical memory narrative that participates in constructing the collective history of Asian Americans. If we read *China Men* and are moved by its evocation of the past—feeling empathic recognition of the way Kingston's ancestors struggled with exclusion and alienation—we envision a specific history of Asian immigrants in America important to the formation of Asian Americans as a race group.

In this regard, *China Men* not only takes part in recounting the history necessary to understand Asian America as a racial formation but also implies affects involved in remembering that articulate a critical structure of feeling in Asian American works. Tan's drawings portray experiences of disorientation, placelessness, and estrangement for the migrant and use extracted images from US immigrant history to illustrate these experiences, and the stories in *China Men* do the same. The extractions in Kingston's narrative reflect the historical experiences of early Chinese immigrants who became alienated and excluded by cultures of anti-Asian sentiment.

Tan's works are also, among other things, historical memory narratives. They remember migrants and travelers arriving, exploring, and living in imaginary countries, cities, and lands. And like *China Men*'s elliptical narrative, Tan's works play creatively with contexts of history, setting, and place. As in *The Arrival*, time frames are indeterminate; the stories could take place in the past, present, or future. However, in interviews and comments available on his website and at the end of his books, Tan gives political and historical context to his stories. For instance, in one interview, he comments that Australia is a "nation that is still coming to terms with a problematic history as well as a changing contemporary landscape" ("Conversation" 45). Australia's national government, Tan observes, has been slow to recognize and remember its past of discriminating against Aboriginal people and Asian immigrants. This "problematic history" refers to the country's era of racism against Chinese immigrants and Aboriginal people under the White Australia Policy, which unofficially began in the 1850s and legally ended in 1973.[1]

Under the White Australia Policy, Chinese immigrants endured discrimination and exclusion on the basis of the nation's perception of the Chinese as too racially different from Europeans to assimilate into its white society. In his graphic narratives, Tan implicitly represents his country's problematic history of the White Australia Policy. His drawings mediate a critical awareness to unearth Australia's past of racially excluding and discriminating against Chinese immigrants. His art allegorizes the social remembering and recognition of Australia's problematic history through its images of landscapes that are metaphors for emotions. In his concluding comments to *Lost and Found*, a recent collection of illustrated stories, Tan explains that his idea to visualize "emotions as landscapes" is a way to describe "intangible feelings using visual metaphors: monsters, sunlight, rainbows, storm clouds" (126). He wants to "illuminate something that is often invisible" (126), a complex understanding and awareness of how the present and the future are created from histories that are increasingly made invisible and forgotten in modern capitalist societies.

One of these histories is the immigration of Asian people to the Western world from the nineteenth to the mid-twentieth century. Tan uses his emotions as landscapes as a visual conceit not only to bring into relief this history of immigration but also to create awareness of how Australia's history of anti-Chinese racism and other problematic histories have become disremembered in the present.[2] A good example of this visual conceit that illustrates the historical memory of Asian immigrants and provokes awareness of this memory's invisibility in modern societies is the two-page grid of immigrant faces that opens *The Arrival*. It bears repeating that Tan drew these faces "based on photographs taken at Ellis Island, New York, from 1892 to 1954." Although the faces belong to people whom Tan knows or has made up, their haunting resemblance to immigrants processed at Ellis Island evokes a specific history of international migrants arriving in America in the late nineteenth and early twentieth centuries. The emotions of recognizing and remembering this history—*feeling in historical memory*—stir and enable us to imagine placing this history in the setting and time frame of Tan's international migration fantasy. As a visual conceit for feeling in historical memory, the novel's grid of faces provokes our awareness of Asian immigrant histories in other countries of the Western world, such as Australia, and in other cultural works, such as *China Men*. As Kingston's narrative provokes us to ask questions about how and why problematic histories of racial exclusion and containment become forgotten and unrecognized in the present, Tan's graphic narratives with their emotions as landscapes do the same, especially if we read them alongside a work that enables remembering an early period of Asian immigrant history in the Western world and recounts this history necessary to understanding the racial formation of Asian Americans.

This chapter reads Tan's work alongside *China Men* to show how this pairing allows us to interpret Kingston's narrative and its representation of an early period of Asian American history in new critical contexts. To read Tan's work as allegories of remembering immigrant history alongside Kingston's *China Men* highlights three key points important to this book's argument that artists and writers of Asian descent articulate a critical structure of feeling. First, this juxtaposition allows us to interpret *China Men* as a narrative about the exploitation and containment of racialized Chinese immigrants in a global frame. Reading Tan's international migration fantasy alongside *China Men* registers, I argue, the collective history of racialized Asian Americans that Kingston's text narrativizes as a global development, a construct shaped and defined by transnational cultures of Asiatic racial sentiments. Second, by understanding Tan's emotions as landscapes to be a visual conceit that illustrates alienation, placelessness, and disconnection as the problem of forgetting in modernity, we can envision this conceit operating in *China Men* to see that it, too, signifies the problem of disremembering histories of Asian immigrant experience in modern societies that have been globalized. In this way, we can understand Kingston's *China Men* as a narrative that allegorizes a characteristic feature of emotional life in modern Western societies: the attempt to over-come alienation and cognitively map historical and social contexts in a culture of forgetting. And third, when we comparatively read Tan's stories alongside *China Men*, we might see that both affectively register Asian American racialization because they contain extracted iconic images of Asian immigrant history that provoke empathic feeling in the memory of Asian immigrant experience throughout the Western world. This histori-cal memory, which we can envision dynamically and collectively in *China Men* when reading its stories with Tan's graphic narratives, has meaning and context, I further argue, in a cosmopolitan vision that articulates awareness of comparable histories of anti-Chinese racism in Australia and America and mediates an ethical or imagined openness, direction, and connection to an integrated and shared lifeworld. If comparatively reading Tan's stories in juxtaposition with *China Men* allows us to place Kingston's imaginary depiction of Asian American history in both a global frame and a cosmopolitan vision, we can *reimagine* this collective history to be illus-trated in the emotions as landscapes that appear throughout Tan's work.

## The Violence of Forgetting

To show how Tan's stories mediate a history of Asian immigrant experi-ence, I turn to another of his graphic narratives, *Tales from Outer Suburbia* (hereafter *Tales*). One of the stories in *Tales*, "Our Expedition," ends with a breathtaking image of two boys who, having finished an adventure in the outer suburbs, sit in the middle of the road with their legs hanging over the edge where it breaks off (see Figure 1.4). The two boys are brothers who leave their home on a quest to determine if a street directory they have found in their father's car is accurate. The directory mysteriously stops at Map 268, indicating that nothing else exists beyond this final page. The younger brother who narrates the story says, "*Obviously* certain pages had fallen out. Map 268 itself was packed full of streets, avenues, crescents and cul-de-sacs, right up to the edge . . . it's not like it faded off into noth-ing. It made no sense" (84, original italics). Yet the older brother disagrees, arguing that the map is "literally correct, because it would otherwise have 'joins Map 269' in small print up the side. If the map says it is so, then it is" (84). The two brothers bet each other twenty dollars on who is right, and they go to find the exact location in the directory. They take a bus to the outer suburbs. They get off near their destination and hike through streets, parks, and malls that they think will be unaccustomed landscape like "a desert or jungle wilderness" (89). Yet as they venture farther they find that

FIGURE 1.4. Two brothers hang over the edge in Shaun Tan's "Our Expedition," *Tales from Outer Suburbia*. Copyright © by Shaun Tan 2008. (Reprinted by permission of Shaun Tan)

"everything looked the same, as if each new street, park, or shopping mall was simply another version of our own, made from the same giant assembly kit" (89). Finally, when they reach the exact location in Map 268, the older brother walks some distance ahead and plops down "right in the middle of the road, *with his legs hanging over the edge*" (89, original italics). The younger brother sits down next to him and realizes he has lost the bet.

This final image in "Our Expedition" is an allegory for the problem of disremembering the past in a manufactured place such as suburbia, whose uniform and sprawling topography can make its inhabitants feel displaced and alienated. In this last image of the two brothers who reach the very end of suburbia and find it literally cut off from the rest of the world, Tan illustrates how the past becomes overlooked in an environment that has been rapidly developed into outer suburbs. Before vast areas of Australia's wilderness were turned into suburbs, Aboriginal people inhabited the lands for sixty thousand years. Some of these lands were occupied by tens of thousands of Chinese immigrants who arrived in Australia in the 1850s to work as miners and field laborers. For the Asian people who lived on these lands, life was a struggle against European Australians who discriminated against them and forcibly removed them from their homes and settlements.

For nearly seventy-five years, Chinese immigrants endured racial exclusion and discrimination under the White Australia Policy. As I noted earlier, Tan refers to this particular era of anti-Chinese racism as Australia's problematic history, and he is deeply concerned about the forgetting of it.

Australians who disremember their country's era of anti-Chinese racism, Tan suggests, are cut off from a significant historical period whose cultural remembrance has produced what Pierre Nora calls "minority memories" (439). For racial and ethnic minorities, remembering past struggles and hardships under racism has traditionally expressed "a marked emancipatory trend among peoples, ethnic groups and even certain classes of individual in the world today; in short, the emergence, over a very short period of time, of all those forms of memory bound up with minority groups for whom rehabilitating their past is part and parcel of reaffirming their identity" (439). If Tan's art can be understood as a social document that reflects the historical memory of his country's past racism under the White Australia Policy, it also can be seen to revive and reconstruct a history of this racism as a defining feature in the composition of minority memory for Chinese Australians.

Comics artists represent time in ways that visually collapse, extract, and refract it on the pages of their work. They depict unconventional arrangements of time to visualize historical moments, often by abstracting these moments, as we can see in the grid of faces that opens *The Arrival*. By illustrating history through unusual arrangements of space and time, comics artists reconstruct historical memory in their work (Jeff Adams, *Documentary Graphic Novels* 62). "By introducing time into the equation," Scott McCloud explains, "comics artists are arranging the page in ways not always conducive to traditional picture-making. Here, the composition of the picture is joined by the composition of change, the composition of drama—and the composition of memory" (115). In their illustration of how modern Australia forgets and renders lost its memory of problematic history, Tan's stories depict unconventional arrangements of space and time to portray the rapid changes caused by modernization, capitalist development that has generated feelings of loss and anxiety: "an accelerated precipitation of all things into an ever more swiftly retreating past" that shatters the unity of historical time (Nora 438), producing feelings of displacement and distance for the inhabitants of suburbanized Australia.

Another way to understand the problem of not remembering in modern Western societies, as Tan depicts it, is that the minority memory of anti-Chinese racism under the White Australia Policy complicates and contradicts the country's celebration of multiculturalism as a narrative of Australian national identity. Having developed their nation in a global market economy, Australians today enjoy cultural diversity as the commercially managed coexistence of different ethnic groups. Multiculturalism in this liberal capitalist context is about the aspirational norms of diversity in global commerce and the everyday shopping habits of consumers. The development of rural lands for suburban living produces, in turn, consumer multicultural desires among the ethnically diverse residents who live, work, and make their homes in the suburbs. The sociologist Amanda Wise has coined the term *sensuous multiculturalism* to describe the interactive roles of "emotions, affect and habitus in the experience of cultural diversity" among residents in Australia's suburbs (917). European Australians in the suburbs today show their desire to "embrace diversity" by interacting amicably through commerce with nonwhite residents who are increasingly Chinese immigrants (917). The consumerist celebration of diversity in Australia's suburbs has produced, according to Wise, "sensuous and embodied modes of being that mediate intercultural interactions between long-term Anglo-Celtic elderly residents in the [suburbs] and newly arrived Chinese immigrants and their associated urban spaces" (917). Following Wise, if we understand multiculturalism in Australia's suburbs as a consumer phenomenon that gratifies desires and has strong sensory appeal for commodities, then such multiculturalism is a production of liberal capitalism that commercializes and produces affective experiences in people.

Sensuous multiculturalism, as a current mode of capitalist production that narrates and represents Australian national identity, both commodifies and generates emotional experiences as a form of "affective labor." According to Michael Hardt and Antonio Negri, affective labor is an institutionalized form of "immaterial labor," such as the labor of consumption necessary in liberal capitalist societies that depend on consumerism and that make people relate to commodities as consumers through the emotions (*Empire* 292–93). A form of work for the consumer, affective labor structures a certain state of the body along with a certain mode of thinking to create aspirations for an everyday life of consumerism. Affective labor thus produces or manipulates affects to express and structure subjectivities for consumerism.

As an emotional production in suburbia, however, sensuous multiculturalism is unreceptive to the minority memory of anti-Chinese racism. As Ien Ang points out, the problem with "the discourse of multiculturalism as it has been constructed in Australia" is that it represses the country's problematic history of racism (100). Multiculturalism in its consumer and commercialized forms "is incapable of providing a convincing and effective narrative of Australian national identity because it does not acknowledge and engage with a crucial ideological concern in the national formation's past and present, namely that of race" (100). In particular, sensuous multiculturalism's everyday practice by middle-class suburbanites entails *overlooking* the history of the White Australia Policy, whose disregarding stems in part from privatizing and developing the lands where Chinese immigrants once lived, worked, and struggled during Australia's era of racism. As Tan shows in his art, these lands have been transformed and commodified into suburbs at the cost of rendering forgotten the laws that excluded and contained Chinese immigrants and that produced an important period in Australia's history of race relations.

While downplaying and overlooking its problematic history has been important to Australia's commercialization of diversity, this consumer-based multiculturalism attenuates a critical understanding of the historical forces—the racist laws of the White Australia Policy—from which an Asian immigrant population emerges as a racial group, and it becomes understood as a racial form through its documentation of racism in literature, film, art, and social movements. *Racial form*, as Colleen Lye puts it, refers to the emergence of "race as form" that develops from historical forces and active social relations ("Racial Form" 95). An Asiatic racial form was brought into historical being in the twentieth century "across a variety of registers" (95) and, in particular, as a problematic question of the relationship between "race understood as representation and race as an agency of literary and other social formations" (99). Lye's materialist analysis of Asiatic racial form is a forceful account of Asian racialization in the United States. Yet her conceptualization of it may be extended comparatively and transnationally, I contend, to examine this racialization in Australia and to depict it as a minority memory by a comics artist such as Shaun Tan. In Australia today, the tension between, on one hand, the minority memory of the White Australia Policy that contributed to the historical emergence of an Asiatic racial form and, on the other, the forgetting of this problematic history in consumer multiculturalism—an everyday culture of forgetting—is precisely what Tan shows in his art.

Shaun Tan was born in 1974, one year after Australia ended its 1901 Immigration Restriction Act, which legally allowed whites to discriminate against nonwhites as well as restrict their immigration. As Ien Ang explains, this act became the basis for the country's era of racism under the White Australia Policy (101). Growing up in the wake of discriminatory practices that legislatively enforced the White Australia Policy, Tan experienced in his own life a separateness caused by the racism that white Australians perpetrated against the Chinese. "Being a half-Chinese at a time and place when this was fairly unusual may have compounded this [disconnectedness]," Tan discloses.

> I was constantly being asked "where are you from?" to which my response of "here" only prompted a deeper inquiry, "where do your parents come from?" At least this was far more positive attention than the occasional low-level racism I experienced as a child, and which I also noticed directed either overtly or surreptitiously at my Chinese father from time to time. Growing up I did have a vague sense of separateness, an unclear notion of identity or detachment from roots, on top of that traditionally contested concept of what it is to be "Australian," or worse, "un-Australian" (whatever that might mean). ("Comments on *The Arrival*")

To be sure, Tan's feelings of "separateness" and "detachment from roots" inform his desire to identify with Asian immigrant forbears. But his art also documents his feelings of detachment from history and ancestry by referencing his childhood experiences with isolation and displacement. In interviews, Tan comments on the estrangement he felt as a child, his sense of feeling separated from origins that he portrays in his work. "I notice that a lot of my paintings depict figures in alienating landscapes, often with an undercurrent sense of a troubled identity, or at least a displaced one. I think that has a lot to do with growing up in an outer suburban environment with little historical memory, in the world's most remote capital city [Perth]" ("Conversation" 45).

Here we might consider that Tan's memory of isolation and displacement in suburbia references the White Australia Policy in relation to America's history of anti-Chinese sentiment, and does so in contrast to today's neoliberal politics of "post-race" in both countries.[3] For his stories compel us to recognize and remember this history and to realize why it becomes forgotten in consequence of capitalist development. By referencing Australia's history of anti-Chinese racism, Tan's art alludes to America's history of anti-Asian racism as a transnational minority memory against our putatively color-blind moment in neoliberalism.

To address this allusion, we need to consider the problem with remembering in liberal capitalist societies in the setting of Tan's stories, as well as in the historical context of an Asiatic racial form that emerged, in part, from transnational histories of anti-Chinese racism in both Australia and America. Australia's history of anti-Chinese racism bears similarities to such history in the United States from the 1850s to the mid-twentieth century. Exclusion acts, antimiscegenation laws, and discriminatory legislation that specifically targeted the Chinese and other Asian immigrants have constructed Asian populations in both countries as a race group. Moreover, as I will discuss later in this chapter, there's an indication of anti-Chinese discourse from Australia—for example, the racist phrase *Chinaman's chance*—that made its way to America in the nineteenth century. The purported migratory passage of this phrase from Australia to America allows us to interpret Kingston's depiction of anti-Chinese racism in her narrative as a critique of discriminatory practices against the Chinese on a global scale. When we read *China Men* comparatively alongside Tan's stories, we'll see that Kingston's text evokes Asian American racialization in a global frame by reflecting the problem of not remembering history under forces of liberal capitalism's modernization.

By *modernization* in the contexts of both Kingston's and Tan's works, I refer to the contemporary societies of America and Australia in which consumerism and commodification in neoliberal multiculturalism make feeling cut off from history a characteristic feature. If alienated labor was a characteristic feature of nineteenth-century capitalism for Chinese migrants who toiled as indentured laborers and coolies in America, in today's era of economic liberalism we understand that alienation at work has transmuted into alienation in consumerism. Tan's concluding comments to *Lost and Found* that Australia has been slow to recognize and remember its problematic history, and his representation of this problem in his stories, can be understood in light of his other statements about economic policies that dehumanize people (125). These are policies of capitalist liberalization such as neoliberalism in which financial deregulation and the governing role of the private sector produce and exacerbate human displacement, alienation, and emotional disconnection.

Though concealed and made invisible in capitalist liberalization, the history of early Asian migrants as Tan depicts it haunts the present. His pictures of landscapes as metaphors for emotion imply remembering the past evocatively by conjuring the presence of Chinese migrants who once inhabited rural lands before these were developed into outer suburbs. If, as the sociology of memory scholar Barbara Misztal explains, memory is "closely connected with emotions because emotions are in part about the past and because memory invokes emotions" (80–81), we might see that Tan's graphic narratives are an allegorical form that *revives* memory through the artistic rendering of emotions. We can appreciate, in other words, his stories as visual depictions of affects in the form of landscapes that contain extracted iconic images from history, as in the opening pages of *The Arrival*. These emotionally charged graphic forms are metaphors for remembering history. They are feeling in historical memory.

In *Lost and Found*, Tan explains that his basic idea to represent emotions as landscapes is a way to visualize alienation from the natural world. This alienation is conditioned by forgetting in modern capitalist societies, a feeling of disconnection and dislocation as the effect of an amnesiac consumer culture. Materialist concepts of reification and commodification help explain how forces of capitalism cause forgetting, and an awareness of the causes of forgetting informs Tan's revival of historical memory through his landscape drawings that depict alienation. His illustrations evoke historical memory and imbue it with deep feeling. But also his pictures depict forgetting history in suburbia, where the land has been transformed and commodified for housing developments.

Implied as an atmospheric mood in his landscape drawings, Tan's attempt to "illuminate something that is often invisible" aptly depicts one of the thematic contexts of reification developed by Georg Lukács. Through reification, a process that Lukács called "the necessary, immediate reality of every living person in capitalist society" (History 197), human beings and relations transform into thinglike objects and abstractions, which do not act in a human way but perform according to the laws of the thing-world.

As Paul Connerton formulates it, reification may also be understood as commodification. It is quite reasonable, Connerton maintains, "to describe the process most frequently diagnosed as reification or the fetishism of commodities as a process of forgetting" (52–53). Reification is, moreover, a primary capitalist force in transforming and developing land. In his analysis of urban destruction by the acceleration of capitalist modernization, Connerton writes: "Both our urban hierarchies and our transport systems demonstrate the acceleration in the pace at which our produced landscapes are transformed. Capitalism continually restructures our urban landscapes through suburbanization, deindustrialization, gentrification and urban renewal. And capitalism annihilates space through its fixed investment in rail, road and port systems, because at some point the impulsion to continue to annihilate space must make these initial investments obsolete and redundant" (119). Following Connerton's argument about how reification annihilates space and erodes historical memory, I suggest this is a condition that both Tan illustrates and Kingston depicts in their stories of international migration. For Tan and Kingston, forces of commodity reification that cause people to forget are part of the alienating systems of liberal capitalist societies.

An assessment of reification in Tan's emotions as landscapes gives us insight into how capitalism, through the aspiration for an everyday "normal" life, causes people to overlook and disremember history. If it can be understood that to "feel normal" in liberal capitalism requires optimism for achieving the good life, as Lauren Berlant would put it (167–68), we see how everyday life in capitalism requires, in turn, the suppression and concealment of painful histories such as Australia's anti-Chinese laws and discriminatory practices in the last century. This is a problematic history utterly contradicting aspirations for a color-blind world order that are attributable to the so-called triumph of capitalism in Western liberal democracy.[4]

We might further understand such optimism as the yearning to belong and feel normal by acquiring a postracial sensibility, which is an aspiration in the everyday life of consumer or sensuous multiculturalism. "I realise that I have a recurrent interest in notions of 'belonging,'" Tan divulges, "particularly the finding or losing of it" ("Comments on *The Arrival*"). As Tan implies in his drawings and comments, the tendency to find (feel) and to lose (forget) belonging essential to reification has much to do with the corporate ownership of the media. An amnesiac culture is a consequence of corporate consumerism, which conditions forgetting the primal recognition that human beings accord each other in a process of intersubjective interaction (Jay 8). What Tan figuratively depicts in the visual conceit of his emotions as landscapes is, I further suggest, "a primal dimension of the human relation to the world" that gets lost in reification (Jay 8).[5]

In "The Amnesia Machine," a two-page story in the middle of *Tales*, Tan illustrates the control of everyday life by the market forces of commodification (see Figure 1.5). These forces produce an emotional disconnection from the past and the distortion of truth in the present. They render the connection between people and their relation to history ever more abstract, effectively neutralizing time and space because of the commodities people consume. The story appears as a newspaper article about a machine driven through the streets of an unnamed suburb. The machine resembles a nuclear missile that has commonly appeared in military parades throughout the world. Accompanying the machine is a colorful van playing a "catchy jingle." People in the suburb can receive a free ice cream from this van at the cost of their memories. Surrounding the story in the newspaper are other articles entitled "Truth overrated, explains Minister" and "Meltdown not so bad after all" (74). The story's narrator is blasé about the dishonesty of politicians and corporate control of the media. He reads "a newspaper article about the recent election result, an

FIGURE 1.5. The control of everyday life by the market forces of commodification in Shaun Tan's "The Amnesia Machine," *Tales from Outer Suburbia*. Copyright © by Shaun Tan 2008. (Reprinted by permission of Shaun Tan)

unsurprising government victory, and some other stories about media ownership, missing government revenue, corruption, and so on, all quite boring" (74). But what most interests him in the newspaper is how "every page features a full color advertisement for a new, bright pink ice cream" (74). Tan explains that "the phrase 'amnesia machine' or 'amnesia factory'" had long been in his mind as a way to describe political campaigns and electioneering. "It's not so much an issue of conspiracies, but rather a failure of critical vigilance, and public apathy" ("Comments on *Tales*"). Again, we can infer that Tan is concerned about people in consumer capitalism who no longer have the ability to reflect complexly on the past, a capacity for deep remembering necessary for people to think critically about the present and their intricate relation to space and time (history).

Insofar as politics and politicians have become commodities in liberal capitalist societies, people have become consumers in a capitalist totality, estranging them and rendering them insentient to a primal relation with place and history. Such a mentality of indifference largely reflects the alienation of modern everyday life from economic processes of extraction and production. In his concluding comments to his stories in *Lost and Found*, Tan explains that he wants to portray the "social apathy and dehumanizing economic policies advocated by some governments and bureaucrats" (123). These neoliberal policies of privatization and property ownership effectively drive the homogenizing forces of global capital that render people indifferent to place and history. An apathetic citizenry lose the ability to reflect deeply, becoming incapable of grasping global capitalism's effects on their memory and consciousness. The story's narrator explains that he cannot recall and evaluate his own "dream about that thing, that machine, but even now the details are elusive and my mind feels more and more like any emptying room" (74). Through the narrator here, we see the disturbing consequences of capitalist totality's power: its production of a hegemonic consumer culture that erases one's ability to cognitively map for oneself a meaningful context within space and time. For it is the present that concerns the narrator, not the past. He's aware only of the flavor of the "ice cream cone right here in my hand, melting. Is it meant to be strawberry or raspberry?" (74). There's nothing else for the narrator, it seems, outside the capitalist totality that has structured human subjectivity for a modern identity in which the most important concerns are the commodities for purchase and consumption.

Another way to understand such totality is that it is the fully administered world of modernization, as T. W. Adorno conceptualized it, in which modern identity is a product of the totalizing system of commodity exchange. The principle of this modern identity originates in the logic of equivalence and exchange in the capitalist system (Jameson, *Late Marxism* 28). Here we can understand Adorno's critique of modern identity to interpret the narrator in Tan's story as a subject whose identity is a product of liberal capitalism's totalizing social relations. With an identity produced by the capitalist logic of equivalence and exchange, the narrator is himself a commodity who cannot see his existence outside the rationalized object-world of consumerism and commodity relations. Ultimately, we can understand Tan's story to reflect the way capitalism has transmuted alienated and abstracted workers into alienated and abstracted consumers. Capitalism coerces people to comply with their own abstraction (i.e., commodification) in a totalizing system that creates *"the reduction of human labor to the abstract universal of average working hours"* (Adorno, *Negative Dialectics* 146). Workers are a commodity, Marx argued, insofar as they "must sell themselves piece-meal" under the relations of capitalist production, "exposed to all the vicissitudes of competition, to all the fluctuations of the market" (Marx and Engels, *Manifesto* 479).

In the process of commodity exchange, unequal things get exchanged as if they were equal—hence profit extraction by the accumulation of surplus value. In this sense, the abstraction of human labor is the defining feature of commodity exchange in capitalism's profit motive, a process from which modern identity originates. This process by which ideology produces the coercion of identity to make people comply with commodification in exchange relations shows why the narrator in "The Amnesia Machine" assimilates and has confidence in what Tan calls "dehumanizing economic policies" facilitated by neoliberalism. For assimilation is the material process by which people are coerced into aspiring for a modern identity, an identity premised on manipulating and abstracting affects—on affective labor—to express and structure liberal personhood and individualism.

Such identity is what the narrator in Tan's story has become: a person who cannot reflect critically and evaluate his own dream in a hegemonic consumer culture. Without critical awareness it becomes difficult to remember the past and to imagine continuity with and emergence from a natural world that contains a living history of ancestors and forebears. What's at stake in losing history and memory because of social apathy is, then, the imagination. This is an imagination important to creating art, writing poetry, and telling stories, as Kingston would put it, which not only contradicts alienated labor and estrangement in consumerism but also expresses one's abiding connection to the past and an empathic and affiliative relation to people and places in history.

In this regard, both Kingston and Tan bring to mind Georges Didi-Huberman's term *disimagination machine*, which is the problem to "imagine for ourselves" in a "world, full, almost choked with imaginary commodities" (3). Didi-Huberman coined *disimagination machine* to explain the difficulty of representing the Holocaust through images—specifically archival photographs of mass killings in Nazi concentration camps—in a contemporary world oversaturated with pictures and photos. Here, I suggest, Kingston's and Tan's narratives figuratively engage with Didi-Huberman's disimagination machine to show us how a politics of disimagination both generated and used in liberal capitalist societies undermines the ability of people to recognize and realize a critical sense of remembering, agency, ethics, and collective resistance (Giroux).

One of the final stories in *China Men*, "The Brother in Vietnam," offers an account of forgetting and its negative impact on the imagination in a modern society overdeveloped by consumerism and commercialization. Kingston, the narrator, explains that the Vietnam War has begun and that her younger brother is "old enough to be drafted" (277). The story dovetails the war with capitalism's economics to depict the contradictions in a modern society whereby corporations profit from social domination, a totalizing corporatism that people accommodate throughout the entirety of society. Her younger brother takes a job as a high school teacher while trying to avoid enlisting in the military and going overseas where he would have to kill other Asians: "Chinese Americans against Chinese. . . . 'Orientals' belonged over there fighting among their own kind" (277). Disturbingly, the brother's students, mostly African Americans and Latinos in special education classes, are insensitive to the barbarities committed in the war: "During Current Events, he told his class some atrocities to convince them about the wrongness of war. The students looked at the pictures of napalmed children and said, "Sure, war is hell." Where had they learned that acceptance? . . . The brother felt that it was *self-evident* that we ought to do anything to stop war. But he was learning that upon hearing terrible things, there are people who are, instead, filled with a crazy patriotism" (278, italics added). To the brother, it is "self-evident" that war and corporatism function together to create social division and exploit an underprivileged class of racialized minorities. He tries to help the students understand this, but he's working against structures of domination that make the students incapable of realizing their own exploitation, containment, and marginalization by the corporate capitalist system. To be sure, the brother believes he has a "teachable moment" when a student asks: "Who owns the electricity?" The brother says electricity, like water, gas, and oil, "originally belonged to nobody and everybody. Like air. 'But the corporations that control electricity sell it to the rest of us'" (278). Yet the student replies that he sees nothing wrong with corporations owning and controlling the natural elements. As in "The Amnesia Machine," where the narrator loses the ability to reflect critically and is powerless to interpret his own dreams, Kingston's story implies the problem of people not being able to orient themselves in critical relation to the ideological totality of corporate capitalism. The students who are poor and marginalized as racialized minorities cannot imagine their "real conditions of existence" as subjects whose abjection and alterity by capitalist structures function to enable modern society as a war economy (Jameson, *Postmodernism* 51). They can see only their existence as subjects abiding in the familiar and rationalized object-world of consumerism. The brother asks the student what poor people are supposed to do when they cannot afford to pay for utilities: "'Whoever discovered it deserves to be paid for it,' said the stubborn boy. 'It's Communist not to let him make all the money he can.' Although the students could not read or follow logic, they blocked him with their anti-Communism, which seemed to come naturally to them, without effort or study. He had thought it was self-evident that air, at least, belongs to all of us. The students' parents were on welfare, unemployment, and workmen's compensation, but they defended capitalism without knowing what it was called" (278). That the students "defended capitalism without knowing what it was called" reflects the way people exist in an everyday culture of forgetting, an existence in which they cannot cognitively map their position in a totality of modern capitalist relations. The inability to cognitively map one's orientation and position in "the world space of multinational capital," in Jameson's terms, betokens a crisis of imagination in which subjects are not able to grasp their position as "collective subjects and regain a capacity to act and struggle" (*Postmodernism* 54). In this sense, the inability of people to cognitively map a position and orient themselves in relation to the ideological totality of capitalism is a lot like their overlooking the past and disremembering history. As "The Amnesia Machine" illustrates, in ways that supplement our reading of the modern everyday in "The Brother in Vietnam," the ability of the imagination to contradict alienation and offer a credible vision for an alternative order is at stake when everyday life is structured by a homogenizing corporate-consumer culture. The imagination fosters deep remembering and critical awareness that enable people to revive and reconstruct the past and articulate an affiliative sense of belonging in, as well as emerging from, other people and places in history. But without the imagination it's not possible to conceive and construct the collective historical memory important not only to forming an identity that is constituted by critical awareness but also to positioning oneself associatively and *empathically* in the realm of a common humanity.

When the brother does enlist in the military, Kingston reflects whether there is any alternative to war and the capitalist system structuring a modern identity. To the brother, it is self-evident that being in the military and being a civilian are the same thing. They are both about existing as a subject who assimilates and conforms to the mechanization of an everyday life organized by corporate capitalist structures—a life in modernity that's become fully administered, managed, and machinelike, as Tan shows us.

When he joins the navy, the brother performs work that is mindnumbingly repetitive and emptied of any meaningful indicators that would differentiate one moment from the next. The work is, in other words, devoid of anything that would stir his imagination to make meaningful connections, distinctions, and differences. The brother complains: "They get us up at five-thirty before our brains can start functioning. . . . My brain feels like wet cement. I can't see. Here I'm getting up, and I didn't even go to sleep yet. I didn't even have any dreams. Sorry. No dreams to tell. . . . They're turning us into housewives. Make beds. Fold clothes. Shine shoes. Sweep. Swab. . . . Foot blisters. Bone bruises. Shin splints. Slave labor" (287). As the brother experiences it, the everyday routine of the military's segmented and delegated labor allows no criti-cal reflection—"No dreams to tell"—that would enable soldiers to connect and position themselves within a common humanity, because such con-nection and positioning contradict the purpose of vanquishing the enemy in war. When he's at work during the heaviest US bombing of Vietnam, "his job of flipping switches and connecting circuits and typing was the same as on land, the numbers and letters almost the same" (296). The dis-connected and alienated labor in the military's fully administered world mirrors the disconnection and alienation in an ordinary life of consumer-ism in America. The brother explains, "When we ate a candy bar, drank grape juice, bought bread . . . wrapped food in plastic, made a phone call, put money in the bank, cleaned the oven, washed with soap, turned on the electricity, refrigerated food, cooked it, ran a computer, drove a car, rode an airplane, sprayed with insecticide, we were supporting the cor-porations that made tanks and bombers, napalm, defoliants, and bombs" (284). The experience of war is indistinguishable from an everyday life of consumption in America because they constitute an interlinked system in a capitalist totality. And as Tan's "The Amnesia Machine" illustrates, our fully administered world has created an ever widening gap between people as consumers and a primal relation to the natural world. This is a con-sequence of the transnational corporate practices that Kingston exposes by showing us the very real connections between critical reflection (deep remembering) and modern identity (liberal personhood), specifically cor-porate consumerism and a patriarchal military industry.

Since America operates on a war economy, every commodity we pur-chase and consume allows corporations to reap profits used to make war weaponry. The brother further says: "Everything was connected to everything else and to war. The Peace Movement published names of board members of weapons factories; they were the same people who were bankers and university trustees and government officials. Lines connected them in one interlocking system. The Pacifists' boycott lists included so many ordinary things, we couldn't live day-to-day American lives with-out adding to the war" (284). As Ernest Mandel has argued, one of the hallmarks of corporate capitalism is the private accumulation of wealth through war weaponry and military expenditure. Following Mandel, we can see that Kingston's story critiques the commodification of violence by a military industry generating profit in a "permanent arms economy."[6] It links America's consumer economy to the validation of atrocity in warfare. The interlocking system of war and corporate capitalism that produces weapons for the military is fundamental to "feeling normal" by aspiring for a liberal personhood that has its basis in property ownership. "The Brother in Vietnam" portrays corporate capitalism as a totalizing system forcing people to accommodate atrocity and violence in war, rendering such violence an everyday condition of modern identity. America's history of exclusion and violence against immigrants, racialized minorities, and Native Americans informs both Kingston's and Tan's depictions of modern identity in a war economy, because Americans have rationalized warfare as fundamental not only to the capitalist system but also to the US national ethos of freedom and its attendant aspiration to achieve liberal personhood.

## *Suburbia*'s Specters and *China Men*'s Ghosts

If a primal recognition in feeling connection and belonging goes away in commodity reification, does it ever come back? If history and the imagination are denied by a culture of forgetting in corporate consumerism, where do they go?

As we've seen in "The Amnesia Machine," Tan portrays in his pictures of landscapes the effect of an alienating modern society that uses "strategic rationality and abstract steering mechanisms such as money" to transform the world increasingly in the grip of commodification (Jay 8–9). Growing up alienated in the outer suburbs of Perth, Tan represents this feeling in his illustrated emotions as landscapes. His visual conceit depicts the sense that history as a felt experience has been "lost" and that with it a primal connection to ancestral people and land has been forgotten in a modern world organized and structured under commodity reification.

If Tan's illustrations narrate the effect of commodity relations in capitalism to neutralize critical awareness and the ability to "imagine for ourselves," they simultaneously provoke us to realize and recover the "lost thing" that is history. To show how Tan recovers and revives this history, I turn to his book *The Lost Thing*, a luminous graphic novel about amnesia in everyday life. "*The Lost Thing*," Tan explains, "is a humorous story about a boy who discovers a bizarre-looking creature while out collecting bottle-tops at a beach. Having guessed that it is lost, he tries to find out who owns it or where it belongs, but *the problem is met with indifference by everyone else*, who barely notice its presence. Each is unhelpful in their own way; strangers, friends, parents are all unwilling to entertain this uninvited interruption to day-to-day life. In spite of his better judgement, the boy feels sorry for this hapless creature, and attempts to find out where it belongs" ("Comments on *The Lost Thing*") (see Figure 1.6). Tan's graphic novel is an allegory about historical amnesia, "where people have essentially lost their imagination, and every aspect of life is industrialized and departmentalized" (Tan, "Conversation" 45). This forgetting resonates meaningfully as an affect within *The Lost Thing*. "Suffusing it is an anxiety," Tan further explains, "that somehow finds apt expression in the phrase 'the lost thing': *a vague sense of forgetting something important*, losing the inspirations of childhood, or being worn down by the pressure of adult pragmatism and cynicism" ("Comments on *The Lost Thing*," italics added). This anxiety saturating Tan's story can be understood as an emotional quality that not only illustrates the process of reification but also may be seen as an affective "moment" expressing the rupturing of forgetting, a powerful experience of recognition and realization through an object, setting, or place that can transform the ordinary and the everyday into conditions of possibility for imagining an alternative or a different way of life. In the words of Henri Lefebvre, "'Moments' are those instances of intense experience in everyday life that provide an immanent critique of the everyday: they are moments of vivid sensations of disgust, of shock, of delight and so on, which although fleeting, provide a promise of the possibility of a different daily life, while at the same time puncturing the continuum of the present" (qtd. in Highmore 115–16). In Tan's story, we can see that the creature—the lost thing—illuminates an affective moment of becoming aware of everyday forgetting and indifference, a mindfulness of social fragmentation and apathy in modern capitalist societies. Personifying the vague sense of forgetting something important, the creature characterizes both the loss and the return of our primal recognition. This embodied return contradicts the commodity relations absorbing everyday life and denying the deep remembering of emerging from and belonging in the natural world, of connecting to histories of immigrant generations, diasporic ancestors, and indigenous people.

Through such affective moments—"vivid sensations" in everyday life that allegorize the disruption of forgetting history and a primal relation to the natural world—Tan's story mediates a critical awareness to uncover and recover Australia's past of racially excluding and discriminating against Aboriginal people and Asian immigrants. Using images of settings and places that are metaphors for emotions, *The Lost Thing* demonstrates through illustrated racial feelings experiences of placelessness,

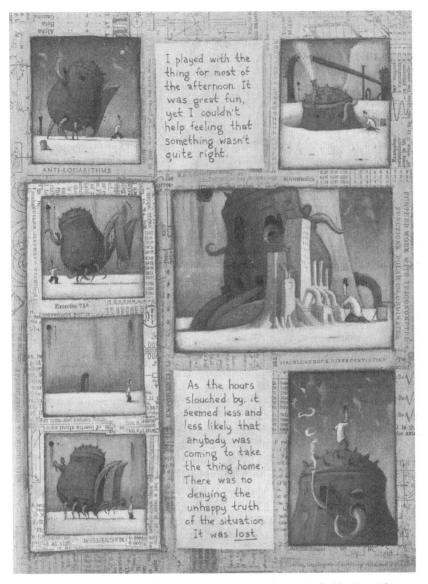

FIGURE 1.6. The anxiety of forgetting history in Shaun Tan's *The Lost Thing*. Copyright © by Shaun Tan 1999. (Reprinted by permission of Shaun Tan)

disconnection, and isolation, implying the problem of disremembering history as a transnational corporate practice. And its images of human indifference in modernity—of disaffection caused by economic processes of affective labor and emotional extraction in a corporate capitalist system—diagnose our current modern era as a totality in which people are alienated in rapidly manufactured environments, estranged from the natural world by suburbanization and urban renewal.

The history of early Asian migrants as Tan depicts it accordingly haunts the present. His pictures of landscapes as metaphors for affective moments and racial feelings imply remembering the past evocatively by conjuring the presence of racialized others who once inhabited rural lands before these were developed into suburbs. In this sense, we see how Tan's stories are a popular cultural form reviving memory through their graphic representation of a critical structure of feeling. We understand, in other words, that comics not only depict but actually *produce* affects as metaphors for feeling in historical memory. Further, if we conceptualize racial form as that which is produced and sustained by its representation and expression in Asian American literature, then comics art as a genre of this literature depicts Asian American racialization by referencing and revising an Asiatic racial form, historically developed from a distinctly US version of Orientalism that emerged alongside US imperialist incursions in Asia. This emotional production of racial form as memory through comics art recovers history not only as resistance to forgetting but as a contradiction to capitalist modernity and its everyday culture of forgetting.

Insofar as the hapless creature in Tan's story personifies our affective moments experienced as sensory contradictions to the everyday, it signifies the return of our primal recognition. In this manner, the lost thing connotes the reemergence of problematic histories overlooked and disremembered in modern societies—for instance, the history of Chinese immigrants in Australia who were excluded and discriminated against under the White Australia Policy. The Immigration Restriction Act of 1901 that enforced the White Australia Policy allowed whites to discriminate against the Chinese as well as to restrict their immigration.[7] This law was intended to reduce the numbers of Chinese immigrants who sought to enter the country for work and economic opportunities, and it succeeded. Australia's Chinese population declined from 29,900 in 1901 to 6,400 in 1947. For nearly seventy-five years, Australia enforced the Immigration Restriction Act under a racially divisive campaign of nation building. This policy encouraged mass European immigration to Australia to preserve a dominant white culture that many Australians with British ancestry believed to be "fragile" and endangered by Asians and other non-European immigrants (Fitzgerald 11). As John Lack and Jacqueline Templeton explain in their study of Australian immigration, "From Federation in 1901 Australians insistently proclaimed their British identity. Convinced of their vulnerability as a remote and lightly populated outpost of Empire in close proximity to Asia, and in dread of the rising power of Japan, Australians clung to the notion of a British Australia, legislated boldly to preserve their racial identity, and strengthened it with regular transfusions of British blood" (xiii). Australia's history as a nation begins with its origins as an outpost of British Empire established to populate the continent with white settlers who would colonize its lands, displace Aboriginal people, and exclude Asian immigrants. The preservation of Australia's nationalized racial identity as the "blood" and culture of Britain was to be secured by encouraging European immigration to maintain a white majority ruling over a nonwhite minority. Hence, European Australians would establish their cultural identity as British by maintaining a dominant white culture and restricting nonwhite immigration as well as containing and removing nonwhites from the land.

In the early twentieth century when Australia instituted its anti-Chinese laws, the United States had already legislated its own immigrant restrictions that targeted the Chinese. In a chapter called "The Laws" in the middle of *China Men*, Kingston provides a time line from 1868 to 1978 of the immigrant acts and Supreme Court decisions that restricted and regulated the numbers of Chinese in America and their possibilities of settlement. In 1882, writes Kingston, "the U.S. Congress passed the first Chinese Exclusion Act. It banned the entrance of Chinese laborers, both skilled and unskilled, for ten years. Anyone unqualified for citizenship could not come in—and by the terms of the Nationality Act of 1870, Chinese were not qualified for citizenship" (153). As Kingston shows in her listing of the exclusion acts, white Americans specifically targeted the Chinese as a group unqualified for citizenship on the basis of their perception of them as racial others. According to Mae Ngai, "The premises of exclusion—the alleged racial unassimilability of Chinese—powerfully influenced Americans' perceptions of Chinese Americans as permanent foreigners. Excluded from the polity and for the most part confined to Chinatown ghettoes and an ethnic economy, Chinese Americans remained marginalized from mainstream society well into the twentieth century" (202). The exclusion acts led to the passage of Alien Land Laws beginning in California in 1913. These laws prohibited land and home ownership by persons ineligible for citizenship. "Though the Chinese were filling and leveeing the San Joaquin Delta for thirteen cents a square yard, building the richest agricultural land in the world," Kingston further writes, "they were prohibited from owning land or real estate" (153).

To be sure, in passing the exclusion acts, the US courts relied on the notion of the Chinese as racially unassimilable to deny them citizenship and the rights of land ownership. Yet they attempted to render invisible the racial logic embedded in passing the exclusion acts so as to *obscure* the perception of America as a nation whose ideals and customs were white and European. Australia, however, did not try to hide the constitution of itself as a white nation. From the beginning of its immigration restriction acts, Australia sought to construct its sovereignty as a nation on the basis of the containment and removal of nonwhites to preserve its racial identity as European and white. To maintain the Australian nation as culturally British, the white majority instituted European ethnocentric practices that led to their own internal colonization. In psychoanalytic terms, we can understand this internal colonization as the white majority's attempt to preserve its "whiteness" by legislatively excluding and marginalizing Aboriginal people and the Chinese. Anti-Chinese laws make up Australia's problematic history that, in the first quarter of the twenty-first century during Australia's economic and social progress as a multicultural capitalist nation, is being forgotten. In this collective forgetting of legalized discrimination to preserve dominant white identity, Australia's past of anti-Chinese hostility is, to some extent, comparable to America's history of excluding and forcibly removing indigenous people and Chinese migrants on the basis of white supremacist ideals. And like the United States, Australia produced a liberal personhood for European settlers according to white supremacist cultural ideals—a self-possessing individualism premised on racially excluding and containing the Chinese and other nonwhite people.

By institutionalizing the preservation of white identity through legislative acts and discriminatory practices, European Australians sought to protect themselves from what they perceived to be a potentially hostile Asian way of life and the threat of contamination from racial others (London 5).[8] Yet as Eric Lott has explained, whiteness as a nationally instituted culture often entails psychological disorder (476). To maintain and preserve whiteness as a national culture is an undertaking constantly in danger of compromise. Amid its propagation of racial exclusion and marginalization, a white nationhood needs to have its "purity" affirmed continually, and done so by negation through segregating, marginalizing, and excluding racial others deemed threatening to the nation's whiteness. The preservation of whiteness as a dominant culture, Lott contends, "depend[s] on mastering the other at home—and in oneself: an internal colonization whose achievement is fragile at best and which is often exceeded or threatened by the gender and racial arrangements on which it depends" (476). For those of European descent at home in the Australian nation, internal colonization required not only being "one's own master" but also purging from oneself what was believed to be the racial and cultural contamination of the Chinese. Again in psychoanalytic terms, the historical purging of the Chinese through exclusion and forced removal becomes an unresolved mourning in the present, a condition of racial melancholia. The forgetting of this history—a history unassimilated in the nation's collective memory—haunts the nation's consumer-multicultural society. And it does so because the national ideals of progress and freedom, which are premised on the liberal capitalist logic of equivalence and exchange, cover over and disavow problematic history. As Anne Cheng contends, dominant white identity in America operates melancholically as an elaborate identity system that "appears in different guises. Both racist and white liberal discourses participate in this dynamic, albeit out of different motivations. The racists need to develop elaborate ideologies in order to accommodate their actions with official American ideals, while white liberals need to keep burying the racial others in order to memorialize them. . . . Both violent vilification and the indifference to vilification express, rather than invalidate, the melancholic dynamic" (11–12). Following Cheng, we further see that both Australia *and* America as progressive multicultural nations have become amnesiac about their pasts of excluding and containing those whom they've historically identified as racial others.

Yet as we have seen in the extracted images and symbols of US immigrant history in Tan's stories, these racial others come back to haunt the modern nation as ghostly figures of an Asiatic racial form: specters of racialization from the unassimilated history of anti-Chinese discrimination and violence. The stories reflect the forgotten restriction acts of the White Australia Policy that forcibly drove out the Chinese from the country's rural lands. These are lands that have been cleared away to create suburbs for a growing ethnically diverse and immigrant population. Today's development of suburbia into a diverse place where many Asian immigrants live, work, and make homes alongside whites is a primary way that Australia manages and commercializes multiculturalism. But through this topographic commodification, the historical presence of the Chinese and the traumas they suffered gets repressed as part of a shared amnesia among the residents living in these suburbs.

In his stories, Tan depicts suburbia as a strange place. In *Tales*, a site as mundane and banal as a bare lawn in a front yard is the location at which to commemorate ancestral heritage and the history of Asian migrants who were driven off the land because of racist violence and legalized anti-Chinese discrimination. According to Tan, suburbia is "a place of subconscious imaginings" where remembering history can happen as a haunting contradiction to stultifying routine in everyday life ("Comments on *Tales*"). In the story "Stick Figures," which Tan says represents the immediate environment of his own childhood in the sprawling northern suburbs of Perth, we see eerily quiet suburban streets, sidewalks, lawns, parking lots, and bus shelters (see Figure 1.7). Although suburbia is a place generating sensuous multiculturalism, it cannot ultimately contain history. As Tan shows us, suburbia is a natural location—a living environment—for imagining dead ancestors emerging from the earth as phantoms, wandering the land in search of home and belonging. Suburbia's specters hence defy the developed and commodified bush country that conceals these ancestors, rendering them forgotten.

However, the spectral presences haunting suburbia are not really ghosts in the conventional sense of being evil spirits. Rather, they are innocuous stick figures made of twigs and branches from native flora. In the story's first paragraph, Tan writes that the stick figures "are not a problem, [they are] just another part of the suburban landscape, their brittle legs moving as slowly as clouds. They have always been here, since before anyone remembers, since before the bush was cleared and all the houses were built" (65). As they appear in the story, the figures look familiar because they are from natural elements with limbs made of undergrowth and dead plants. But they come from a bush country that no longer exists, having been removed to transform the wilderness into new roads, homes, and shopping malls. The removal of the bush to develop Australia's suburbs, Tan implies, has created an amnesiac culture, making human inhabitants such as the two boys in "Our Expedition" alienated because they've become detached from a natural world that has always been there surrounding them. "Too often things seem to be built without a proper acknowledgment or empathy," says Tan. "It is simply swept aside as if it never existed, replaced by an amnesiac culture" ("Comments on *Tales*"). Such alienating detachment from the natural world makes it difficult for suburbanites to remember and feel connection to the indigenous people who also populated the bush country and were forcibly removed from it, along with the Chinese who lived and worked on these lands.

Yet suburbia's amnesiac culture produces its own racially melancholic contradiction. Insofar as the stick figures in Tan's story trouble

FIGURE 1.7. History haunts suburbia in
Shaun Tan's "Stick Figures," *Tales from
Outer Suburbia*. Copyright © by Shaun
Tan 2008. (Reprinted by permission of
Shaun Tan)

the suburbs—"standing by fences and driveways, in alleyways and parks,
silent sentinels" (65)—they are reminders of early Chinese migrants who
were attacked and driven from the land by race riots. Tan implies this history in his story.

> Some older boys take great delight in beating [the stick figures] with
> baseball bats, golf clubs, or whatever is at hand, including the vic-
> tim's own snapped off limbs. With careful aim a good strike will
> send the head—a faceless clod of earth—flying high into the air. The
> body remains passively upright until smashed to splinters between
> heels and asphalt. This can go on for hours, depending on how many
> the boys can find. But eventually, it stops being amusing. It becomes
> boring, somehow enraging, the way they just stand there and take it.
> What are they? Why are they here? What do they want? (66–67)

The dismemberment of the stick figures here conjures up images of white
mobs that pillaged Chinese encampments in the nineteenth century. The
mobs rampaged through the camps, maiming Chinese miners who fled
for their lives and hacking limbs from victims beaten unconscious. In the
Buckland Riot of 1857, white rioters attacked Chinese encampments in the

goldfields of Victoria, Australia. Shouting, "Come on and let us drive the long tailed devils off at once" (Hoban), the rioters robbed, beat, and drove out from their homes approximately two thousand Chinese miners. The rioters cut off the limbs of victims to remove jewelry from their corpses. Although crime police arrested thirteen men accused of injuring and murdering the Chinese miners, empaneled juries acquitted the accused men of their offenses (Willard 24–26). In the Lambing Flats riots of 1861, mobs of white men attacked Chinese workers and drove them from the gold mines and fields in the Burrangong region of New South Wales (Connolly 35). The mobs trampled through the Chinese encampment, hunting and knocking down the Chinese with the butt ends of their whips and scalping off the queues of those killed in the rampage. Some of the rioters displayed the queues as trophies on banners, waving the scalps to foment hatred and violence. They set fire to every tent in the camp, leaving it a heap of smoldering ruins after driving away all the Chinese.

In Tan's story, the boys' "delight" as they beat the figures "with baseball bats, golf clubs, or whatever is at hand, including the victim's own snapped off limbs," effectively references Australia's history of anti-Chinese antipathy. The story alludes, furthermore, to the banality of this racial hostility, whose perpetrators were acquitted of their crimes by juries that quickly made decisions without any critical judgment or stirring of conscience. The juries responded favorably to crowds who cheered to free the accused. They made decisions thoughtlessly because there were no laws to recognize the rights of the Chinese and protect them from harm. "But eventually, [the violence] stops being amusing," writes Tan. "It becomes boring, somehow enraging, the way they just stand there and take it." To the extent that living in outer suburbia means feeling cut off and alienated from any critical awareness of the past, such violence becomes banal, Tan suggests, because it is a consequence of dehumanizing alienation, born out of an inability to cognitively map one's historical location within a thoroughly commodified society.

Australia's problematic history of violence and struggle, however, refuses to be forgotten. In "Stick Figures," history comes back in its haunting of a contemporary place and time, an everyday modern society denying the historical memory of anti-Chinese racism, rendering it invisible. "Are they here for a reason?" the story's narrator asks about the stick figures. "It's impossible to know, but if you stop and stare at them for a long time, you can imagine that they too might be searching for answers, for some kind of meaning. It's as if they take all our questions and offer them straight back: Who are you? Why are you here? What do you want?" (69)

(see Figure 1.8). These questions the narrator imagines the figures asking us—people who live in modernity both today and in the future—are about why they have been overlooked and why their history has been rendered unmemorable. If the figures are metaphors for past crimes and injustices against the Chinese who once lived and worked on these lands, such questions thus echo what whites would have asked the Chinese with hostility to drive them out. In this regard, historical memory is, according to the story's ghostly metaphors for anti-Chinese racism and violence, like apparitions of historical materialism: specters of past and future histories that continually haunt the present (Derrida xix). Insofar as modern capitalist societies have, in their current neoliberal manifestations of affective labor, consigned to oblivion the memory and force that have historically produced an Asiatic racial form, race has been abstracted from history to befit "the spirit of neoliberalism," masking current modes of racial violence and exploitation (Melamed 1). Yet this history and this memory trouble the present as a racial *revenant*. The historical memory that informs race haunts the present as a testament not only "to a living past" but also "to a living future, for the *revenant* may already mark the promised return of the specter of living being" (Derrida 123).

In *China Men*, we might construe a "specter of living being" as the historical memory of Chinese men who were indentured laborers in Hawaii's sugar plantations and workers in the construction of America's transcontinental railroads in the nineteenth century. In the story "The Great Grandfather of the Sandalwood Mountains," Kingston describes being in Hawaii, where she "stood alongside the highway at the edge of the sugarcane and listened for the voices of the great grandfathers. . . . The winds blowing in the long leaves do not whisper words I hear. Yet the rows and fields, organized like conveyor belts, hide murdered and raped bodies; this is a dumping ground. Old Filipino men die in abandoned sheds" (88). For Kingston, the ghosts of ancestors are not visible in the sugarcane "to bend the eyes" (88). But the shift to first person here designates this landscape as the site of problematic history, a history refusing to be forgotten and, like suburbia's specters for Tan, coming back in its haunting of a contemporary place and time that denies being disremembered in modernity.

By telling us that the sugarcane is "organized like conveyor belts," Kingston implies that the commodification of Hawaii's natural environment has origins in the abstracted and alienated labor of Chinese men. Yet to people today who have become habituated to consuming vast amounts of processed sugar in their food and drink, these origins are not seen because of the mechanized production of commodities. Kingston's linking of the way modern society forgets problematic history to an implication of commodity fetishism is striking for its generative referencing and complexity. Her linking invokes Marx, who explained the commodity as "a very queer thing" because it appears "mysterious" to consumers who cannot perceive the physical labor of workers who produced it (*Capital* 47). The mechanization of food, in particular, conceals a powerful moral and social cost because it denies both goods and people their place, their history. Hence the historical alienation of the Chinese immigrant laborers who worked the cane fields is imperceptible to modern society's eyes.

As Kingston implies, the abstracted and racialized labor of Chinese men in the past transmutes into the alienation of consumerism in the present. Consumers who are habituated to an everyday consumption of processed sugar are estranged from the fact that they are, in effect, ingesting a past of violence and struggle that is part of the collective history of Asian Americans. That this landscape has been transformed into a killing field—a "dumping ground" for concealing "murdered and raped bodies"— indicates a further linking to the brother's story about the interlocking system of war, mechanization, and consumer capitalism—an interlocking system that sublates the imagination important to positioning oneself within a realm of common humanity. By her shift to first-person narration, then, Kingston directly tells us that we, in modernity, commodify and consume acts of violence and atrocity that not only happened long ago but take place now. She tells us to imagine her own experience of listening to the voices of ancestors in the cane fields as a provocation to uncover and recover the historical memory important to the history of Asian Americans, "for whom," again in the words of Pierre Nora, "rehabilitating their past is part and parcel of reaffirming their identity."

Kingston has explained that her stories "come out of the land. You have to listen to the land with your imagination to hear them. The imagination can take you to the place where you will find the history that is really there" (Kingston, lecture). The imagination is in the natural elements, in the landscapes where history has taken place, where the pasts of ancestors can be found, their presence felt, and where the "lost thing" that is historical memory may be recovered. Kingston's emphasis on the power of the imagination to enable and animate the return of historical memory suggests a way to revive the primal recognition in feeling connection and belonging. This primal recognition, I suggest, is important to an empathic sense of connection and belonging in collective humanity. It is, moreover, important to projects of justice and fairness for a common humanity not only in the present but in the living future. Again, Derrida's extraordinary

FIGURE 1.8. Suburbia's specters query their being forgotten in "Stick Figures," *Tales from Outer Suburbia.* Copyright © by Shaun Tan 2008. (Reprinted by permission of Shaun Tan)

account of our responsibility to pursue justice for those "beyond the living present in general" bears repeating; the history of class struggle and conflict is "always still to come and is distinguished, like democracy itself, from every living present understood as plenitude of a presence-to-itself, as totality of a presence effectively identical to itself. . . . A ghost never dies, it remains always to come and to come-back" (123). In this sense, the specters of historical materialism that Tan implies in "Stick Figures" inspire us to imagine them in *China Men* as ghosts of Asian immigrant ancestors who hold the present accountable not only for the future remembering of their own histories but also for future projects of justice and fairness.

If anxiety is an affect of "forgetting something important" suffusing *The Lost Thing*'s story about the way people both forget history in everyday modernity and yet experience an affective moment as a rupturing contradiction to forgetting, then for Kingston in *China Men* this affect is evident in the narrative's abstracted moments of Chinese immigrant history. These moments articulate the recovery and reconstruction of collective

Asian American history. Moreover, in their indication of early Chinese migrant workers—"China Men"—who protested their unjust and unfair treatment under harsh labor conditions, these moments express poignant contradiction to the racial exploitation and containment these workers experienced. These affects—a critical structure of feeling—in Kingston's memoir document Asian American racialization because they reference significant events in the US history of Chinese immigrant experience.

The story of Bak Goong, the Great Grandfather of the Sandalwood Mountains, is Kingston's depiction of another important moment in America's history of Asian immigration: the experience of Chinese men in the mid- to late nineteenth century who endured oppression and alienation while working as racialized laborers in Hawaii. The Great Grandfather's story is Kingston's abstraction of a significant but unrecognized history of Chinese migrant workers, whose exploitation as coolies and indentured servants enabled a modern racialized division of labor that was indispensable to the construction and definition of liberal ideals and concepts such as freedom and the pursuit of happiness in modern Western societies (Lowe, "Intimacies" 192). Because the story is an abstracted part of the American history of early Chinese migrants in *China Men*'s imaginary and elliptical narrative, it invites reading and interpreting Bak Goong's experience in comparative relation with the genealogy of Chinese workers in the global historical contexts of their exploitation as coolies and indentured servants.

The story alludes to a history of Chinese migrants who resisted their exploitation as workers in its characterization of Bak Goong as a chronic talker. After spending three months at sea onboard a ship with other Chinese passengers, who were "locked belowdeck though they were not planning to escape," Bak Goong arrives in Hawaii to take his job in a sugar plantation. Other workers who arrived earlier "said that the plantation had a rule that they not talk at work, but this rule was so absurd, he thought he must have misheard tones" (99–100). The monotony of Bak Goong's work to clear land for the plantation while obeying the rule of silence angers him, provoking him to complain incessantly: "He worked for that day and the next and the next without saying anything, but got angry, chopping as if cutting arms and legs. . . . 'You go out on the road to find adventure,' he wanted to say, 'and what do you find but another farm where the same things happen day after day. Work. Work. Work. Eat. Eat. Eat. Shit and piss. Sleep. Work. Work'" (100). Bak Goong's anger is a vehement moment in the story that contradicts his alienation and critically evaluates the orderly repetitions of the everyday. His complaints and utterances express his sense of self-worth against white "demon" plantation owners and overseers who considered the Chinese to be naturally servile and obedient. "He withstood the hours; he did the work well, but the rule of silence wrought him up whenever a demon rode by. He wanted to talk about how he sawed through trunks and the interlocked branches held the trees upright. He suddenly had all kinds of things to say" (100). When he starts to sing while working, the white overseers, Bak Goong ponders, "must have thought he was singing a traditional song when he was really commenting and planning" (101).

In conjunction with another moment when Bak Goong considers the plantation as "some kind of a slave labor camp" because his long overdue payment "came out short" (102), the story's characterization of his singing invites comparison with enslaved Africans in America, who sang while working on plantations to protest their abjection and to articulate powerful emotions that registered their humanity against their bondage (C. Yang 75). In his autobiography, Frederick Douglass recorded how slaves "would make the dense old woods, for miles around, reverberate with their wild songs, revealing at once the highest joy and the deepest sadness. . . . The thought that came up, came out—if not in the word, in the sound—and as frequently in the one as in the other. They would sometimes sing the most pathetic sentiment in the most rapturous tone, and the most rapturous sentiment in the most pathetic tone" (262). As sentiment protesting his subjugation under racialized plantation labor, a slavelike structure of domination, Bak Goong's talking and singing position him comparatively in the historical contexts of slavery. But as he sings and talks, he suddenly hears "a bang or crack next to his ear": "The demon was recoiling his whip. 'Shut up, Paké.' He heard distinct syllables out of the white demon's moving mouth. 'Shut up. Go work. Chinaman, go work. You stay go work. Shut up.' He caught every word, which surprised him so much, he forgot to grab the whip. He labored on, muttering, 'Shut up. Shut up, you.' He found a cut on his shoulder" (101). Bak Goong's resistance through talking and the violence he suffers from the white overseer form an abstracted moment in early Asian American history that indicates the constitution of America's transnational capitalist system through racial exploitation and containment. In stories such as Bak Goong's in Hawaii and the younger brother's in Vietnam, we see Kingston's depiction of violence against her ancestors to represent the modernization of America as a global process enabled by racialized divisions of labor that were maintained through violence and subjugation.

In *China Men*'s "The Grandfather of the Sierra Nevada Mountains," the story of Ah Goong references America as a country that became modern through the alienation of Chinese migrants whose labor in railroad construction was racialized by violence. The Central Pacific Railroad hires Ah Goong "on sight," believing that "chinamen had a natural talent for explosions" (128). The railroads and mining companies considered the Chinese to be expendable and delegated them to do the dynamiting and exploding. Helping to blast through mountains for the railroads, Ah Goong witnesses the injury and death of fellow Chinese as an everyday occurrence. "Nitroglycerine exploded when it was jounced on a horse or dropped. A man who fell with it in his pockets blew himself up into red pieces. . . . Human bodies skipped through the air like puppets and made Ah Goong laugh crazily as if the arms and legs would come together again" (136). Kingston's gory depiction of Chinese men's bodies blasted into pieces and raining down is a disturbing yet passionate moment in her portrayal of those Chinese workers who died by the hundreds when constructing the First Transcontinental Railroad. The physical and mental violence these men suffered stays indelibly etched in the natural environment like the "smell of burned flesh remain[ing] in the rocks" (136). Kingston limns the landscapes of her narrative with the blood of Chinese men to reflect their exploited working bodies as racialized violence that was "indispensable labor" in the making of modern America (140).

Just as suburbia in Tan's story is a place where specters of Chinese migrants emerge from the earth to contradict their being forgotten, the railroad in the story of Ah Goong sends forth ghosts of Chinese workingmen who died while on the job, faceless and placeless by the racialized abstraction of their labor and the alienation of their bodies. Kingston writes:

> Spring did come, and when the snow melted, it revealed the past year, what had happened, what they had done, where they had worked, the lost tools, the thawing bodies, some standing with tools in hand, the bright rails. "Remember Uncle Long Winded Leong?" "Remember Strong Back Wong?" "Remember Lee Brother?" "And Fong Uncle?" They lost count of the number dead; there is no record of how many died building the railroad. Or maybe it was demons doing the counting and chinamen not worth counting. Whether it was good luck or bad luck, the dead were buried or cairned next to the last section of track they had worked on. "May his ghost not have to toil," they said over graves. . . . "Maybe his ghost will ride the train home." (138)

As Tan's stick figures remind Australia's suburban inhabitants of the early Chinese migrants who were attacked and driven from the bush by race riots, Kingston's specters prompt us to realize America's melancholic history of violence against Asian migrants. The ghosts of dead China Men contest the white railroad officials who considered the lives of Chinese workingmen expendable—"demons" carelessly "doing the counting" of killed Chinese, callously deciding their bodies "not worth counting." These ghosts remind us of the central place the Chinese occupied in racialized divisions of labor that allowed America to become an industrialized nation in a transnational context with the exploitation of globally migrant workers. For Tan and Kingston, then, histories of racial violence emerge as ethereal contradictions in liberal capitalist societies that formerly sought to preserve and maintain whiteness as a national culture. And the covering over, disavowal, and forgetting of anti-Asian hostility for the sake of affirming Western modernity's progress worldwide is clearly a condition of racial melancholia.

In this imaginative way of the raconteur to influence our mode of thinking about the past, Kingston depicts Asian American racialization as a mnemonic development—a process arising from America's problem of misrecognizing its history of anti-Chinese exclusion and violence. That is, racialization is brought into being as an abstracted and reified form in Kingston's obfuscated referencing of America's white racial state. Her China Men's ghosts signify the melancholic condition of US liberal individualism and the whiteness upon which this individualism is historically premised. As *revenants* of unfinished mourning, they register liberal democratic concepts of freedom and the pursuit of happiness to be both haunted and enabled by our disremembering the Driving Out of Chinese migrants and other acts of racial violence in the nineteenth century.

Traditionally, violence has functioned in US liberal democracy to distinguish the citizen from racialized others who are perceived to be too different and foreign to assimilate into dominant white culture. In America's history of racialized migrant labor, Euro-American workers and their families in the West and throughout the Pacific Coast region used violence against the Chinese to assert their own inclusion and belonging in America both as citizens and as normative persons. The many instances of race riots against the Chinese demonstrate this violence as an avowal of inclusion and exclusion, freedom and containment, equality and disparity for whites and Asians respectively. As I noted earlier, the yellow peril fears that structured the racialized perception of Asians as threats to white producer economies and working-class identity provoked white Americans to riot against the Chinese. Anti-Chinese exclusion and discriminatory cultural practices legislatively endorsed by the government encouraged white mobs to storm Chinese settlements and encampments. The mobs burned Chinese homes and looted shops to drive out the Chinese from lands that whites claimed as their territory and private property. They lynched and scalped those Chinese who remained, branded their corpses with hot irons, and cut off body parts. Kingston references the Driving Out in her depiction of Ah Goong after he completes work on the railroad.

> He was lucky not to be in Colorado when the Denver demons burned all chinaman homes and businesses, nor in Rock Springs, Wyoming, where the miner demons killed twenty-eight or fifty chinamen. The Rock Springs Massacre began in a large coal mine. . . . The outnumbered chinamen were shot in the back as they ran to Chinatown, which the demons burned. They forced chinamen out into the open and shot them; demon women and children threw the wounded back in the flames. . . . The hunt went on for a month before federal troops came. The count of the dead was inexact because bodies were mutilated and pieces scattered all over the Wyoming Territory. (148)

To be sure, the bodies of the Chinese who were "mutilated and pieces scattered all over" reflects the violent extremes of white racial fear. Yet such violent extremes of anti-Chinese sentiment are also evident in the racialized segmentation and abstraction of labor that dehumanized Chinese workingmen. And insofar as this violent division and alienation of Chinese labor in the past invokes today's habituation among Americans to commodify and ingest violence, it indexes racial fear as a historical force centrally operating in the constitution and maintenance of American personhood: the basis of this personhood on the white citizen's claiming land as private property (territorialization) in the nineteenth century.

## "Cheap John Chinaman" and "Chinaman's Chance": Transnational Anti-Asian Discourse

Kingston's story of her grandfather reflects another important event in the early period of Asian American history with its depiction of Ah Goong joining the Chinese workers' strike for fair wages. In June of 1867 thousands of Chinese workers who were engaged in tunnel work in the High Sierra went on strike. "Demanding wages of forty-five dollars a month and an eight-hour day, 5,000 laborers walked out 'as one man'" (Takaki 86). In her story, Kingston describes the Chinese workers making their demands in one collective voice as "China Men": "All the while the English speaking China Men, who were being advised by the shrewdest bargainers, were at the demons' headquarters repeating the demand: 'Eight hours a day good for white man, all the same good for China Man.' . . . 'Cheap John Chinaman,' said the demons, many of whom had red hair. The China Men scowled out of the corners of their eyes" (141). In this passage, Kingston describes the Chinese workers referring to themselves in the two-worded inclusive plural *China Men* against white coworkers who repeatedly refer to them with the single-word term *Chinaman.* Like Bak Goong's talking and singing, the Chinese workingmen's declaration of themselves as "China Men" articulates identity and agency against white racialized perceptions of the Chinese as naturally servile and obedient. Their assertion as "China Men" voices their protest against being infantilized as if by striking they were behaving like disobedient children. It expresses, furthermore, their resistance to the derogatory term *chinaman*—a racial epithet commonly uttered by whites to insult the Chinese.

When Kingston breaks her story's third-person narration to describe the moment when she stood by the cane field listening for the voices of ancestors, she mentions remembering her own experience with the *chinaman* epithet: "I had only encountered that slurred-together word in taunts when walking past racists. (They would be the ones loafing on a fence, and they said the chinaman was sitting on a fence '. . . trying to make a dollar out of fifty cents')" (88). This anti-Chinese rhyming taunt brings to mind anti-Asian sentiments in the nostalgic popular songs and poems that were performed and shared among whites in nineteenth-century California. These songs and poems made up an emotional popular culture that represented a racial form of white identity that operated melancholically. This identity's ideals of prosperity, freedom, and individualism were to be secured by racially interpellating the Chinese as obstructions to the pursuit of happiness for whites in California.

Kingston's description of "chinaman" as a "slurred-together word" also calls to mind the historical and social contexts of the phrase "Cheap John Chinaman." The phrase refers to Chinese men in the nineteenth century who were building the transcontinental railroad and went on strike to demand payment equal to that of whites. Yet the phrase also interpellates the Chinese as different and inferior in their labor and in their cultural and ethnic identity as people from China. In mentioning that she encountered the phrase in "taunts when walking past racists," Kingston emphasizes the performative force of bigoted language to construct a person of Asian descent as alien and inferior by negation. In her argument that gender is a social construct performed and regulated by "utterances," Judith Butler contends that bigoted language is the "forcible citation of a norm" imposed on those perceived by a dominant majority to be different and contradictory to the norm (231–32). When Kingston remembers encountering "racists" who uttered the taunt "chinaman . . . sitting on a fence trying to make a dollar out of fifty cents," she indicates its linkage to a history of anti-Chinese racism and exclusion. Bigoted language attempts to negate, exclude, and abject a subject by the force of interpellation. "The interpellation *echoes past* interpellations," Butler explains, "and binds the speakers, as if they spoke in unison across time" (226, italics added). The racists whom Kingston encountered uttered anti-Chinese insults to assert their own inclusion within a dominant majority. They avowed themselves as conforming to a norm and a prototype linking them to a dominant white majority of the past. Since *chinaman* is, Kingston implies, an anti-Chinese taunt expressing anti-Chinese taunts from the past, it has the interpellative force of racially abjecting Asian Americans in the present by linking them to the history of anti-Chinese abjection in the nineteenth century. The phrase carries the weight of the past when white Californians in the 1850s defined and maintained white identity as normative by excluding and containing the Chinese. The taunt reverberates past anti-Asian antipathy, echoing and reflecting other anti-Chinese insults and variations of the *chinaman* slur—for instance, the commonly known idiomatic expression *Chinaman's chance*.

Although Kingston doesn't specifically mention *Chinaman's chance*, it is clearly invoked in her memoir as another abstracted moment from the early period of Asian American history. In this regard, the invocation of *Chinaman's chance* here raises questions. What does this anti-Chinese expression further signify in the context of Asian American racialization? Where does this phrase putatively originate? Does it have anything in common with other anti-Asian racial feelings such as yellow peril fears?

When white men in California in the nineteenth century wanted to mock the futility of another man's attempt to accomplish something difficult, they would say: "Not a Chinaman's chance!" (Ambrose 150). The historical circumstances of this phrase and the discriminatory laws that actualized it have been well documented. In the American West, the phrase reputedly originated during the years when Chinese migrants worked in the California gold mines (1848–55) and risked their lives to build the First Transcontinental Railroad (1863–69) (Ambrose 150–53).

In this historical context of racialized labor, the phrase *Chinaman's chance* underscores the widespread anti-Asian sentiment among white workingmen in the American West during the nineteenth century. Laboring as itinerant workers, Chinese migrants were routinely attacked by white men who felt they had free rein to brutalize and rob them because no laws protected the Chinese from maltreatment and injury. On the contrary, the United States at this time passed discriminatory laws that singled out the Chinese for exclusion and containment.[9] As Kingston suggests in her chapter "The Laws," America's history of immigration exclusion acts, legalized discriminatory practices, and Supreme Court decisions that regulated and curtailed the possibilities of Asian American settlement and cultural expression were structured by popular anti-Asian discourse. Exclusion acts forcibly removed the Chinese from the lands on which they worked and the towns where they made their homes. Because of legalized discrimination, Chinese immigrants were denied civil and political rights and even recognition as fellow human beings. The legislated denial of rights and recognition for the Chinese effectively confirmed a racial climate so hostile to them that it became customary among white Americans to assume for over a century that Chinese immigrants were logically disqualified from getting justice for harm done to them on the basis of their race.[10] The discriminatory laws assured a cultural logic of US citizenship to be premised on white privilege and the exclusion of Chinese immigrants from the right to equality and protection.

Other accounts of *Chinaman's chance* report that this pejorative expression originated with white Australians who immigrated to California just after the discovery of gold in the early nineteenth century. In his 1965 article on the cultural origins of *Chinaman's chance*, the folk-etymologist Peter Tamony wrote that the phrase "has its base in British boxing usage. . . . In florid accounts of prizefights a hundred and fifty years ago, this figure of speech became an allusion to the non-chance a fighter could expect under the heavy blows of a rough-and-tumble opponent. Current American analogues are *glass jaw*, *crockery chin*, and *china chin*" (203, original italics). English pugilists, according to Tamony, used the phrase as an insult to suggest the ease with which a boxing opponent could be defeated by hitting and breaking his face into bits as if it were delicate chinaware (203). The English brought the phrase with them to Australia, to which they came both as immigrants and as convicts who were transported to various penal colonies by the British government. Australian professional boxers picked up the phrase from the British and brought it with them to California, where they competed in boxing matches in San Francisco. The phrase then found its way in the mouths of white American men who worked in the mines and fields throughout the West. In adopting the expression to disparage the futility of another man's attempt to accomplish a difficult task, white men referred to the perceived worthless and expendable lives of the Chinese who worked alongside them.

Following Tamony's account, *Chinaman's chance* is transnational in both its development and its persistence because it made its way across three continents during the nineteenth century. Its migratory passage from Europe to Australia and to North America suggests the cross-cultural exchange of discriminatory practices against the Chinese on a global scale. In this transnational historical context, *Chinaman's chance* is a metaphor for the onerous hardships borne by the Chinese in both Australia and the United States at roughly the same time. Originating in the nineteenth century and enduring in the present, the phrase articulates how greatly Chinese immigrants suffered from the discriminatory laws and practices perpetrated by whites in both countries.

These laws and practices of anti-Chinese bigotry instantiated the historical alienation and dehumanization of Asians within the United States, a nation whose long history of racial strife and violence has engendered prevailing stereotypes about Asians as perpetual foreigners and unassimilable aliens. Yet violence against Asians in the United States and abroad in the countries, territories, and continents of the Pacific where America has been involved because of its interests in imperial and colonial powers, capitalist expansion, and war has historically produced and characterized the *transnational* American body politic. The reputed Australian origins of *Chinaman's chance*, like *yellow peril*'s purported origins in Europe, reflect the way anti-Asian discourse and racial sentiment have shaped Asian American history as a global development. In this sense, Asian America as a racial formation, shaped by exclusion acts and discriminatory practices, has been constituted and set in motion by economic and political forces that have traversed national borders.

We can, therefore, conceptualize Asian America's racial formation as transnationally conditioned by anti-Asian sentiment and discourse from Europe (*yellow peril*) and Australia (*Chinaman's chance*). This allows us to rethink an Asian American text such as *China Men* as a cultural work that articulates a critical structure of feeling to deflect and redirect a set of racialized discourses and tropes that have constructed an Asiatic racial form. These are discourses and tropes shaped by anti-Asian cultural practices from other countries and continents. For instance, by titling her book *China Men* and referencing the intercontinental utterance of the pejorative expression *chinaman*, Kingston offers a way to construe Asian American racialization as a transnational process. In this regard, and in a comparative reading with Tan's referencing of anti-Chinese discourse in his stories, we can rethink her narrative in a global frame.

Memoir and autobiography are cultural productions of Asian Americans that represent the racial identity category of "Asian American" as it has emerged from the protest movements and activist struggles of the 1960s to the 1990s. As themselves ongoing formations, Asian American criticism and literature update and remake aspects of Asian American racialization in the continuing and changing contexts of global economic forces that drive the diasporic migrations of Asian people. The conceptualization of Asian American literature as both a historical document and a theory of racialization has been forcefully argued in Asian American literary criticism. My objective here is not to rehearse these arguments but to reference them to suggest that Asian American literature may be understood to articulate racialization as a transnational process. This literature characterizes an Asiatic racial form, in Lye's terms, that emerged from and is continually updated by the affectively charged perception of Asians as figures of economic opportunity and threat.

Asian American literature's documentation of the exclusion and containment of Asian immigrants not only shows this history as the product of global economic forces but also suggests how these material forces make their way across national borders to produce the history and formation of Asians as racial subjects beyond North America. By documenting this history of transnational racialization, Asian American literature depicts "race" as a geopolitical construction and, in this representational manner, creates a transnational racial form for Asian Americans. As cultural works whose provenance is transnational, then, Asian American literature may be understood to narrate and produce comparatively the history and racialization of Asians outside North America.

In this transnational context, moreover, we can understand that a historical memory narrative such as *China Men* represents Chinese immigrants in the collective history of Asian American racial formation beyond the United States. If the history of Asian American racial formation in *China Men* is shaped and determined in part by discriminatory laws and practices from societies *outside* North America, Kingston's narrative may be read, in turn, to reflect a history of Chinese immigrant experience and the emergence of an Asiatic racial form in other "foreign" countries that implemented similar discriminatory laws and practices to exclude and contain Asians within their territories. These are anti-Chinese legislative acts and cultural practices such as those in Australia under the White Australia Policy, which resemble the discriminatory acts and white supremacist ideologies that targeted the Chinese in the United States from the 1840s to the mid-twentieth century. By this transnational process of racialization in Western modernity, Australia's past of excluding and containing Chinese immigrants as Tan represents it in his work may be compared with America's exclusion and containment of the Chinese by referencing this history in the stories that make up *China Men*. In this regard, I suggest that the memory of Chinese exclusion and containment figuratively shared between Tan in Australia and Kingston in America is discursive. We may construe this discursive relation between their works by realizing the transnational historical contexts of Asian American racialization and the representation of an Asiatic racial form in literature and cultural criticism.

In their host countries and adoptive homelands, Asians have encountered and endured similar discriminatory laws and cultural practices. The legislated exclusion and containment of Asians, especially in the way they have been perceived as yellow peril threats and impediments to modernization in European and Western discourses, are historical forces that have politically articulated and formed them as racialized minorities. This similar racialization of Asians through Western discourses of capital and economic exchange is especially striking in the United States and Australia: two countries whose discriminatory laws and cultural practices specifically targeted Asians for exclusion and containment on the basis of their racial difference from white citizens. As Lisa Lowe points out, the racialization of Asians, particularly as economic threats in Western historical contexts, emerges from a "dialectical struggle between, on the one hand, the racial state that serves the economy and facilitates its needs for

exploitable labor by racializing through the law and repressive appa-
ratuses, and, on the other, the social movements, collective projects,
and cultural practices that continually redefine racial meanings in
ways that seek to reorganize those racialized and gendered capitalist
relations" ("International" 79). Following Lowe, we can understand
the racialization of Asians in the Western world as a transnational
process emerging from the racial projects of Europe and America.
And keeping in mind Okihiro's examination of yellow perilism in
both Europe and America, we might see these racial projects also in
the context of Australia.

If the probable foreign origins of *yellow peril* and *Chinaman's chance*
allow us to conceptualize Asian American racialization as a process
structured by transnational racial sentiments, then we can position
*China Men* globally as a historical memory narrative that is, among
other things, about remembering, however obliquely, the racialized
labor of early Asian immigrants as well as the racialized containment
of their mobility and settlement. The expression *Chinaman's chance*
that Kingston implicitly invokes in her narrative is a focal point for
positioning *China Men* in a global frame, which we can do by reading
it comparatively with Tan's figurative depiction of anti-Chinese antipathy in an ideology of white nationhood—a problematic history—in his
graphic narratives.

If this focal point pivots on the fact that America and Australia
implemented similar discriminatory laws and cultural practices against
Asians and exchanged racialized perceptions of Asians as economic
threats for over a century (1840s to mid-1900s), then the global setting
in Kingston's referencing of anti-Asian discourse becomes apparent.
Following Tamony's account of *Chinaman's chance* as originating in
Australia, we have conceptualized this phrase as a discursive sign to
register the transnational racialization of Asians in the United States
and Australia. To the extent that white Australians purportedly brought
the expression with them to America when they arrived in California
in the nineteenth century, the etymological origins and migration of
it, as Kingston implies in *China Men*, may historically contextualize
the transnational process of capital and labor in Asian American racial
formation. If we understand the exclusion and containment of Chinese
immigrants in America during the nineteenth century as historical
context for Asian America's racial formation, it is important to realize the transnational effect of this racialization produced, in part, by
a cultural logic of exchanges of anti-Asian sentiment and other racial

feelings between the United States and Australia in their emergence as modern liberal capitalist societies.

Clearly anti-Asian sentiment has had a far-reaching emotional impact on racialized perceptions of Asians in the Western world. In this affective geohistorical manner, the racially discriminatory laws and cultural practices that excluded and contained Chinese immigrants in America are, I suggest, influenced by discriminatory practices against the Chinese in Australia. As the effects of globalized racial feelings, then, the economically based discriminatory laws and cultural practices that constructed Asian Americans as a race group are historically informed, in part, by the anti-Chinese sentiment of white Australians.

Kingston's account of the exclusion and containment of Chinese immigrants in America through her referencing of anti-Chinese discourse can thus be reimagined in a global frame to register a history of anti-Chinese antipathy in Australia. We can reimagine her referencing here as a transnational history by reading it comparatively with Tan's graphic narratives and their haunting remembrance of anti-Chinese racism in Australia. In their mnemonic referencing of the past exclusion and containment of Chinese immigrants and the forgetting of this problematic history in Australia, Tan's narratives figuratively illustrate, we might also imagine, Asian American racialization because they contain abstracted images and signs of US immigrant history important to Asian America's racial formation. By way of memory's ability to arouse other memories that make up a collective Asian American history, Kingston's mnemonic representation of Chinese immigrants becomes globally contextualized when we envisage it to invoke the historical memory of early Chinese immigrants in Australia and throughout the Western world.

## Memory's Cosmopolitan Vision

Insofar as the racial form of Asian Americans is transnational because of the historical simultaneity of Asian immigrants' victimization by similar exclusion laws and discriminatory practices in Australia and America, this racial form is also *cosmopolitan* because its representation in *China Men* expresses a critical awareness of the past that is global, collective, and dynamic. If the history and memory giving rise to this racial form are transnational, such history and memory entail a cosmopolitan mode from which to mediate an Asian American racial form in other contexts outside America. In other words, it is through a cosmopolitan openness and inclusiveness of remembering that we understand the invocation of Chinese immigrant history in Tan's picture books through Kingston's work. Here an ethnic *and* a minority memory arises as an emergent response to transnational processes of an Asian American racial form.

This memory of racial form invokes cosmopolitanism as Susan Koshy conceptualizes it, imbricating the minority subject and cosmopolitanism with the objective to trespass and break through boundaries of culture, discipline, and nation. *Minority cosmopolitanism* refers to "translocal affiliations that are grounded in the experience of minority subjects and are marked by a critical awareness of the constraints of primary attachments such as family, religion, race, and nation and by an ethical or imaginative receptivity, orientation, or aspiration to an interconnected or shared world" ("Minority Cosmopolitanism" 594). In a similar attempt to recognize and engage with the generative possibilities of disregarding national borders and hierarchies of difference, Michael Rothberg offers the concept of "multidirectional memory" as a way "to draw attention to the dynamic transfers that take place between diverse places and times during the act of remembrance. Thinking in terms of multidirectional memory helps explain the spiraling interactions that characterize the politics of memory . . . and acknowledges how remembrance cuts across and binds together diverse spatial, temporal, and cultural sites" (11). Through Rothberg's multidirectional memory and Koshy's minority cosmopolitanism, remembering immigrant history as told through ethnic narrative can be understood to produce in part, as well as to emerge from, an Asian American racial form that is itself global in scope and provenance.

The Asian American as a racial form is represented and produced in ethnic literary works that are themselves influenced by the ever-shifting and boundary-defying forces of globalization. For example, the migratory contexts of *yellow peril* and *Chinaman's chance* and the Asiatic racial form these terms manifest implicitly inform themes of history and memory in works as seemingly disparate as Kingston's *China Men* and Tan's graphic narratives. In this border-transgressive context, the racial formation of Asian America is a result of globalization, represented by Kingston and Tan when we read their stories comparatively across the divides of nation, geography, and genre. By way of memory that is transnational and cosmopolitan in its multidirectionality, Kingston's remembrance of Chinese immigrants in *China Men* shapes our understanding of Tan's remembrance of early Chinese immigrants in his narratives. In this cosmopolitan and multidirectional remembering, therefore, the memory of early Chinese immigrants in the United States transfers to and links across national borders with the historical remembrance of Chinese immigrants in Australia.

We can imagine a cosmopolitan and multidirectional remembering in Tan's stories about suburbia. As in *The Arrival*, the story "Eric" in *Tales* evokes an empathic feeling in the historical memory of Asian international migration. In this story, a foreign exchange student comes to live with an Australian family in the suburbs. The student resembles a small fragile leaf, prefiguring the ghostly stick figures made of native vegetation that appear later in *Tales*. The family finds "it very difficult to pronounce [the student's] name correctly," so he tells them "to just call him 'Eric.'" A child in the family narrates the story, describing Eric's polite and inquisitive nature: "Eric was very curious and always had plenty of questions" (10) (see Figure 1.9). The child explains that he wants Eric to feel comfortable in his family's home and happy in his country. The family takes Eric on weekly excursions "to show our visitor the best places in the city and its surrounds" (12). After living with his host family for some time, Eric suddenly departs "early one morning, with little more than a wave and a polite good-bye" (14). Although Eric's unexpected departure leaves the family with an "uncomfortable feeling [that] hung in the air, like something unfinished, unresolved" (17), they are enchanted to discover a thank-you gift from Eric in their pantry: a garden that will thrive and delight them for years to come (see Figure 1.10). With its evocative images of an immigrant character whose curiosity and sincerity oblige the narrator to imagine "what it might be like for him here in our country" (10), "Eric" stirs the reader's imagination to recognize and recall the feeling of being a stranger in an unfamiliar place. Tan's story incites us to identify empathically with migrant people in the past, present, and future, making us recall our own travels to foreign places or unfamiliar locales, and experiencing the feeling of being surrounded by basic but imprecise notions of things, artifacts, objects.

Figuratively a *revenant* of past Asian migrants who were driven out of Australia by racial prejudice that purportedly made its way transnationally to North America, Eric as a racial specter offers a way to remember and imagine a history of Asian migrant experience and racialization anew. In his story, Tan thus engages with an ethics of cosmopolitanism (Koshy) and memory (Rothberg) by imbuing his images with the potential to push our imagination and animate the images with our own story line. In doing this, we articulate the migrant's attempt to grasp an unfamiliar language and a way of life in another country. Our imagination here might then encourage empathy for the migrant: an empathic feeling that, as Tan puts it, "plants the reader more firmly in the shoes of an immigrant character" ("Comments on *The Arrival*"), and imparts to us the migrant's subjective experience of becoming accustomed to and belonging in another country. We might also feel a sense of responsibility for the migrant by admitting him into our world and valuing the difference the migrant introduces into our own lives (Palumbo-Liu, *Deliverance* 14). Tan's visual metaphors for empathy and belonging—so loaded with the imagination's potential to interpret and configure migrant subjectivities—illustrate an ethics of cosmopolitanism and minority memory that affirms the humanity of others. His emotions as landscapes, in this graphic context, elaborate the transnationalism of Asian American racialization by making us feel and remember a history of Asian migration that happened long ago but that takes place now and in the future.

*China Men* also affirms the humanity of others. In her book's final story "On Listening," Kingston is at a party hearing one of the guests, a Filipino scholar, tell a story about the Chinese who purportedly arrived in the Philippines in March of 1603 to look for the Gold Mountain. Young Chinese American men at the party also listen to the scholar. But his story is full of gaps, fragments, and obfuscation, befitting *China Men*'s elliptical narrative and its mystified references to important events in Asian American history. Kingston writes:

> Because I didn't hear everything, I asked him to repeat the story and what he seemed to say again was "They found a gold needle in a mountain. They filled a basket with dirt to take with them back to China."
> "Do you mean the Filipinos tricked them?" I asked. "What were they doing in Spain?"
> "I'll write it down in a letter, and mail it to you," he said, and went on to something else.
> Good. Now I could watch the young men who listen. (308)

Kingston does not fully understand the scholar's story, and she does not tell us if he ever did write the story down and mail it to her. In this sense, an inconclusiveness of meaning in both the scholar's story and Kingston's narrative invites us to rethink progress, determinacy, and conclusion. As in Tan's art, this inconclusiveness enables us to imagine

FIGURE 1.9. A foreign exchange student in Shaun Tan's "Eric," *Tales from Outer Suburbia*. Copyright © by Shaun Tan 2008. (Reprinted by permission of Shaun Tan)

our own story line to shape the narrative's meanings anew. In effect, Kingston ends her book with a tone and gesture of generative openness that we can describe as a cosmopolitan vision: a receptivity to intercultural encounter and to the transformative possibilities of such encounters. This tone and gesture in "On Listening" demonstrates the way feeling in historical memory can be reimagined for an ethics of encounter that is about linkages across home and the world, between self and other. A cosmopolitan vision, as Kingston implies it, proposes a way to become critically aware of contradiction and to cognitively map a position and orientation within totality. If *cognitive mapping* refers to the "mental patterns people construct as a means of apprehending the world around them" (Roberts 141), then by reimagining Kingston's *China Men* with Tan's graphic narratives we might understand this comprehension to be realized through their articulations of cosmopolitanism. They do not give a complete excavation of the past or an evident redemption of Asian immigrant history. Instead, they *reflect*

FIGURE 1.10. An enchanting thank-you gift dispels uncomfortable feeling in "Eric," *Tales from Outer Suburbia*. Copyright © by Shaun Tan 2008. (Reprinted by permission of Shaun Tan)

the distortions and omissions of the Asian migrant's experience with living and working in global modernity's culture of forgetting, and its emotional productions of estrangement and disconnection. In their reflections of the migrant's experiences with alienation and placelessness, Kingston and Tan orient us in relation to an alternative totality that is about affiliation and mutual recognition. The feeling in historical memory of Asian international migration in their works enables us to envision a common and collective humanity, offering an empathic remembering to contradict disaffection and affirm worldly intimacy.

## 2 /  Happiness for Hire: The Anger of Carlos Bulosan as a Critique of Emotional Labor

Nineteenth-century anti-Asian sentiment powerfully modeled the racialization of Filipinos in twentieth-century America. As can be seen in the writings of Carlos Bulosan, capitalism's economics produced an Asiatic racial form that shaped racialized perceptions of early Filipino migrants on the US Pacific Coast. Yet these perceptions were paradoxical: white Americans perceived Filipinos through stereotypes about black men as hypersexual predators of white women. But whites also associated Filipinos with the Chinese, who were thought to have an unusual capacity for exploitable labor—for performing servile work that, in the eyes of whites, rendered Filipinos subservient and childlike.

In 1930, at age seventeen and roughly eleven years before he would achieve recognition as a great writer, poet, and activist, Carlos Bulosan left his native Philippines and migrated to America as a "noncitizen national" (Espiritu 47).[1] Bulosan left the Philippines as part of a migration wave of over 120,000 Filipinos who came to the United States and Hawaii during the 1920s and 1930s to work in fish canneries and agriculture. Traveling by ship, he landed in Seattle, Washington, where he immediately found himself in a desperate situation to find work at the beginning of America's worst economic crisis, the Great Depression. In his semiautobiographical *America Is in the Heart* (henceforth *America*), Bulosan recounts his life as a migrant laborer through the hardship and despair of his alter ego, Carlos. Arriving with big dreams to make a home in America but with only twenty cents in his pocket, Carlos is eager to get a job. He finds one in a fish cannery in Alaska. A hotel owner sells him for five dollars to a Filipino contractor who makes his living by tricking young migrants into working in factories as indentured laborers. Betrayed by compatriots in another country that is rife with racial hostility against Filipinos, Carlos begins a tough life of toil, strife, and alienation. "It was the beginning of my life in America," he says, "the beginning of a long flight that carried me down the years, fighting desperately to find peace in some corner of life" (101). Carlos's "long flight" to "find peace" amid constant fear and humiliation—negative emotions created by racial hostility and violence against Filipinos—articulates his struggle to accommodate America's contradictory perception of Filipinos both as servile workers and as threatening racial others.

This perceptual contradiction reflects the racialization of Filipinos by their subjection to the discriminatory laws and cultural practices of US imperialism that existed in immigration policy while the Philippines was under US colonial rule (1899–1946). As Mae Ngai explains, "Filipino migration lay bare the contradictions between the insular policy of benevolent assimilation and the immigration policy of Asiatic exclusion, which had fully matured by the 1920s, and domestic racism generally" (97).[2] When Filipinos arrived in the United States in relatively small numbers in the 1900s to early 1920s, Americans took little notice of them because their nation's project to colonize the Philippines had largely become forgotten "through the myth of historical accident and benevolence" (97). In the mid-1920s, however, Filipinos began arriving in the United States in much larger numbers, and Americans were forced "to confront their colonial subjects, the objects of their tutelage and uplift" (97). In direct confrontation with the bodily evidence of US colonial policy and practice in the Philippines, Americans started to perceive Filipinos as threatening others who were competing with white men for employment and for the erotic attentions of white women. A rising tide of anti-Filipino hostility thus emerged in the late 1920s as tens of thousands of Filipinos arrived in America looking to find work and make homes for themselves. Race riots throughout the Pacific Coast in which white mobs attacked, maimed, and killed Filipinos at dance halls and in labor camps were the most visible and infamous expressions of a pervasive anti-Filipino sentiment. This anti-Filipino feeling was wrought by the perception that Filipinos would be hired over whites because they were slavishly willing to be used as cheap labor, as well as the belief that Filipino men were hypersexual and that their relations with white women would cause race mixing and would undermine "the racially exclusive, presumptively [white] heterosexual, nuclear family" (106–7).

Yet this perception of Filipinos as "hyper" in their apparent enthusiasm for low-wage jobs and in their sexual desires for white women was fueled by long-standing anti-Asiatic politics and antiblack attitudes. The development of anti-Filipino feeling therefore began with "a tradition of anti-Oriental racism that was eighty years in the making" (109), and antiblack typecasting joined with anti-Asiatic politics to generate the anti-Filipino hostility that was pervasive along the Pacific Coast.

In his writings, Bulosan represents this anti-Filipino feeling as an emotional paradox that caused his alienation at work and, more pervasively, humiliated and estranged him throughout his life in America. His freedom to travel and make a home for himself in America was adversely affected by contradictory racialized perceptions. Such perceptions informed exclusionary laws that targeted Filipinos and sought to alienate them because of their purported resemblance to black men as sexually aggressive, on one hand, and their racial classification with the Chinese as docile laborers, on the other. In *America*, Carlos feels humiliation and estrangement each time he is subjected to anti-Filipino antipathy. In one telling scene, he and his brother, Macario, are hired to work as house servants for a wealthy white couple in Los Angeles. Carlos overhears the husband say to his wife: "You can hire these natives for almost nothing. . . . They are only too glad to work for white folks" (141). His wife responds that she will not have a Filipino in the house when their daughter is home because she believes that all Filipinos are "sex-crazy" (141). The racialized perception of Filipinos both as gladly servile and as sexually threatening has been well documented.[3] According to Allan Isaac, Filipino men who came to the United States in the early to mid-twentieth century found themselves stereotyped in a racial order that was perpetuated, in large part, by white perceptions of black men as "brutish and oversexed" and Asians as docile and asexual (126). The position of Filipinos in this racial order, Isaac explains, "oscillates between the two figures and takes on either or both characteristics, depending on the fears and desires of the [white American]" (126). Because of their vacillating location within this construction, Filipinos represented a particular racial anxiety for white Americans in their apprehension of an Asiatic racial form. Contradictory perceptions of East Asians both as exemplary agents of capitalist modernity (the model minority stereotype) and as dreadful figures of ruinous invasion (the yellow peril threat) are the historical consequence of the US identification of the Asiatic as the sign of globalization. "The antinomies of Asiatic racial form," Colleen Lye asserts, "reflect the pattern of a modernizing China and Japan changing places as US friend and enemy. At any given point in this history, their opposite status was necessary to the maintenance of US security" (*America's Asia* 10). However, as Isaac suggests in his argument that the oscillatory Filipino characterizes a racial form that is unlike other Asian racializations, whites' perception of Filipino men as at once subservient and predatory offers a twist in an emotionally charged Asiatic racial form. This is an Asian American racialization process that began in the early twentieth century and constructed Asians through capitalist and imperialist discourses both as economic exemplars and as threats in the US national imaginary.

Yet the racialization of Filipinos, because of their position as US colonial subjects in a racial order that associated them with stereotypes about black men as sexual predators and Asians as models of capitalist production, might be understood to constitute a particular racialized affect— anti-Filipino feeling—from a set of relations between emotions and race that construct, in part, an Asiatic racial form. As Sianne Ngai contends, African Americans have long been perceived by Euro-Americans as affectively volatile in a process of racial subjection that attributes a "kind of exaggerated emotional expressiveness" (94)—what Ngai calls "animatedness" (94)—to the bodies of African Americans. The depiction of black people as overly animated reinforces fears about stereotypically impulsive and subversive black bodies whose freedom of movement must be regulated, manipulated, and contained. American culture has since the nineteenth century represented and perpetuated the perception of African Americans as affectively excessive in ways that racialize their emotions and subjectivity through visual objectification. "Yet it is the cultural representation of the African-American," Ngai further explains, "that most visibly harnesses the affective qualities of liveliness, effusiveness, spontaneity, and zeal to a disturbing racial epistemology, and makes these variants of 'animatedness' function as bodily (hence self-evident) signs of the raced subject's naturalness or authenticity" (95).

While US culture has stereotyped African Americans with a high-spiritedness that is simultaneously naturalized and manipulable (e.g., the impetuous Topsy and the overly sentimental Uncle Tom in Harriet Beecher Stowe's *Uncle Tom's Cabin*), Asian Americans at the opposite end of this affectively charged racial spectrum have been typecast as emotionally unreadable and menacingly impassive (e.g., the sinister, affectless face of Fu Man Chu in Hollywood's film adaptations of the Sax Rohmer novels). To be sure, American perceptions of Asians as quietly compliant and industriously obedient have also perpetuated the racial stereotype of Asian Americans as model minorities. Yet for Filipinos at the time when Bulosan arrived in the United States, the racialized sexual stereotyping of Filipino men and fears of race mixing that were coupled with anxieties about Filipinos competing with whites for jobs largely reflect white American perceptions of Filipinos as exceedingly emotional. As Mae Ngai reports, "A social worker in southern California [in the 1930s] said: '[Filipinos are] very emotional. Women are their weakness. Filipinos are easy prey for women who can pick up any Filipino on the street. . . . Filipinos are too sentimental for words'" (113). Perceived to be too sexually exuberant in their bodily comportment and especially in their stereotyped desires for white women, and simultaneously wanted by whites for their readily exploitable labor, Filipinos accordingly found themselves caught in a racial arrangement with the overemotional and oversexed black subject on one end and the emotionally inscrutable and docile East Asian on the other.

To say that Filipinos were "caught" in a racial construction in which a primary condition of African American and Asian American racialization was their subjection to perceptions that characterized them as racially marked underscores two important points in Bulosan's writings, where we can discern how emotions shape a Filipino racial form. First, Bulosan documents a racially exploitative labor system that generated and used fear as an affective form of economic violence to abstract the labor of Filipinos and alienate their bodies. Particularly in *America*, Bulosan portrays the alienation of Filipinos as a primary historical force of their racialization. Second, and more implicitly, Bulosan documents numerous acts of violence against Filipino migrant workers by white men who sought to control and arrest their movement because they perceived Filipinos as threats. In his portrayal of this violence, Bulosan shows that the suppression and containment of Filipinos begin with white fears of Filipino expressiveness, both in their sexuality and in their labor, and that the most disturbing effect of this fear is violence to discipline and control Filipino bodies.[4] According to Bulosan, a Filipino racial form wrought by a violent set of relations between emotions (fear and anxiety) and race emerged from a racial order that the US capitalist system historically produced and maintained. In the early to mid-twentieth century, a capitalist emotional culture of possessive individualism generated racial feelings that upheld a discriminatory logic of equivalence and exchange—a white racial logic defining citizenship through an exclusionary system of property ownership and relations. A Filipino racial form that was created by perceptions of Filipinos both as readily exploitable for cheap labor and as sexually threatening was thus an affectively charged contradiction—an emotional paradox that Bulosan struggled to accommodate and document in his life as a migrant laborer.

In *America*, Bulosan takes great pains to expose the exploitative practices of the canning and agricultural industries that relied heavily on cheap Filipino labor. He describes, for instance, the cannery's hazardous conditions that frequently injured and maimed workers. "The lighting system was bad and dangerous to our eyes," explains Carlos, "and those of us who were working in the semi-darkness were severely affected by the strong ammonia from the machinery" (102). Despite these horrific conditions, Carlos and his fellow workers cannot complain or protest. They do their jobs with hushed restraint because they fear henchmen who "saw to it that every attempt at unionization was frustrated and the instigators of the idea punished" (101). Carlos's emotional control in submitting to the factory's environment of fear and intimidation is disturbingly evident when he witnesses a horrific accident while he is washing beheaded fish in water diluted with lye: "One afternoon a cutter above me, working in the poor light, slashed off his right arm with the cutting machine. It happened so swiftly he did not cry out. I saw his arm floating down the water among the fish heads" (102). That Carlos quietly observes the severed arm of his coworker drifting by as he does his job conveys an ironic tone of detachment characterizing the experience of alienation at work. His disturbing indifference here exemplifies the way labor for him becomes detached from any meaningful personal context. He sells his body for labor merely to survive and subsist. And though the accident's gruesome violence is clearly upsetting, more troubling is the fear and intimidation that have forced Carlos and other laborers into compliant silence. Compelled to work in oppressive and demeaning conditions, they become alienated from themselves and from each other.

In his writings, Bulosan describes his labor struggles as an experience of affective control and isolation, articulating the concepts of emotional labor and alienation in the workplace. The historian Moishe Postone explains that "alienation is the process of the objectification of abstract labor" (162). In capitalist production, the abstraction of labor that leads to alienation is the expenditure of work to create value, produced from the commodities the worker makes in the organization of labor. In the early to mid-twentieth century, alienation in the US workplace happened especially in the assembly lines of factories and in the fields of agricultural industry, where workers were regimented in a complicated manufacturing process broken down into its many segments. Assembly lines were developed as an apparatus for the objectification of abstract labor. Regimented labor produced conditions to objectify and alienate workers under technologies of control and surveillance that treated them as identical and interchangeable.

According to Arlie Hochschild in her classic study of the commercialization of human feeling, emotional labor is a regulatory condition in which a worker modifies her feelings in accordance with organizational or company display rules for affective expression while on the job (7).[5] In Marx's theory of alienation, people who are exploited laborers in manufacturing jobs become alienated when they are forced to comply with the requirement that they express only labor that gets abstracted for profit. When a worker is forced to modify his feelings while at work, he controls and contains his feelings as a by-product of his abstract labor. In this sense, emotional labor is the abstraction of labor that alienates the worker from the products of his own work and from human life. Emotional labor and alienation thus characterize industrial workers who become objectified in the capitalist production process, which estranges them from their own labor and from their fellow workers. Both concepts diagnose the worker's emotional self-manipulation as the necessary managing and feigning of feelings for opportunistic reasons.

I want to suggest that Bulosan's descriptions of alienation allow us a way to understand how racism and racialization were bound up with the last century's capitalist modes of production. By situating Bulosan's depictions of alienation within the conditions of regimented manual labor and Fordism, a twentieth-century corporate system of mechanized production, we can historicize emotional labor in the US capitalist system for an early period in Asian American literature. Asian American writings of this period are marked by the explicit use of racial categories to oppress predominantly Asian male immigrants and materialist depictions of the migrant worker's racialized objectification and alienation. Through close attention to materialist concerns in Bulosan's scrutiny of racial exploitation as a causal factor in alienated labor, we can see how racialization intersects the alienation of the worker's body and subjectivity. Moreover, his critique of alienation at work allows us a way to realize how Marxist critical theory can comprehend the racial and emotional character of capitalism and therefore come to grips with the dual process by which affective and economic relationships come to define and shape Asian American racialization.

For Bulosan, the struggle against racism overlaps with the worker's consciousness of objectification and simultaneous recognition of the suffering of others. His anger about alienation at work underscores how the labor abstraction of racialized minorities in America manifested a relationship between emotions and race—a relationship that US capitalism as a system of emotional reproduction causally underlies and continues to generate in an era of economic globalization. In this regard, Bulosan's anger not only critiques his alienation in consequence of labor exploitation but also articulates a critical structure of feeling in his writings. His concerns are to underscore through anger how the abstraction of his own labor required the objectification of Filipino bodies and the expropriation of their subjectivities because of their racialized minority status. In her classic essay "The Uses of Anger: Women Responding to Racism," Audre Lorde argued that anger is filled with information and energy that racially oppressed women can use as "a language" to respond to "racist attitudes, to the actions and presumptions that arise out of those attitudes" (*Sister* 124). Lorde further contends: "Anger is creative; it works to create a language with which to respond to that which one is against" (133). Following Lorde, we might understand Bulosan's anger as a critical language that reveals the dehumanizing exploitation of Filipinos toiling in the assembly lines of Alaska's canneries and in the fields of California's farms. Through his anger-infused critique of emotional labor and alienation, Bulosan articulates a powerful emotion as a discursive tool to make visible the injustice of racialized Filipino labor.

In one of his political essays, Bulosan explains how he began to write his stories, describing the "compelling force that propelled [him] from an obscure occupation to the rewarding writing of short stories" (*On Becoming Filipino* 109). "That *force* was anger," he reveals, "born of a rebellious dissatisfaction with everything around me" (109). Through his anger as a "compelling force," Bulosan depicts social processes by which human bodies and feelings become objectified in exploited and alienated labor. He describes the regulation and objectification of emotions in labor exploitation as features of racial trauma for Filipinos who worked in farm fields and canneries. This trauma, generated by a racially exploitative and discriminatory work environment, nearly destroys all hope of the American Dream for Bulosan. If the American Dream is, in its conventional sense, an emotionally charged capitalist idea that characterizes optimism for financial success and uplift, then its bitter contradiction is what Bulosan calls "American *reality*." In his essay "My Education," Bulosan shows how the American Dream turns into the nightmare of "American *reality*" in which fear overtakes the psyche of Filipino migrants who are forced to live hand to mouth in a racially hostile and predatory work environment. This fear that US capitalism generates to exploit and subjugate Filipino migrant workers produces, as one of its most nefarious consequences, their alienation, which Bulosan explains is the "feeling of not belonging" in America (125).

According to E. San Juan Jr., one way to understand how America is in the heart for Bulosan is to understand that the "treacherous, alienating, heartless metropolis" of America generates, as an affective contradiction, his anger important to his "self-becoming" (11). "America" in this context of emotion and race operates on and produces fear and anguish for Bulosan, provoking at first his humiliation and then his anger to *protest* his alienation and protect himself from harm. According to Philip Fisher, anger is useful for collective political expression and for communicating the realm of personal worth (193). Oppressed people have historically used their anger to seek justice through social protest and formal legal systems. Through his anger as both criticism and protest Bulosan deals with his suppression and subjugation in ways that affirm and preserve his self. To be sure, we can see how America is in the heart for Bulosan if it is understood that his anger negates his objectification and containment, as he writes about his rage while working under harsh and exploitative conditions. Yet anger is also a compelling force for his self-preservation, insofar as it nourishes his critical awareness and gives him the will to write.

By taking into account the critical function of anger for Bulosan, I argue that we come to understand the enduring relevance of his oeuvre to critique racial oppression through his depiction of the worker's containment and alienation in a process I call the *emotional labor of racialization*. By describing his struggles to manage emotional distress and suffering, Bulosan trenchantly critiques racial exploitation and inequality in the work environment within the historical contexts of regimented industrial labor, in which unskilled and semiskilled minority workers were segregated and alienated in their industrial jobs. Through his angry depictions of work exploitation, Bulosan articulates a materialist analysis of the emotions that foregrounds emotional objectification in racialization. His subjective experiences underscore how racialization is bound up with theoretical accounts of alienation at work and scrutinizes the emergence of a Filipino racial form.

In his essays from the prose collection *On Becoming Filipino*, Bulosan explains social processes by which human bodies and feelings become objectified in the alienation of labor. He contends that the regulation and modification of feelings are the psychologically injurious effects of capitalism's exploitation of workers to accumulate profit. In his essay "Freedom from Want," for example, Bulosan provides a stirring assessment of how the capitalist profit system—what he calls a "materialistic age" (133)—alienates the bodies of workers and deprives them of fundamental freedoms necessary for thinking critically and creatively:

> But we are not really free unless we use what we produce. So long as the fruit of our labor is denied us, so long will want manifest itself in a world of slaves. It is only when we have plenty to eat—plenty of everything—that we begin to understand what freedom means. To us, freedom is not an intangible thing. When we have enough to eat, then we are healthy enough to enjoy what we eat. Then we have the time and ability to read and think and discuss things. Then we are not merely living but also becoming a creative part of life. (131–32)

By pointing out that exploited workers are not allowed to use "what [they] produce" (i.e., "the fruit of our labor"), Bulosan posits that an oppressive structure such as the capitalist profit system outlaws material human needs in the abstraction of labor and in doing so limits affective needs essential to cultivating and preserving the self-worth of workers. As Rosemary Hennessy contends, capitalism's alienation and commodification of workers restricts their potential to develop their intellectual and creative capacities (210). "As a species," Hennessy explains, "humans have many capacities—for intellect, invention, communication; the capacity for sensation and affect and for affective social relations. . . . Affective needs are inseparable from the social component of most need satisfaction, then, but they also constitute human needs in themselves in the sense that all people deserve to have the conditions available that will allow them to exercise and develop their affective capacities" (210–11). As a vital human need, affective social relations allow people to achieve satisfaction and well-being when they experience fulfillment in their labor *and* when they feel that these relations are met while they are at work. Moreover, for workers to fulfill their affective capacities is, as Bulosan puts it, for them to realize their conditions of possibility for knowledge and self-worth, which can nourish their intellect and motivate them to become "a creative part of life."

Audre Lorde has described the psychological toll of emotional labor and estranged labor on the lives of workers. For the working class especially, alienation and unmet affective needs render work joyless in a profit system that reduces labor to subsistence and survival. In her classic essay "Uses of the Erotic: The Erotic as Power," Lorde writes:

The principal horror of any system which defines the good in terms of profit rather than in terms of human need, or which defines human need to the exclusion of the psychic and emotional components of that need—the principal horror of such a system is that it robs our work of its erotic value, its erotic power and life appeal and fulfillment. Such a system reduces work to a travesty of necessities, a duty by which we earn bread or oblivion for ourselves and those we love. But this is tantamount to blinding a painter and then telling her to improve her work, and to enjoy the act of painting. It is not only next to impossible, it is also profoundly cruel. (*Sister* 55)

According to Lorde, the "erotic" is an affective human need that is shared among women laborers as a "depth of feeling" (53). The "emotional components of that need" are realized as individual fulfillment from the work women do. The erotic is, in other words, a "sense of satisfaction and completion" that women derive from their labor performed collaboratively with other workers (54–55). Yet the capitalist profit system, which is dominated and controlled by men in a patriarchal order, demeans and discounts the erotic by exploiting and alienating women in their labor (53). One of the terrible consequences of estranged labor for women is that patriarchy compels them to suppress the erotic and subsequently denies them an affective need important "as a considered source of power and information" for knowledge and self-worth (53). Effectively modeled by patriarchy, then, the profit system is profoundly cruel because it controls and represses the erotic from the work women perform in exchange for meager wages, for barely enough compensation to survive and subsist.

In his essay, too, Bulosan portrays a profit system that dehumanizes workers by denying them a sense of satisfaction and well-being. The profit system is profoundly cruel for Filipino migrant workers because it objectifies and dehumanizes them by denying them the right to use what they produce and thereby, as Lorde puts it, "reduc[ing] work to a travesty of necessities." That the exploitation in abstract labor makes Filipino workers live hand to mouth and feel trapped by their jobs—that it makes them feel objectified and dehumanized while laboring under wage-slavery conditions—registers the felt consequences of their alienation at work. As Adorno argued, the profit system's ideology, which serves the interests of the property-owning capitalist class, forces workers to comply with their own abstraction (i.e., objectification) and to reduce their labor "to the abstract universal of average working hours" (146). Workers who feel exploited and dehumanized, as Bulosan did, articulate feeling as if they are merely parts within a machine, because they are constituted as things or commodities in regimented and estranged labor.

When Bulosan uses the word *freedom* in his writings, he refers to the individual fulfillment the worker feels when he receives fair payment for his labor and takes part in collectively owning the means of production. The worker's right to bargain collectively and partake in managing the production process (i.e., the freedom to "use what we produce") should be, according to Bulosan, the premise of democracy: "We recognize the mainsprings of American democracy in our right to form unions and bargain through them collectively, our opportunity to sell our products at reasonable prices" (32). For Bulosan, freedom in this democratic socialist vision is the worker's self-worth in collaboration with his coworkers, and hence his liberation from wage slavery. In this sense, too, the worker's freedom is a necessary condition for knowledge that enables him to become "a creative part of life," which is the antithesis of fear. As Bulosan reveals in *America*, capitalists use fear to alienate workers and force them to comply with their exploitation and subjugation. Yet in an alternative economic system whereby workers have a stake in collectively owning the means of production, their freedom to "think and discuss things without fear" can create what Bulosan contends is an ideal social order of "economic peace," an aspirational norm in his socialist vision: "Everywhere we are on the march, passing through darkness into a sphere of economic peace. When we have the freedom to think and discuss things without fear, when peace and security are assured, when the futures of our children are ensured—then we have resurrected and cultivated the early beginnings of democracy. And America lives and becomes a growing part of our aspirations again" (133). Bulosan here argues passionately about hope as a human need in a democracy built and maintained by the "aspirations" of intellectual and creative "freedom." His concept of "economic peace" as a social order achieved collaboratively suggests a compelling point in Hennessy's argument about the cooperative way in which individual human needs are met: "No matter how they are historically met, however, human needs have an individual corporeal dimension and a social one in that meeting them is always a historical, collective practice" (210). Hennessy's argument clarifies the worker's *fulfillment* as a human need in Bulosan's socialist vision for "economic peace." In other words, the satisfaction and well-being of workers, which are affective human needs, have an "individual corporeal dimension and a social one" when workers collectively own the means of production.

As concepts representing the worker's fulfillment in labor, Bulosan's "freedom" and "economic peace" imply a critical framework for theorizing emotions as human needs. For example, the empowering and collective feeling of fulfillment in labor—exemplified in Bulosan's terms by the bonds realized and shared by an underclass of workers—carries the potential to negate structures of oppression and social domination. When felt and realized by the working poor, this fulfillment scrutinizes all aspects of their existence and implicitly foregrounds an otherwise given and seemingly invisible profit system, whose oppressive ideology must be realized to be transcended. According to Bulosan, if oppressed working people understand that emotions have a critical dimension, they have them by way of dialectical negation. For affects of empowerment and fulfillment negate their own restriction in a profit system that produces and then negates them as the contradictions of consumption and mass production. This is to say that Bulosan's critique of alienation allows us a way to understand the central operative of oppressions in capitalist modes of production. In particular, his critique of emotional labor is relevant to critical theories of consciousness and subjectivity in a modern capitalist society.

## Creating Anxiety, Hiring Happiness

The time during which Bulosan produced his writings encapsulates a period in the mid-twentieth century when Americans felt much anxiety in a modern society changing rapidly from technological development and the global expansion of capitalism. An intensification of commodity relations—driven by the use of technology to enable mass production and the seemingly endless accumulation of profit—reified the social relations of Americans and regimented their working lives.[6] This period's anxieties about the controlling influence of machines and markets to alienate people from themselves and each other persisted well into the late twentieth century.[7] America's ongoing imperialist incursions in the Asia-Pacific, technologization of warfare and mass destruction, and globalization of commodity production are historical forces and consequences of Western capitalist modernity's growth and private accumulation.

In *America*, Bulosan refers to the estrangement and loss of self in capitalist modernity as "the turmoil of modern industrialism" (245). He describes an advanced industrial society whose development of machines for war, mass destruction, and human exploitation creates anxieties and fears in everyday life that alienate people from themselves and each other. These are machines of modern industry, moreover, that manual laborers operated and that hurt and injured them, damaging their bodies for life. Consider, for instance, Bulosan's essay "I Am Not a Laughing Man," in which he rails against the hazardous working conditions of canneries. Alienating his body while performing the repetitive motions of assembly-line labor, Bulosan suffered the paralysis of his right hand.[8] This injury made it difficult for him to do his work and keep his employment in agriculture and factories during wartime in the 1940s.

> Well, it started with the war. I was working at a fish cannery in San Pedro, California, when it came. Then my friends started going away, some to the armed forces and others to wartime industries. I was lonely. This was the beginning of my anger.
>
> Then my right hand was paralyzed; perhaps a relapse induced by the cold water where I washed the fish heads at the cannery. I could not work fast any more. I was fired. This time my anger took a definite shape, not that I had not been fired before from other jobs. I was fired many times and in many places. (*On Becoming Filipino* 138)

That Bulosan's anger began to take "a definite shape" at the start of America's involvement in World War II suggests how alienation, which Bulosan had long felt as an effect of emotional labor in his working life, was now pervasive in his social life. Believing in their cause to purvey and spread Western civilization in the Pacific through colonization of the Philippines, US imperialists expected Filipinos to comply with the subjective rationality of American patriotism during wartime. "I was lonely," Bulosan laments, suggesting how this patriotism compelled Filipinos to enlist in the armed forces, taking them away from the US mainland and fragmenting Filipino communities throughout the West Coast. Filipinos who alienated their bodies laboring under exploitive conditions because of the racialized perception that they were happy to serve white people were now expected to defend America in the war. Yet despite Filipinos' enlistment in the military and other wartime industries they continued to endure abuse in their jobs and experience racial hatred in US society at large.

That Bulosan says his anger stems from getting fired from a factory job suggests, moreover, how his anger arises from his struggle to accommodate the contradictory perception of Filipinos as both happily servile and menacing. This perception continued unabated during the war, when rights to naturalization were granted only to those Filipinos who enlisted in the armed forces. Many Filipinos who enlisted understood the moral discrepancy of their being granted citizenship solely because the US military needed to exploit their labor in wartime. The irrationality of their being allowed to naturalize only if they enlisted and risked dying in combat angered them. In her study of Filipino men in America, Linda España-Maram interviews a Filipino veteran of World War II who tells her that this irrationality infuriated him and other Filipinos: "'Why now, major?' he asked his commanding officer, who had urged him to become a citizen. 'Why that privilege now? When we were . . . private citizens [and] we ask[ed] . . . and they don't like us. In fact they brand us. Why now . . . are [citizenship rights] given . . . when we are soldiers? And at the same time why do they have to give [them] only to the soldiers rather than to all [Filipinos]?" (153). The anger of Filipinos during the war articulated their resistance to the illogical perception of Filipinos both as subservient colonial subjects and as threats. In accord with this resistance, Bulosan's anger took shape as the initial stirrings of his radical consciousness at the start of America's involvement in the war. His indignation, like that of the Filipino veteran who heatedly questions his commanding officer about the citizenship inconsistency, underscores the paradox within this perception.

According to Bulosan, anger can be channeled as a force to critique the exploitation of Filipinos who worked as soldiers in the military and as laborers in canneries and farm fields. As noncitizen nationals whose work either in the armed forces or in factories registered their subservience as colonial subjects, Filipinos performed labor not only as commodities for subsistence but also in subjection to their perceived status as embodiments of service and compliance. Here the imbrication of Filipino racialization, emotional labor, alienation, colonialism, and the intensification of commodity relations in modern capitalism may be understood. That white Americans perceived Filipinos as eagerly compliant workers indicates this perception as an *expectation* in which Filipinos would perform happiness as a commodity to demonstrate compliance with their colonized status and, more implicitly, to express an emotional labor of racialization in their jobs as servants and manual laborers. Filipinos were, according to this racialized perception, objects of commodity happiness: figures of "happiness for hire" who white Americans expected would perform glad submission while on the job.

For Bulosan, the expectation that Filipinos express and produce happiness as an emotional commodity is an irrationality premised on racialized perceptions, and this angers him deeply. For example, in his essay's beginning paragraphs he fumes about white critics who praise his writings for their apparent cheeriness and simplicity:

> I am mad. I am mad because when my book, *The Laughter of My Father*, was published by Harcourt, Brace and Company, the critics called me "the Pure Comic Spirit."
>
> I am not a laughing man. I am an angry man. That is why I started writing. I guess you will have to be angry at something if you want to be a writer. (138)

Published in 1944, *The Laugher of My Father* was Bulosan's first book of stories about his origins and family history in the Philippines. In a letter to his publisher, Bulosan explains that his book is an "indictment against an economic system that stifled the growth of the primitive . . . making him decadent overnight without passing through the various stages of growth and decay" (qtd. in San Juan 7). Although the target of Bulosan's critique in his book is the Philippines' feudal capitalist system, American critics who reviewed *The Laughter of My Father* interpreted its stories as comedy. They labeled them "commercialized folk humor" and "local 'exotic' color" (7) and considered Bulosan an amusing yet unsophisticated author. In their egregious misreading of Bulosan's objective to critique feudal capitalism in the Philippines and in their pat generalizations of him as a writer of childlike simplicity, these critics expressed the racialized perception of Filipinos as highly spirited, infantile natives. In another essay, "The Worker as Writer," Bulosan contends that "the writer [of stories] is also a worker" and that "the stories he creates are commodities" (143). But critics who dubbed Bulosan "the Pure Comic Spirit" did so because they considered Filipinos to be overemotional. And they ascribed to Bulosan and his work the racialized affect of "animatedness"—in Sianne Ngai's terms, an overstated expressiveness among black Americans who were racially stereotyped with childish exuberance. Bulosan's critics expected him to personify this racialized affect in his position as a colonial subject and to reproduce it in his work as a writer. By referring to him as a guileless writer of humorous folklore, these critics articulated the attitude of US imperialists who expected Filipinos to perform as colonized native subjects, eagerly performing servility as evidence of their noncitizen and migrant-worker status. The imperialist and white supremacist expectation that Filipinos gladly comply with their subaltern status was, then, a causal condition of the emotional labor that Filipinos performed in their jobs as house servants and manual laborers. And it was, in particular, this naturalized assumption of Filipino servitude and subjection among Bulosan's white employers that enraged him, compelling him to channel that rage into his critical writings.

In another of her essays about capitalism's repression of emotions, Lorde contends that "there must always be some group of people, who, through systemized oppression, can be made to feel surplus, to occupy the place of the dehumanized inferior" (114). If, as Lorde contends, the profit system causes oppression and subordinates affective human needs by dehumanizing and rendering "surplus" the poor and the marginalized, it would also be the case, as an extension of Lorde's argument and as reference to Bulosan's anger about the Filipino worker's performance of glad servility, that profit is extracted through an emotional labor of racialization—a process that restricts the bodies *and* feelings of racialized minority workers to the operation of capitalist production. As Bulosan implies in his critique of emotional labor, the profit system denigrates and renders excessive (i.e., "surplus") an immense underclass of racialized working poor and Third World people who are excluded from the social and economic privileges of this system.

Yet what especially angers Bulosan is how the naturalized assumption of Filipinos as subalterns—who are "only too glad to serve white folks"—is coupled with the expectation that Filipinos put aside their "differences," as Lorde would put it. Members of racially oppressed, objectified groups are expected to accommodate the oppressor's ideology in order to assimilate into a hegemonic profit system and maintain its status quo. That an underclass of racialized workers in America are objectified through an emotional labor of racialization, a process of negation requiring them to relinquish "positive" affirmation of their difference, is the result of capitalism's oppressive ideology, which divides and fragments all of society. Lorde elaborates on this argument:

> Institutionalized rejection of difference is an absolute necessity in a profit economy which needs outsiders as surplus people. As members of such an economy, we have all been programmed to respond to the human differences between us with fear and loathing and to handle that difference in one of three ways: ignore it, and if that is not possible, copy it if we think it is dominant, or destroy it if we think it is subordinate. But we have no patterns for relating across our human differences as equals. As a result, those differences have been misnamed and misused in the service of separation and confusion. (115)

The organized rejection of difference to create profit, Lorde asserts, requires the disparagement of human social differences as an "absolute necessity," a process that renders minority difference "surplus" in order to negate and dispense with it. The system of profit extraction hence maintains its dominant position for "the oppressors" through the "separation and confusion" of difference. This is the social division and fragmentation that is fundamental to the perpetuation of class society.

In the capitalist process of alienation, which is analogous to the function of the Universal "to strip away the particularities of [minority] identity" in order to make the minority conform to white ideals and cultural norms demanded by the Universal (Palumbo-Liu, "Universalisms" 202), the profit economy coerces racialized minority workers to negate their "human differences." These differences are the historical particularities and forces of racial oppression, and their avowal would signify recognition of this oppression. And such recognition would take place in an alternative system—for example, Bulosan's democracy of "economic peace"—in which differences would be recognized through another process that would render them "positive" for the oppressed subject's affirmation of self and identity, instead of negative, "misnamed and misused" for exploitation in a profit economy that has institutionalized the rejection of difference. We might extend, then, Bulosan's democratic socialist vision to encompass this affirming social process, which, in turn, would enable recognizing the consciousness of racially oppressed people to realize their conditions of possibility for knowledge and self-worth.

For Bulosan, the knowledge that informs and stirs consciousness entails recognizing that capitalism's profit system dehumanizes people by negating and abstracting their differences under the objectification process, interpellating them as "outsiders," insofar as they fall outside the institutionalized norms of the ruling class. Yet how specifically is it to be understood that the profit system extracts and exploits social differences in the labor that oppressed workers perform? As Bulosan implies in his critical writings, the profit system dehumanizes racialized laborers as an underclass by objectifying them as commodities and as inferior racial others. Racial minority differences are disparaged and relegated to inferior status—rendered "surplus"—in order to maintain the profit derived from divisions of labor. Through Lorde's arguments here, we can surmise that Bulosan declares alienation at work to be an underlying cause of oppression in the formation of the racialized minority subject, insofar as the implicit goal of the profit system is to appropriate surplus value by institutionalized mechanisms of denigrating racial "difference" and exploiting this difference for financial gain. Consequently, to realize how it feels to be objectified in terms of "feeling surplus," as a racially oppressed worker whose minority status (his "difference") is disparaged and abstracted by his employer, is to imply a Marxist critique of racial oppression that, in turn, suggests the necessary expression of negative feeling, particularly anger, to structure and form the worker's consciousness.

This materialist critique informs the radical visions of both Bulosan's "freedom from want" and Lorde's "life appeal and fulfillment," which are derived from the ability of workers to participate in the collective ownership of their own labor. It is important to note, however, that Lorde implies her radical vision for collective labor through her depiction of shared emotions between racially oppressed women workers and that these emotions are components of their consciousness. And to actualize this consciousness so that it transforms society to satisfy human needs, instead of the pursuit of profit for a ruling class, requires struggle and hard work. More specifically, it requires the intellectual labor of collaborative criticism to confront racism and gender discrimination as a form of resistance in political struggle. As Sara Ahmed observes, developing consciousness as "a form of political struggle" is an arduous task impossible to achieve without physical and mental pain (*Promise* 84). "Lorde argues throughout her work," Ahmed explains, "that we should not be protected from what hurts. We have to work and struggle not so much to feel but to notice what causes hurt, which means unlearning what we have learned not to notice. We have to do this work if we are to produce critical understandings of how violence, as a relation of force and harm, is directed towards some bodies and not others" (215–16). Ahmed perceptively elaborates on Lorde's argument about the "hard labor" necessary for "becoming conscious" not only as an act of self-preservation, in the effort to defend oneself against the violence of bigotry and exploitation, but also as a way to restructure society so that it respects discrete ways of life and implements social equality. "We need to examine the ways in which our world can be truly different," Lorde proposes. "I am speaking here of the necessity for reassessing the quality of all the aspects of our lives and of our work, and of how we move toward and through them" (55). Here the shared expression and collaboratively charged feeling of minority workers in "our work"—implied in Bulosan's first-person-plural point of view in "we" workers—provides the framework to envision a credible alternative to the present order of exploitation, displacement of human needs, fragmentation of community, and the disparagement of differences evident in a socially divisive society. Against the profit system's objective to extract surplus value by rendering inferior an underclass of racially oppressed workers, Bulosan channels his anger into his critique of capitalism's alienation of workers and their objectification in emotional labor. Through his materialist evaluation of the emotions as both political and critical, he imagines a more humane world in which human consciousness can be liberated from the incessant want of unmet needs.

## Racial Fear in America

If the "minoritized body" is, as Arjun Appadurai has argued, both "the mirror and the instrument of those abstractions we fear most" (47), then today's fears about racially minoritized bodies in the United States have historical origins in American fears about Filipinos from the 1920s through the 1940s. In its most common interpretation, fear is an emotional response to an approaching and identifiable threat.[9] In their perception of Filipino migrants as threats, whites on the US Pacific Coast passed anti-Filipino legislation to make racially identifiable a migrant worker minority group on which to fix their fears of impending unemployment and economic loss during the Great Depression. As Bulosan shows in his writings, white fears about Filipinos were based on perceptions of them as sexually primitive and menacing. The bodies of Filipino men were minoritized abstractions that whites construed in threatening opposition to their dominant social norms.

In *America*, nowhere is the enmeshment of capitalism and the emotions to control and contain the bodies of minorities more evident than in what Bulosan calls the "racial fear" of Filipinos. Whites feared Filipino migrants as a dangerous labor force that threatened to overtake them in competition for jobs and the accumulation of capital. If US capitalism is an emotional system of reproduction (Pfister 1136), insofar as it generates emotions that have regulated, abstracted, and alienated the bodies of immigrants and minorities, then we can see how a capitalist culture of emotion has operated in conjunction with the interests of the US state to maintain a white national citizenry bound by race, language, and culture. As in past racial fears about the Chinese as a yellow peril invading and overtaking America in the nineteenth century, capitalism and the state have operated together to constitute the "whiteness" of the US nation by concentrating wealth and power in its white citizenry. A capitalist culture of emotion in mid-twentieth-century America, which was itself a production of wealth preservation and the racial interests of the US nation-state, generated and exploited fears about Filipinos as a growing labor force that threatened capital accumulation by whites. White fears about Filipinos as an expanding minority group informed and produced legislation that targeted Filipinos for exclusion and discrimination. Bulosan's critique of racial fear underscores how capitalism and the US nation-state collaborated in the interests of wealth accumulation to exploit fears of Filipinos, leading to the passage of anti-Filipino discriminatory laws.

Capitalism's production of racial fear, which abstracted and minoritized the bodies of Filipinos, was specific to "the genesis, presence, and legacies of American colonialism in the Philippines" (Rodriguez 184). White American fears of Filipino migrants in the early to mid-twentieth century were produced as racial feelings in a capitalist emotional culture—a culture bound up with the politics of imperialist white supremacy, manifested by America's military occupation and colonization of the Philippines. As Bulosan shows in his anger-infused criticism, a Filipino racial form thus emerged, in large part, from the racial fear of Filipinos, which was itself generated by the collaborative discourses of white capital accumulation and the white supremacist constitution of the US empire-state.

In *America*, Carlos's indignation at being continually denied housing, refused service in restaurants, fired from jobs, and brutally attacked while looking for work registers his struggle to accommodate America's contradictory perception of Filipinos as servile colonial subjects and as threatening racial others. His ire against many instances of degradation underscores how this perceptual racial antinomy mirrors what he eventually comes to understand as "the paradox of America" (147): a country at once cruel and kind. This affective paradox exemplifies what I've described as a violent set of relations between emotions and race that America's imperial and exploitative capitalist order produced in the early to mid-twentieth century. Economically based racial feelings during the Great Depression fueled the anti-Filipino sentiment pervasive among white Americans on the Pacific Coast from the late 1920s through the 1940s. This racial fear led to the passage of discriminatory laws such as the Tydings-McDuffie Act of 1934 and anti-intermarriage legislation such as the amendment of California's antimiscegenation law in 1933 to unambiguously include Filipinos within its reach.

Anti-Filipino legislation constrained the ability of Filipinos to travel and migrate within the territorial jurisdiction of the United States. In particular, the Tydings-McDuffie Act literally alienated and constrained the bodies of Filipinos in America. As Mae Ngai contends, the act transformed Filipinos as "nationals" within their status as colonial subjects into "undesirable aliens" as citizens of a Philippine nation (96–97). It was authored in the Seventy-Third US Congress by Senator Millard Tydings of Maryland and Representative John McDuffie of Alabama and was signed into law by President Franklin D. Roosevelt. By passing this law, the United States recognized the Philippines as a commonwealth and set a ten-year transition period to full independence. However, America's granting of Philippine independence reproduced many features of its colonial relationship. Filipinos were now officially labeled citizens of the Philippines, but they continued to owe allegiance to the United States, even though the Tydings-McDuffie Act rendered them aliens and reduced their annual immigration quota to fifty, "the lowest in the world" (97). As Ngai explains, "The Philippine quota was a gratuitous gesture meant to degrade Filipinos to a status something short of nationhood, their American tutelage placing them just barely above the fully excludable Asiatic races" (119–20). Even more degrading was the law's effect on trade between the United States and the Philippines. It allowed Americans unobstructed entry into the Philippines long after the country would achieve independence on July 4, 1946. Bidirectional free trade between the two countries was replaced by a one-sided agreement that "subjected Filipino products to the same tariff schedules that applied to all other countries yet which granted American capital and products continued free access to the Philippine market" (M. Ngai 120). In effect, the law benefited American capitalists by forcing Filipinos to *remain* in the Philippines, saddling them with debt incurred by losing protection of the trade tariff. A writer for a Filipino newspaper in California criticized the Tydings-McDuffie Act as "bait to entrap us. . . . It restricts our liberty of action. We cannot send our products [into] American markets. We cannot come to the United States. We must stay home and slave to pay off principal and interest on bonds held by foreign capitalists" (qtd. in M. Ngai 120). Yet for Filipinos living and working in the United States, the act put them in a precarious and vulnerable position—a consequence of their abrupt change in status from nationals to aliens in America. Although Filipinos who arrived in America before the law's passage on May 1, 1934 were deemed to be aliens, they were not subject to deportation for any act or condition that existed prior to that date. However, they were "subject to deportation for deportable acts committed after May 1, 1934" (M. Ngai 120).

In *America*, Bulosan depicts the experiences of Filipino men confronting widespread anti-Filipino sentiment intensified by racially discriminatory laws. In 1933, three years after arriving in Seattle at the onset of the Great Depression, Carlos explains how Filipinos in the midst of prevalent anti-Filipino violence were experiencing not only alienation at work but also hostility from whites throughout the entirety of society. The change in their perceived status from compliant laborers to racial menaces structured the feeling among Filipinos that they had to accommodate in their social lives the alienation they had long felt at work. It was now, in other words, the job of Filipinos to live in fear and to work even harder to appear unassuming so as not to be detected and assaulted by vigilantes who sought to arrest and punish Filipinos because they perceived them as racially marked for exclusion and removal. Bulosan explains in great detail how Filipinos were forced to live in a constant state of anxiety about their vulnerability to hostility and violence, which produced in them a bitter and destructive cynicism. "My distrust of white men grew," Carlos reveals, "and drove me blindly into the midst of my own people; together we hid cynically behind our mounting fears, hating the broad white universe at our door. . . . Was it possible that, coming to America with certain illusions of equality, I had slowly succumbed to the hypnotic effects of racial fear?" (163–64). As Carlos realizes, the racial fear of whites has negatively acted upon Filipinos individually by affecting them *collectively* as a minority group that has been rendered illegal and unassimilable by discriminatory legislation. His question about succumbing to the "hypnotic effects of racial fear" articulates his anxiety that his own vision for equality and freedom in America is transmogrifying into an intense cynicism—a vehemently negative emotion alienating and isolating Filipinos not only from each other but also from all of society.

By transforming Filipinos into unassimilable aliens, California's anti-miscegenation laws and immigrant exclusion acts led to the mass alienation of Filipinos in America. In a chapter in the middle of *America*, Carlos explains how his anger began to take shape as a compelling force to critique anti-Filipino hostility. He channels his indignation into a critique that represents the degraded condition of Filipinos at the time of their legislated transformation from nationals into unassimilable aliens—an alteration of their perceived racial status from docile colonial subjects to threatening alien others. "It was now the year of the great hatred: the lives of Filipinos were cheaper than those of dogs. They were forcibly shoved off the streets when they showed resistance. The sentiment against them was accelerated by the marriage of a Filipino and a girl of the Caucasian race in Pasadena. The case was tried in court and many technicalities were brought in with it to degrade the lineage and character of the Filipino people" (143). Here Carlos refers to the 1933 case of *Roldan v. the United States*, in which a Filipino, Salvador Roldan, attempted to marry a white British woman, Marjorie Rogers. California's 1880 antimiscegenation law prohibited marriage between "white persons" and "negroes, mulattoes, and Mongolians," and Filipinos were classified as Mongolians. The case was argued in Los Angeles Superior Court, and the court ruled that Roldan was "Malay," not Mongolian, thus allowing him to marry Rogers. But the court "noted that it ruled only on the law and urged the legislature to align the law with contemporary *'common thought'*" (M. Ngai 115, italics added). By following the court's advice to agree with widespread perceptions of Asians as threats and thus to implicitly validate the inflamed hostilities against Filipinos causing race riots all along the Pacific Coast, the legislature amended California's antimiscegenation law to unambiguously include members of the Malay race within its scope. That the Los Angeles Superior Court sought to align state law with "contemporary 'common thought'" attests to the legalized racial subjection of Filipinos: their official racial classification as "Malays" to deny them the freedom to marry white women and create families with them, a racial grouping premised on emotionally charged perceptions of Filipinos as alien others.

Filipinos were wanted in America for the exploitation of their labor, and their freedom to travel and migrate as nationals and experience the benefits of inclusion in US society had to be constrained in order to maintain their exploitation and to legislatively underwrite America as a nation for white people. In this sense, anti-Filipino hostility, which the court euphemized as "contemporary 'common thought,'" underscores how emotions and race were bound up with US imperialism and a capitalist logic of exploitation to alienate Filipinos and racialize them as threatening others. We may infer from this that racialized perception as "common thought" was materialized by being enacted into antimiscegenation law and was produced and upheld by racial feelings (anti-Filipino sentiment) to inform the historical conditions of anti-Filipino exclusion and discriminatory practices shaping and determining a Filipino racial form in the mid-twentieth century. The significance of racial feelings to produce this racial form is evident with regard to white nativist organizations that lobbied to pass legislation that would prohibit Filipino migration to America on the perception that Filipinos were racially antithetical to a US nation-state of and for the white race, and that they embodied a primitive and predacious sexuality. The racist diatribes of V. S. McClatchy, for instance, who co-owned the *Sacramento Bee* and was one of California's most outspoken white supremacists and nativists, typify the anti-Asian racism that discursively constructed Filipinos as sexual predators on white females. McClatchy presumed that Filipinos were morally the "'worst *form* of Orientals,' because of the 'criminal nature in which we find them engaged in the delinquency of young girls'" (qtd. in M. Ngai 117, italics added). Here the Orientalist stereotyping of Asians as menaces—expressing and generating the threatening side of a Manichaean dichotomy that constituted an Asiatic racial form—was evident in McClatchy's attempts to influence anti-Filipino policy on the basis of his view that Filipinos molest white females. That he ascribed a corrupting sexuality to Filipinos in his characterization of them as predators on "young [white] girls" articulates the white supremacist rhetoric in California, which dovetailed with colonial and anti-immigrant discourses to define the sexuality and gender of Filipino men over against white patriarchal norms.

McClatchy's racist depiction of Filipino men as sexual deviants details a particular racialization process for Filipinos in which they were defined primarily as embodiments of native sensuality *and* rendered racially inferior by white imperialists who considered themselves to be the purveyors of moral order as a natural extension of Western civilization. According to Susan Koshy, anti-immigrant and colonial discourses represented Filipinos as "hypercorporeal" in order to define them as racially incompatible with white American civilization. Along with anxieties about the homosocial nature of the Filipino male workforce, the typecasting of Filipino men as hypercorporeal natives who were incapable of containing their desires for young white females was at the very center of antimiscegenation rhetoric. In her reading of Filipino sexuality and miscegenation in Bulosan's *America*, Koshy argues that the sexuality of Filipinos "constituted an 'unincorporated territory' of desire [for white Americans], designated as being under the jurisdiction of civilizing American norms but deemed unabsorbable within the American body politic" (*Sexual Naturalization* 102).[10] Filipinos who were in America at the time when the Philippines was a US colonial possession had to accommodate to white patriarchal norms of sexuality and gender that informed and determined their assimilation into US society. But such assimilation was illogical, not to mention futile, because these norms were the rationale for white supremacist perceptions of Filipinos as simply too deviant to be civilizable.

Alleged to be "hyper" in their supposed eagerness for menial labor and in their desires for white females, Filipinos therefore struggled to accommodate norms that were entirely paradoxical, insofar as they deemed Filipinos to be unassimilable on the basis of judgments of their sexuality as primitive and overly sensual. However, as Ngai explains, white Americans also made assumptions about the "womanless" and homosocial nature of the largely Filipino male workforce—suppositions that "associated their homosocial condition with a *lack* of masculinity" (111, italics added). These assumptions of Filipinos both as feminized males and as gender deviants have their basis in white fears during the nineteenth century when large numbers of Chinese men arrived in the US Pacific Coast to find work in mining and railroad construction. "The presence of an all-male Asiatic workforce on the Pacific Coast threatened the emerging social order founded upon the 'racially exclusive, presumptively heterosexual, nuclear family.' Since the time of anti-Chinese movement in the late nineteenth century, the Oriental threat was cast as an 'ambiguous, inscrutable, and hermaphroditic' sexuality, a 'third sex'" (M. Ngai 113).

The stereotyping of Filipino men's gender as aberrant and their sexuality as enigmatic was a primary force in the racialization of Filipinos that Bulosan described in his writings. Hostilities against Filipino men who engaged with white women in public were instituted through antimiscegenation laws that legally rendered Filipino men deviant. And this legislated recognition and implementation of white fears about the sexuality of Filipinos affected Bulosan profoundly. Antimiscegenation laws that specifically targeted Filipinos were, for Bulosan, the most acute manifestation of "American reality." The negative effects of these laws on Filipinos brutally contradicted his aspiration to realize freedom and find a place to call home in America. For him, the passage of anti-Filipino legislation was a clear indication that white men who blamed Filipinos for economic problems and were anxious about sexual rivalry with Filipino men had codified their racial fear into laws that turned Filipinos into criminals. Fear-based antimiscegenation laws, for instance, compelled Bulosan to write what would become one of the most oft-quoted passages in *America*: "I came to know afterward that in many ways it was a crime to be a Filipino in California. I came to know that the public streets were not free to my people: we were stopped each time these vigilant patrolmen saw us driving a car. We were suspect each time we were seen with a white woman. And perhaps it was this narrowing of our life into a tiny island, into a filthy segment of American society, that had driven

Filipinos . . . inward, hating everyone and despising all positive urgencies toward freedom" (121). Racial fear, which worked through and on the bodies of Filipinos to construct them as dangerous and to rationalize violence against them if they were "seen with a white woman," contained and apprehended Filipinos in ways that negatively affected their ability to move and inhabit public space. "Fear envelops the bodies that feel it," Sara Ahmed argues, "as well as constructs such bodies as enveloped, as contained by it, as if it comes from outside and moves inward" (*Cultural Politics* 63). Manifested through discriminatory legislation and violence, white racial fear narrowed the lives of Filipinos inexorably. Acts of racial hostility that violated their bodies and constrained their movement had detrimental effects on their psychology. Most disturbingly, white racial fear caused Filipinos to feel this fear as their own. Transformed into fearsome subjects by the exclusion acts and discriminatory laws that ascribed an alien status to them, Filipinos now perceived *each other* as dangerous and *themselves* as racially other.

White racism so humiliated and distressed Filipinos that it made them bitterly cynical, a development that negatively affected their relations with other Filipinos, blocking their feelings of kinship and blinding them from recognizing in one another a common humanity. To be sure, when Carlos first arrives in America he is horrified to witness his fellow countrymen exploiting and beating each other as cruelly as white racists do to them. "I had not seen this sort of brutality in the Philippines," he says, referring to a Filipino farmworker named Julio who becomes enraged when he, Carlos, and other workers learn that the Filipino leader of their crew has absconded with their wages. Julio attacks an elderly Filipino bookkeeper who informs them of the crime. "Julio hit him between the eyes, and the bookkeeper struggled violently. Julio hit him again. The bookkeeper rolled on the floor like a baby. Julio picked him up and threw him outside the house. I thought he was dead. . . . Julio came back and began hitting the door of the kitchen with all his force, in futile anger" (109). Yet after witnessing countless acts of whites exploiting and brutalizing Filipinos and other Filipinos hurting each other, Carlos becomes exceptionally hardened and distrustful. Trying not to internalize and succumb to the fear of white racism, he struggles with an encroaching wariness of his fellow countrymen: "I was not shocked when I saw that my countrymen had become ruthless toward one another, and this sudden impact of cruelty made me insensate to pain and kindness, so that it took me a long time to wholly trust other men" (109). That Carlos admits to feeling "insensate to pain and kindness" indicates a disturbing numbness to the humanity of other Filipinos, born from his experiencing humiliation and shame nearly every day in consequence of white racial fear.

Having internalized this fear, Filipinos not only hurt one another but, in turn, harmed themselves. For Carlos, what is especially painful about racial fear is the destructive toll it takes on his own moral character and sense of self-worth: "We could only pick up fragments of our lives and handle them fearfully, as though the years had made us afraid to know ourselves. I was suddenly ashamed that I could not express the gentle feeling I had for my brother. Was this brutality changing me, too?" (132). As the first-personal plural in Carlos's statement indicates, the threat of white racist violence negatively affected Filipinos individually by compelling them to go on the run and consequently vitiating a sense of community with other migrant workers. Fear was, in this way, an emotional weapon that white racists used to instill in the minds of Filipinos racial inferiority and abjection, which, in turn, would fragment their social reality and deny them a sense of belonging.

There are many instances where Carlos overhears whites refer to Filipinos as "brown monkeys" and sees police officers brutalize and degrade Filipinos as animals. In one such instance, Carlos tells of an educated Filipino named Alonzo who was apprehended by the police for dating a white woman. "'Listen to the brown monkey talk,' said one of the detectives, slapping Alonzo in the face. 'He thinks he has the right to be educated. Listen to the bastard talk English. He thinks he is a *white* man. How do you make this white woman stick with you, googoo?'" (136, italics added). US Marines serving in the Philippines during the Philippine-American War (1898–1902) and subsequently in the period of US colonial rule (1896–1946) used the word *goo-goo* as a pejorative term to mock Filipino speech. David Roediger explains that the derogatory term *gook*, which American soldiers stationed around the world used to refer to all Asians in general, may have originated with the word *goo-goo* used by American imperialists to racially disparage Filipinos (50–54). The phrase "had a specifically racial dimension, with the term applied particularly to those natives who had no mixture of European 'blood'—a particularly despised (or pitied) category which imperialists freely predicted would die out as 'progress' occurred" (50). That it is police officers—embodiments of white male authority and power—who arrest Alonzo and humiliate him with racial epithets shows that a white majority attempted to maintain its dominance as a *masculine* authority by referring to Filipinos as animals and "googoos." In using a term that originated with US troops in the Philippines to degrade Filipinos, then, white police officers signified their inclusion in America's imperialist project to secure white patriarchal control and domination in the Philippines through the rhetorical use of racial fear.

As Carlos's anger tells us, a discourse of white male supremacy described an innate primitiveness and subservience as characteristic features of Filipino racial inferiority that were ostensibly natural to Filipinos through their legislated classification as unassimilable aliens. Using fear to disseminate and publicize racist discourses that naturalized Filipino racial inferiority, white supremacists attempted to put Filipinos in the position of seeing and interpellating themselves as abject minorities through these ideological terms.[11] The "desperate cynicism" to which Carlos fears he might succumb reflects this fear as mediated discourse through which Filipinos felt themselves to be debased as racial others. "Please, God, don't change me in America!" (126), Carlos exclaims after running into his brother Amado in California and immediately noting Amado's cynicism, which has hardened him to the crimes he has committed in order to survive. Carlos's worries about becoming hardened and cynical from internalizing racism and looking upon his own brother and countrymen as fearsome and distrustful indicate the ideological objective of white supremacists to maintain their power and privilege as a majority group by dividing, containing, and immobilizing Filipinos through racial fear. For this white majority, however, to produce and perpetuate racial fear in the political aim of racially identifying a Filipino minority as threatening suggests this majority's anxiety to maintain its hegemony. "The very idea of a majority is a frustration," Appadurai explains, "since it implies some sort of ethnic diffusion of the national peoplehood. Minorities, being a reminder of this small but frustrating deficit, thus unleash the urge to purify. . . . In a sense, the smaller the number and the weaker the minority, the deeper the rage about its capacity to make a majority feel like a mere majority rather than like a whole and uncontested ethnos" (53).

Following Appadurai's argument that the majority constitutes a "frustration" because it finds itself having to defend the perimeter of its ethnic purity to maintain its hegemonic status as the feeling of evident power and domination, we can see this as a characteristic feature of the white patriarchal majority in *America*, which uses racial fear to express a "frustration" about immobilizing and containing Filipino bodies. As an affective political weapon to maintain the white majority's "purity" and masculine authority, racial fear was a tactic of white business owners to suppress Filipino workers by segregating them from other Asians in order to prevent any collaboration for labor strikes and activism. "Japanese workers were also arriving from San Francisco," Carlos explains, "but they were housed in another section of the farm. I did not discover until some years afterward that this tactic was the only way in which farmers could forestall any possible alliance between the Filipinos and the Japanese" (146).

The movement of Filipinos within a social milieu, whose openness and availability waned with the spread of violence against them, became further constrained as they were forced into flight from racial fear. Hence Carlos's assertion that the lives of Filipinos narrowed "into a tiny island, into a filthy segment of American society." His description of Filipino migrants who were enclosed and made vulnerable by the fear of white Americans reveals how this fear produced the racial subjection of Filipinos by an abstraction process that minoritized their bodies in order to mark them for containment visually. The racial subjection of Filipinos by this fear historically contextualizes Ahmed's claim that "fear involves shrinking the body; *it restricts the body's mobility precisely insofar as it seems to prepare the body for flight.* Such shrinkage is significant: fear works to contain some bodies such that they take up less space" (*Cultural Politics* 69, italics in original). The power of fear to immobilize the minoritized body, as Ahmed conceptualizes it, by restricting some bodies through the movement or expansion of others registers the white occupation and regulation of space as a violent objective of white racism. Yet this objective is premised on contradiction: whites' use of racial fear to mark Filipinos racially as threats forced them to go on the run so as to avoid detection and apprehension. But also white male mobs attacked Filipinos to make them afraid of trespassing on "white" territory, injuring their bodies so badly they were rendered immobile, hindered from further movement.

Although Carlos attempts to travel beyond and between geographical spaces where white racism detects him and compels his removal, this range of movement does not in any way provide freedom. Instead, this mobility is an imprisonment. That Carlos is forced to run to avoid becoming a target of anti-Filipino mob violence shows how mobility becomes a force of inhibition and containment, not autonomy and liberty. "I had been fleeing from state to state," an exasperated Carlos explains, "but now I hoped to gather the threads of my life together. *Was there no end to this flight?*" (149, italics added). Here Carlos's infuriated questioning of the racial fear that forces him to flee incessantly returns us to Sau-ling

Wong's argument about the politics of mobility in Asian American literature. Themes of detainment, incarceration, and enforced mobility in mid-twentieth-century Asian American writings, Wong claims, demonstrate "acute contradictions at the heart of American cultural clichés" (*Reading* 136). To the extent that the subjective experience of freedom and the pursuit of happiness are primary features of the American Dream, they can be further understood as "clichés" that not only have long thrived at the heart of the US cultural imaginary but have done so by the contradictions of exclusion, containment, and coerced movement of Asians in America during the nineteenth and twentieth centuries.

Racial fear compels Carlos to flee from detection within a geographical space that whites have territorialized and restricted Filipinos from entering. We might understand such space in affective terms as the freedom and happiness of possessive individualism that traditionally have been the distinction and preserve of Euro-Americans. Racial fear, following Ahmed's claim that white fears of racialized bodies contain and regulate these bodies by both restricting their mobility and coercing them into flight, produced the contradictions of Filipino exclusion, containment, and enforced movement. These contradictions historically enabled whites who were hostile to Filipinos to maintain and protect for themselves the "cultural clichés" of the American Dream: the comfort, security, and contentment largely making up the subjective experience of freedom. By his enraged questioning of whites who racially perceive Filipinos as threats, then, Bulosan in his narrative articulates a critical structure of feeling distinctive to Asian American writings in the early to mid-twentieth century.[12] And his interrogation of white racism *exacerbates* contradictions not only by voicing criticism but also by being the racialized and gendered embodiment of contradiction itself.

## Transcending Paradox

Carlos's indignant questioning of racial fear not only protests how such fear racially objectified Filipinos as embodied contradictions to American freedom but also positions us to understand the emotional contradiction that constitutes the American Dream. Another key scene in the middle of *America* shows, for example, how racial fear compels Filipinos to flee from detection of their perceived criminality. Carlos and two other migrant workers, Frank and José, try to outrun detectives who have caught them hopping aboard a moving freight train. As the three men escape by leaping from car to car, José loses his footing and falls under the train's wheels. Carlos and Frank jump off the train to help their friend, whose feet have been severed in the accident. They carry José a short distance to a highway and try to hail a car to take him to a hospital. But "the motorists looked at us," Carlos angrily explains, "with scorn and spat into the wind" (147). Eventually, someone does stop to help, and at the county hospital where "a kind doctor and two nurses assured [them] that they would do their best for [José]" (147) Carlos wonders about his friend's tragedy and the "paradox of America":

> Walking down the marble stairway of the hospital, I began to wonder at the paradox of America. José's tragedy was brought about by railroad detectives, yet he had done no harm of any consequence to the company. On the highway, again, motorists had refused to take a dying man. And yet in this hospital, among white people— Americans like those who had denied us—we had found refuge and tolerance. *Why was America so kind and yet so cruel?* Was there no way to simplifying things in this continent so that suffering would be minimized? Was there no common denominator on which we could all meet? I was angry and confused, and wondered if I would ever understand this paradox. (147, italics added)

Indeed, it is quite telling that José's nearly fatal injury happens while the three men are desperately searching for work as manual laborers. José's tragedy implies that Carlos's earnest question—"Why was America so kind and yet so cruel?"—must be understood in the context of his struggle to find work while fleeing from white men who are anxious about competing with Filipinos for jobs. In this context, too, his question should be understood within the frame of his democratic socialist vision. As Rachel Lee has argued in her analysis of Bulosan's socialist politics, a tension develops "between a politics aimed at attaining American citizenship and property for Filipinos and a politics of international socialism working toward a global collective labor" (39). If America is for Carlos both kind and cruel, this emotional paradox would indicate that his faith in the American Dream is decidedly *at odds* with his democratic socialist vision.

As I noted in the Introduction, the US capitalist system as the heart and protectorate of America's liberal democratic government is premised on the making and preservation of happiness attained through material acquisition. The pursuit of happiness as stated in the Declaration of Independence is linked to the ownership and defense of private property framed by the liberal political theory of white male individualism. Carlos thus aspires to live for an ideal that is historically premised on liberal capitalist conceptions of white personhood and citizenship rights—a contractarian liberalism underwriting a culture of happiness for Euro-Americans, made and maintained by their racial othering of Asian migrants. His realization of America as an emotional contradiction is, therefore, the consequence of liberal individualism's happiness for white men, which has structured the anti-Filipino sentiments informing anti-miscegnation laws and exclusion acts: racial feelings, in other words, that have shaped a paradoxical Filipino racial form.

For Carlos to achieve his aspiration of living peaceably within a collective and common humanity he must find a way to disentangle his socialist vision from the American Dream of happiness in possessive individualism. Further, he must transcend the destructive cynicism generated by the racial fear that is alienating and isolating Filipinos from one another and from the whole of society. I emphasize this cynicism as *destructive* because Bulosan depicts it as such for Carlos in his many confrontations with racial fear and the brutality that this fear causes among Filipinos. Cynicism is a negative emotion that Carlos grasps as the cause of his dehumanization in association with the transformation of Filipinos from colonial subjects into undesirable aliens. Ultimately, for Carlos to achieve his aspiration he must *transcend* the paradox of America, which, for racially subjected Filipinos, has its roots in the mass alienation of Filipinos during the Great Depression—a consequence of 1930s anti-intermarriage laws and the Tydings-McDuffie Act.

As Bulosan implies in his narrative, cynicism has gendered effects and implications that reflect white racism's embedment in possessive individualism as an oppressive feature of patriarchy. While in a hospital recovering from tuberculosis, for example, Carlos reveals, "I acquired a mask of pretense that became a weapon I was to take out with me into the violent world again" (252). Figuratively, Carlos's "mask of pretense" is like a hardened outer crust that he develops as a form of emotional labor to contain his feelings of vulnerability and masculinize himself; for such feelings are, as Lorde would put it, stigmatized as "a sign of female inferiority" (52). Having become coarsened by racially motivated acts of violence, Carlos feels he must perform white masculinist values of aggression, stoicism, and solitariness to compensate for the perception of Filipinos as feminized because of their presumed homosociality and fervent expressiveness. Covering over this perceived effeminacy, however, forces Carlos to suppress his affective human needs of empathy and kindness in response to white male claims to power—a patriarchal order denigrating gentleness and compassion, subsumed and made secondary by the sexist logic that categorizes expressions of sensitivity as "feminine" and impassiveness as "masculine." Moreover, that Carlos hardens himself through cynicism as a weapon to use against *other* Filipino men directly mirrors the anti-Filipino antipathy of white male racists who used fear as a weapon to instill in the minds of Filipinos subservience and racial inferiority.

A particularly disturbing instance of Carlos's cynicism with potentially destructive consequences for him occurs after the defeat of a bill whose passing would have given Filipinos the right to become naturalized Americans. "But the race-haters in California . . . fought the bill and killed it" (287), Carlos explains bitterly. "And there were other groups against Filipinos: Liberty League of California, Daughters of the Golden West, Daughters of the American Revolution, and the Parent-Teacher Association. These, with the Associated Farmers of California as the sharp spearhead, were instrumental in killing every bill favorable to Filipinos in Congress and in the state Legislature. They worked as one group to deprive Filipinos of the right to live as free men in a country founded upon this very principle" (287). Here Carlos's listing of the many Euro-American political organizations that worked together to ensure the mass alienation of Filipinos registers the crushing violence of white supremacist racial feelings in California at this time. This violence makes Carlos and his brother, Macario, feel overwhelming despair and hopelessness about their condition as a persecuted minority in America—an acute depression that drives Carlos to become violent. For instance, when a man from Macario's place of employment comes to their apartment to order a sickly Macario back to work, Carlos grabs a butcher knife and rushes at this man. After Macario wrestles the knife away from his brother, Carlos wonders, "Why hadn't I killed him?" (288). He then considers returning to a life of crime to protect himself and live for himself only: "Would I go back to the violence of the old days . . . ? I felt the gun in my pocket and the desire to kill for money seized my mind. Was not this weapon a symbol of my past?" (288). But, to his credit, Carlos rejects violence and crime as a way of life. And his awareness of the way white claims to power pivot on the racialized exclusion and subjection of Filipinos—indicated by his comment that white racists "worked as one group to deprive Filipinos of the right to live as free men in a country founded upon this very principle"—implies his emerging, transcendent position as a knowledge-seeking subject.

Carlos's socialist politics and his involvement in the labor movement enable him to negate his estrangement both at work and in his abject status as an unassimilable alien within a hostile and exclusionary society. Because they allow Carlos to negate racial fear and the anti-Filipino feeling at large in society, socialism and organized labor empower his critical consciousness. According to Paolo Freire, critical consciousness focuses on the way oppressed subjects come to understand social contradictions created by exploitative economic and political systems. The cognitive awakening of oppressed subjects affirms their becoming aware of oppression by questioning the nature of their own historical and social situation. By developing an in-depth understanding of their estrangement and dehumanization in processes of exploited labor, oppressed subjects can transcend alienation in capitalism and "be owners of their own labor" (Freire 164). In Freire's terms, then, Carlos's socialist politics and involvement in organized labor depict his transformation into a knowledge-seeking subject. They articulate his critical consciousness as his in-depth understanding of being an oppressed subject who was forced into flight because of white racism.

Lorde's concept of the erotic as the feeling of self-affirmation through collectively produced and owned labor is also helpful to indicate Carlos's transformation from being a dehumanized other to *becoming* a knowledge-seeking subject who understands himself as part of a common humanity. Following Lorde, we can see how the logic of abstracted labor in the alienation of racialized workers' bodies—a form of psychological destruction for Carlos when he is forced to go on the run because of racial fear—is clear from his anger-infused critique of emotional labor, which reflects his awareness of Filipinos as contradictions of white male individualism. Near the end of *America*, for example, Carlos recounts his involvement in the labor movement and the Communist Party. He trenchantly critiques the racism, betrayal, and infighting among members in the labor movement. He chastises the anti-intellectualism of "stupid little men, anti-Filipino," who are in the Communist Party (293). In his final words for the labor movement and the Communist Party, however, he affirms that they "had contributed something definite toward the awakening of Filipinos in the West Coast. Even when it had entirely forsaken them, a few of the more enlightened members had gathered the carcass of their hope in socialism and tried to breathe a new life into it. . . . I would draw inspiration and courage from it to withstand the confusion and utter futility of my own life" (293). Here, in words that affirm his sense of belonging in the labor and socialist movements, Carlos articulates his becoming a distinct kind of knowledge-seeking subject who realizes that his involvement with organized labor has given him meaning and purpose in a life that was previously responsive to fears rendering his existence meaningless, futile, and desperate. He now grasps his oppression under exploitative economic and political systems and understands that Filipinos are excluded from the proprietary realms of the American Dream, as well as the realms of political and symbolic forms of capital shaping and defining this ideal for white Americans.

He most clearly articulates transcendence, though, in his work as a writer and poet. Writing for Bulosan is intellectual work that negates the objectification of his body in alienated labor. In receiving a bound copy of his first book of poems, he describes his elation, but in terms that express the labor of writing as his recognition of oppression and pain—a recognition articulating his critical consciousness. "When the bound copies of my first book of poems, *Letter From America*, arrived, I felt like shouting to the world. . . . It was something that had grown out of my heart. I knew that I would not write the same way again. I had put certain things of myself in it: the days of pain and anguish, of starvation and fear; my hopes, desires, aspirations. All of myself in this little volume of poems—and I would never be like that self again" (320). In this moment when Carlos articulates his consciousness of work that is personally fulfilling—writing as work that negates the alienation of wage slavery and indentured labor—he heralds Lorde's declaration that when "we begin to recognize our deepest feelings, we begin to give up, of necessity, being satisfied with suffering and self-negation" (58). In Lorde's terms, again, Carlos's artistic labor contradicts his estrangement at work that he experienced when first setting foot in America. In his work as a writer, we can see that he articulates a critical structure of feeling that empowers him to fend off incapacitating affects of suffering and self-negation and subsequently to transcend paradox.

In proposing that Bulosan's consciousness enables him to transcend paradox, I turn to Fredric Jameson's concept of dialectical thinking. According to Jameson, dialectical thinking is the ability to reason through both sides of theoretical opposites or disparate phenomena. It is "thought about thought, thought to the second power, concrete thought about an object, which at the same time remains aware of its own intellectual operations in the very act of thinking" (*Late Marxism* 53). Dialectical thinking is, as Jameson further elaborates in *The Political Unconscious*, "the relationship between the levels of instances, and the possibility of adapting analyses and findings from one level to another" (39). The dialectic method thus offers a way to resolve and synthesize the opposing tensions between our individual perception of society as fragmented and the material forces of a coherent social totality. Jameson's concept of the dialectic is helpful for thinking through Bulosan's trope of the "paradox of America" as his critical response to alienation—for example, Carlos's anger when he experiences discrimination and exclusion, as well as the racial fear and anti-Filipino sentiment generated by possessive individualism. For Carlos, who oscillates between contradictory perceptions of Filipinos both as happily servile and as sexually threatening, the dialectic reveals the way these perceptions negate one another in his critical consciousness. The dialectical tension between his alienation in America because of these racialized perceptions *and* his critical awareness of these perceptions as an emotional paradox involve him in negation. Accordingly, in a relationship between these opposing terms of racialization, one cancels the other and lifts it into a higher plane of existence: development of consciousness through resistance and struggle.

As Abdul JanMohamed reminds us, racialization is influenced by economic motives in a regime of capital accumulation that exploits Manichaean oppositions between subjects who are interpellated by racially discriminatory practices and those who cannot appropriately assimilate into the exchange function of capital because of these practices. In referring to JanMohamed's dialectical concept of the racialized subject's formation as a feature of the Manichaean allegory, I further suggest that a critical consciousness emerges for Carlos in contradiction to his racialized subjection in white supremacist imperialism—a culture of US colonialism in the Philippines that has its roots in the proprietary subjectivity of white male individualism. According to JanMohamed, "The dominant model of power- and interest-relations in all colonial societies is the Manichean opposition between the putative superiority of the European and the supposed inferiority of the native. This axis in turn provides the central feature of the colonialist cognitive framework and colonialist literary representation: the Manichean allegory—a field of diverse yet interchangeable oppositions between white and black, good and evil, superiority and inferiority, civilization and savagery, intelligence and emotion, rationality and sensuality, self and Other, subject and object" (63). The racialization of Filipinos by perceptual oppositions between American selfhood and Philippine otherness is, I further suggest, historically located in a Manichaean allegory between the apparent superiority of white male individualism and the collective inferiority of Filipinos. This dichotomy perseveres in racial formations of the Filipino subject as the power relations of racialized perceptions and their structuring by possessive individualism in property ownership, which was globalized in America's imperialist incursions in the Asia-Pacific and its colonization of the Philippines. The racialized Filipino subject and a corresponding Filipino racial form—emerging in America as contradictions of its capitalist profit system—are shaped and defined by this history of US empire.

Bulosan's critical consciousness, we might further understand, articulates his socialist vision of the world in both transcendent and empathic terms. A striking expression of this vision occurs near the end of *America* when Carlos is left alone to realize his common humanity with black Americans after his brother Macario follows Amado to enlist in the military, "the day after Corregidor fell to the Japanese" (323). Before he boards a bus that will take him away to the army reserves, Macario remembers owing money to a black bootblack. He gives the money to his brother to pay the bootblack, and, watching the bus carrying Macario drive away, Carlos ponders: "If I met him again, I would not be the same. He would not be the same, either. Our world was this one, but a new one was being born. We belonged to the old world of confusion; but in this other world—new, bright, promising—we would be unable to meet its demands" (324). In this part of *America*, Carlos describes his estrangement as a Filipino who has been made unassimilable by anti-Filipino exclusion acts and antimiscegenation laws. He comprehends the alienated condition of Filipinos in America now that Macario and Amado have left to join the military. In this manner, Bulosan implies a paradoxical Filipino racial form as a trope to embody the mass alienation of Filipinos, yet also to register the transcendence of this estrangement through a socialist politics of totality. In terms that are transcendent and empathic, then, Bulosan articulates a critical consciousness through his *felt* experiences with conflict in Manichaean oppositions. In his narrative, he imagines his place both in America and in the world to be one within a deep, horizontal comradeship. And ultimately, through the critical consciousness he expresses in his writing, he envisions an empathic concept of universal comradeship, enabling him to reimagine his place in US society as "an integral part of a community of nations" (Srikanth, *Constructing the Enemy* 7)—a homeland in which he can have a sense of continuity with all humanity.

In this part of *America*, too, Carlos experiences recognizable features of brotherhood and humanity in the black American bootblack to whom Macario owes money. When Carlos gives this man his payment, he asks Carlos to join him for a glass of beer in a local bar. Feeling "a ring of sincerity in his voice," Carlos shares one glass of beer with the man. "He offered it to me when he had drunk half of it. I took the glass and drank the rest of the beer" (324). As the two men part, the bootblack tells Carlos: "I'll meet your brother again somewhere, because I got my dime without asking him. But if I don't see him again, I'll remember him every time I see the face of an American dime. Good-bye, friend!" (324–25). Carlos recognizes Macario and implicitly all Filipino migrant laborers in this African American whose hands were "like [his] brother's—tough, large, toil-scarred" (324). In this example of empathy and comradeship, Bulosan demonstrates an understanding of universal fraternity with other men, articulating an empathic socialist vision that transcends America's emotional paradox and its racialized perception of Filipinos as at once servile and threatening. His socialist vision gives him knowledge and a sense of purpose that contradict the racial fear that propelled him into futility and that previously contained, negated, and dehumanized him.

As we can see in his lifelong struggle with alienation and anti-Filipino hostility, Bulosan uses his indignation as a source to awaken his consciousness of life and to write critically about economic and racial exploitation. Although *America* is fiction in large parts, it is also Bulosan's personal account of his transcendent critical consciousness, which was indispensable to his socialist politics. In his narrative, he asserts the fundamental importance of affects to shape and structure him into a knowledge-seeking subject. Near the beginning of *America*, for instance, he describes the emotions important to developing his awareness of economic exploitation and social stratification. When Carlos is a young boy in the Philippines, he works in the fields with his father and brothers to help keep their family out of poverty. Yet no matter how hard Carlos and his family work, they cannot make enough from their meager crops to pay the usurers who have lent the father money at unreasonably high rates of interest.

Carlos's fear and anger turn into the awakening of his critical consciousness as he sees his family slip deeper into debt and poverty. "This family tragedy marked the beginning of my conscious life," Carlos explains, "I became sensitive in the presence of degradation, so sensitive that my unexpressed feelings tempered my psychological relation to the world" (29). One's consciousness of life is, according to Carlos, shaped by emotions, no matter how implicit or unarticulated they are. His ability to be "sensitive in the presence of degradation" informs his awareness of his family's material reality—their debt and abject poverty as the tragic and unjust consequence of the Philippines' feudal capitalist system.

When Carlos arrives in America as a colonial subject, becomes exploited as an indentured laborer, and is rendered an unassimilable alien under the Tydings-McDuffie Act, he remains sensitive to the degradation of himself and his countrymen. This sensitivity allows him to imagine a sense of home, despite the alienation of Filipinos as a function of racial fear. By his feelings of comradeship characterizing his socialist vision, furthermore, he imagines himself belonging at home *in* America. Through this empathic feeling, he affirms as well his belief in the American Dream, redefining it in accord with his transcendent socialist vision. In the last chapter of *America*, it is evident that Carlos has not lost his optimism to strive for this vaunted ideal. Onboard a bus bound for Oregon "to catch the last crew of cannery workers in Portland" (326), he looks out the window to glance at the landscape and discovers

> with astonishment that the American earth was like a huge heart unfolding warmly to receive me. I felt it spreading through my being, warming me with its glowing reality. It came to me that no man—no one at all—could destroy my faith in America again. It was something that had grown out of my defeats and successes, something shaped by my struggles for a place in this vast land, digging my hands into the rich soil here and there, catching a freight to the north and to the south, seeking free meals in dingy gambling houses, reading a book that opened up worlds of heroic thoughts. It was something that grew out of the sacrifices and loneliness of my friends, of my brothers in America and my family in the Philippines—something that grew of our desire to know America, and to become a part of her great tradition, and to contribute something toward her final fulfillment. I knew that no man could destroy my faith in America that had sprung from all our hopes and aspirations, *ever*. (326–27, italics in original)

Bulosan's lyrical rendering of American kindness—here imagined as an earthly human heart opening lovingly to receive him—reaffirms his socialist vision, implied in his narrative's sentimental title. In *America Is in the Heart*'s last paragraph, however, he aligns his socialist vision with the Filipino migrant's tenacious attachment to the American Dream: "the idea that life will get better," as Chris Hedges and Joe Sacco put it in their critique of this hyped ideal, "that progress is inevitable if we obey the rules and work hard, that material prosperity is assured" (226–27). Because Carlos asserts his undying "faith in America" as his last words, it could be argued that *America* ends with "cruel optimism," in Berlant's formulation of this term (24). However, I would not argue this. For as we can see in Bulosan's forceful articulation of critical consciousness in the last half of his narrative, he shows an in-depth understanding of the way white supremacists and their claims to power are enabled by the subjugation of racialized minorities. And his involvement in the labor movement allows him to identify with a democratic socialist totality—an all-encompassing transcendent vision collectively felt and realizable.

Through an inclusive and shared faith in America "that had sprung from all our hopes and aspirations," Carlos foresees overcoming, in time, racialized divisions of class society and imagines himself linked with others in a chain of common humanity: "I felt something growing inside of me again. There was the same thing in each of them that possessed me: their common faith in the working man. I sat with them and listened eagerly. . . . It was in every word and gesture" (310–11). The anger of Carlos Bulosan as a critique of emotional labor is, in the final analysis, an incisive critique of the American Dream. Through his anger about the mass alienation of Filipinos and their emotional labor of racialization, Bulosan scrutinizes the American Dream as a national ethos that is premised on white freedom and privilege—an ideal historically constituted and powered by the denial of belonging to Filipinos in America. Yet his criticism of this ideal negates a negation, ultimately allowing him to disentangle his own socialist vision for total equality from the acquisitive happiness of possessive individualism.

# 3 /  Feeling Asian/American: Ambivalent Attachments in Asian Diasporic Narratives

What has become of the American Dream? For whom does it still matter?

The idea of America as a place of freedom in which anyone can achieve success, realize happiness, and attain a sense of home and belonging remains an important theme in Asian American literature. From the late twentieth century to the present, Asian American writings reflect aspirations to achieve the American Dream, with its good life of wealth, comfort, and well-being, while simultaneously staying grounded in histories of origin, migration, and diaspora. These works represent the attempts of Asian Americans to express a sense of self and claim individualism, evidencing a free life in US liberal democracy. They depict confidence in the promises of equality and equivalence under citizenship—faith in the normative aspiration to belong as ordinary Americans—while concurrently maintaining attachments to particularities of ethnicity and heritage that have their basis in history.

Beginning in the late twentieth century, however, after the passage of the 1965 Immigration and Nationality Act and the incorporation of multiculturalism into liberal humanist principles of modernity, America's ideal as a color-blind society has complicated these attachments. The ideal of Americans as a modern people who maintain a postracial sensibility corresponds with the liberal pluralist vision of James Truslow Adams, who defined the American Dream in 1931 as an ethos of opportunity for each individual according to ability or achievement regardless of the circumstances of birth and social class. This ethos, which registers America's status in the eyes of the world as a nation at the forefront of

Western modernity, strains the Asian American subject's attachments to ethnic identity—an identity grounded in a collective history of racialized experiences.

Through aspirations to achieve success and "make it" in modern America by actualizing its promises of liberal democracy, Asian American writings represent a *tension* between accommodating the ideal of belonging as an ordinary person in America's color-blind society and maintaining attachments to ethnic identity. Articulating contradiction to the American Dream, Asian American cultural works thus express this tension as conflicting feelings, as the Asian American subject's *ambivalence*.

## On Becoming Asian/American: Racialization and Model Minority Normativity

In Asian American literature, conflicting feelings are important to the critique of modern capitalist societies. As we have seen in previous chapters, Han Ong, Maxine Hong Kingston, and Carlos Bulosan—along with Shaun Tan, whose graphic narratives reflect more complexly the transnational frame of Asia American racialization—have all depicted a tension between attachments to ethnic identity and the accommodation to modern capitalism's ideals, which sublate historical grounding and context. Ong, Kingston, and Bulosan reflect this tension, I argue, in affective terms as ambivalence. Investigating this tension has also been central to the work of Asian Americanist scholars. These scholars have examined and documented the experiences of Asian Americans who feel ambivalence in their quest for home and belonging—in their pursuit of freedom, which traditionally has been the distinction and preserve of Euro-Americans and has excluded Asians as foreigners and racial others. The historian Sucheng Chan, for instance, forcefully explains this ambivalence: "Asian Americans, more so than black or Latino Americans, live in a state of ambivalence—lauded as a 'successful' or 'model minority' on the one hand, but subject to continuing unfair treatment, including occasional outbursts of racially motivated violence, on the other" (188). Chan contends that the ambivalence of Asian Americans is the result of their being widely perceived as models of economic success and upward mobility. This perception encodes the Asian American with a model minority status that is both normative and optimistic. The status is normative in terms of its direct relation to the ideals of succeeding and belonging as an ordinary person in America's color-blind society. It registers optimism insofar as it positions Asian Americans as exemplary subjects whose success through hard work without government remedies demonstrates a "model minority thesis" to African Americans and Latinos—a postracial sensibility that race and ethnicity are no longer barriers to upward mobility and social equality.[1] In US society today, the Asian American model minority registers optimism for the way this status signifies confident receptivity to economic processes of globalization. Yet even though Asian Americans are perceived as model minorities, they continue to experience outbursts of discrimination and racialized violence. For Asian Americans, then, accommodating this perception entails a complex psychological process in which conflicting feelings about belonging in America delineate their subjectivity and their racialization.

David Palumbo-Liu trenchantly examines the Asian American subject's psychological transformation from optimism about the American Dream to deep ambivalence about it. In his study of the social distinctions installed between "Asian" and "American," Palumbo-Liu refers to the state of ambivalence for the racially interpellated Asian as an "Asian/American 'split'" (*Asian/American* 1). Because the stereotyping of Asians in America as aliens and threats persists, even in our current era of postrace pluralism, "the proximity of Asian Americans" to the ideal American "should be read as a history of persistent reconfigurations and transgressions of the Asian/American 'split.' 'Asian American' marks both the distinction installed between 'Asian' and 'American' and a dynamic, unsettled, and inclusive movement" (1). Palumbo-Liu's argument about the nearness of Asian Americans to the ideal American can be understood in affective terms. To try and become the "ideal American" is, I contend, to *aspire* for what this identity in its most basic way implies: normativity. To the extent that Asian Americans are construed as model minorities who succeed in their aspirations for upward mobility, which are normative to being an "ideal American," they personify this achievement. As model minority subjects of what Lauren Berlant calls "aspirational normativity" (164), Asian Americans embody a postracial sensibility encoded with post-1960s pluralist discourses of color blindness and, in the present, optimism about accommodating new ways of modern life through economic processes of globalization and the ideology of neoliberal privatization. Here the logic of racialized perception for Asian Americans in a neoliberal capitalist regime construes them as exemplars of upward mobility to befit a model minority normativity more globally conceived.

Insofar as this perception sees model minority normativity as the Asian's ability to succeed without regard to historical matters of exploitation, oppression, and containment—matters that have constructed Asian Americans as economic subjects—it paradoxically *racializes* Asian Americans as prototypes of achievement in a color-blind society. As I noted in the Introduction, the racialization of Asian Americans in this postracial context effectively contains them within the economic form of capital. The racialization of Asian Americans as model minorities thus *immobilizes* them in the forms of capital, denying their ability to convert economic capital into the symbolic form. The Asian American who aspires to become an artist, as in the writings by Don Lee and Ha Jin that this book examines, cannot take for granted the ability to move freely between the forms of capital. In these works, the failure to succeed as an artist reflects a conflict between the Asian American subject who aspires to grasp individualism by acquiring the symbolic capital in creating art *and* the racializing perception of Asians as uniformly economic subjects.

These writings depict, moreover, the experience of Asian migrants and their American-born children who aspire to the American Dream's ideals of success, well-being, and belonging. But this aspiration comes at the cost of relinquishing attachments to an ethnic identity grounded in history. The writings reflect contradictions and tensions of model minority normativity in themes of discomfort, ambivalence, and divided loyalties. As a critical structure of feeling, ambivalence is central to these works' portrayal of Asian migrants who live and labor in America's modern capitalist society—a society facilitated by economic globalization in which all Americans now perform the affective labor of adapting to anxiety and uncertainty so that they may keep aspiring to economic mobility and success.

This chapter argues that conceptualizing Asian migrants' ambivalence—specifically conflicting feelings wrought by aspirations to normativity—is essential to understanding the process of becoming American in Asian diasporic narratives. These narratives reveal that people of Asian descent in America become Asian/American by feeling ambivalence in response to racialized perceptions of Asians as foreigners and aliens, a perception shaped by economic tropes and hegemonic color-blind discourse. Andrew Pham's *Catfish and Mandala* and Ha Jin's *A Free Life* reflect diasporic Asians' process of becoming American through ambivalent attachments to living in America's liberal democracy. Both narratives depict the aspiration of Asian migrant families to normative American lives of material comfort and security. This aspiration is an affect of belonging arranged within modern capitalist culture: the American Dream arises as a feeling that would be produced through upward mobility and economic success. Yet this aspiration is also about *feeling normal*, a yearning to belong in neoliberal America without regard to race, ethnicity, and national origin. Feeling normal is, in this sense, a racialized affect expressed as postracial sensibility within model minority normativity. Pham and Jin critically reflect America's national ethos of freedom and the pursuit of happiness as the basis for an emotional culture in neoliberalism that generates postracial sensibility. In their narratives, they critique the attachments felt for an American Dream at once promised and placed out of reach, contrasting affects of belonging to the contradictory experiences of exclusion and alienation. They show how being subject-to-racialization, amid a neoliberal politics of color blindness, causes the diasporic Asian *to feel* a disabling and disorienting uncertainty about belonging in America. This uncertainty is, I argue, a racial feeling that thwarts the optimistic attachment to the American Dream and turns the aspiration of social belonging into ambivalence. Feeling Asian/American in Asian diasporic narratives is, then, an affective experience of political formation. The process of becoming Asian American through being racialized is in tension with politically naive aspirations to be and feel normal as an ordinary American.

## Cold War Liberalism's Embarrassment: Racism and the Collective Politics of Shame

Asian diasporic narratives not only critique the perception of Asians as models of success and upward mobility but also show how this perception has been instrumental in shaping hegemonic color-blind discourse—a postracial sensibility important to maintaining America's status in the eyes of the world as a modern nation with an exemplary global economy. If these narratives critique this perception in their expressions of ambivalence, it is important to point out that postracial sensibility, which has been popular since the 1990s and comprises today's aspirations to belong and achieve the American Dream, is traceable to America's national ethos of freedom and happiness in a liberal democratic tradition.

On October 3, 1965, President Lyndon Johnson avowed this national ethos when signing into law the Immigration and Nationality Act. Standing at the foot of the Statue of Liberty in New York Harbor, Johnson declared that eliminating national origins quotas remedied a "very deep and painful flaw in the fabric of American justice" (qtd. in M. Ngai 259). The new law "says simply that from this day forth those wishing to immigrate to America shall be admitted on the basis of their skills and their close relationship to those already here" (259). Johnson added that the old system of national origins quotas "violated the basic principle of American democracy—the principle that values and rewards each man on the basis of his *merit as a man*" (259, italics added). Because the act idealized a nondescript "man" who succeeded in America "on the basis of his merit" regardless of the circumstances of birth and social class, it became language that refigured the American Dream to articulate a credo of individualism against the threat of communism in the Cold War era. Its motive was to protect America's position of power and privilege within the global capitalist economy. In the late twentieth century, this nationalist vision for individualism became hegemonic discourse for multiculturalism—a liberal pluralist discourse underpinning postracial sensibility that envisioned America as a color-blind society and maintained transnational economic interests in a neoliberal capitalist regime.[2]

During the Cold War, America sought to overcome its "national shame" over histories of racism and immigration exclusion by envisioning a color-blind society. Cold War liberalism's color blindness has, in our current era, evolved into a neoliberal political philosophy of racial privatization and postracial sensibility—an ideology informing the Asian subject's experiences with racial interpellation and containment. The ongoing racialized perception of Asians as foreigners and threats in US politics is evidence for the persistence of Asiatic stereotyping that suggests its continued production by America's political-economic culture. This culture, which exploits popular anti-Asian sentiment, *updates* yellow peril fears from nineteenth-century Orientalist discourses. The American Orientalist perception of Asians both as economic exemplars and as threats is articulated through affectively charged language to construe a hypersuccessful yet menacing Asian.

This paradoxical form of Asian representation in US Orientalist discourse emerged as a discursive product of America's scramble for power in the new stage of world capitalism during the nineteenth century. As an economic trope to represent America's identification of the Asian as a sign of globalization, an Asiatic racial form developed from the determination of the United States to stake a dominant position in the international markets of East Asia (Lye, *America's Asia* 9). America's imperialist ambitions and relations with East Asia have been encouraged by its manipulation and reproduction of this Asiatic racial form. Although the language that constructs today's Asian American as a racialized subject has undergone significant transformation by the economic processes and historical forces of globalization, any understanding of the contemporary racial formation of Asian Americans is ultimately traceable to this abiding Asiatic racial form, a form generated by America's emotionally charged Orientalist discourses and updated as a *racial abstraction* by politicians in the Cold War between the United States and the Soviet Union.

Nowhere is the manipulation of old yellow peril fears more evident than in recent US geopolitical discourses. As exemplified in the recent election campaigns of American politicians, these discourses, which invoke the affective texture and politics of an abiding Asiatic racial form, show not only that race continues to matter in America through discriminatory practices of racial stigmatization to acquire political power and privilege but also that race persists as an active social relation fundamentally structuring American subjectivities, insofar as it is an emotionally charged commodity aesthetic that America's political-economic culture continually reproduces and exploits.[3]

On the contrary, then, pluralist discourses that envision the United States today as both color-blind and postracial because racial preferences, discrimination, and prejudice apparently no longer happen or matter—discourses that idealize and advocate a postracial sensibility—are in striking contradiction to the anti-Asian sentiments of politicians who exploit yellow peril fears by invoking and fueling today's economic Cold War between China and the United States. But is it really that much of a contradiction? If we trace these political discourses to the first Cold War between the United States as the leader of the so-called "Free World" and the Soviet Union with its communist allies, are these discourses two sides of the same coin? How might today's simultaneously postracial and racializing discourses revise and reproduce, as a yellow peril aesthetic, an affective politics of race from Cold War liberalism? This was a war, we must remember, in which the United States wanted to promote liberal capitalist democracy as the essence of "freedom" and did so framed through the hegemonic discourse of pluralism as well as assimilation into the psychological and subjective conditions of normative life in America.

If, as the proverb goes, "freedom is a state of mind" and if in the context of America's liberal democracy such freedom has been understood collectively as the normative aspiration to a way of life whose principles are "life, liberty, and the pursuit of happiness," this psychological and subjective condition of freedom is the experiential attainment of upward mobility, equality, and comfort inherent in the ideological structure of the American Dream. This dream is itself a consumer product that Americans fetishize as "the primary myth by means of which they mold their interpersonal relations to resemble relations of capitalist production, which are relations among commodities" (Tyson 7). In this sense, the commodity psychology intrinsic to the American Dream is what conventionally defines freedom as the normative aspiration to attain the good life of contentment, security, and equality in America's liberal capitalist democracy.

We might understand this commodity psychology shaping and defining the American Dream to encompass people's affective attachments to fantasies of the good life. Berlant contends that people's desires to achieve the good life reveal the persistence of normativity within these desires (167). These are powerful attachments to fantasies of normal life realizable through hard work, good behavior, and an unflagging belief in the liberal capitalist promises of economic progress, job security, and social and political equality. Today's American Dream is "about the political and affective economies of normativity at the present time, the production as desire of a collective will to imagine oneself as a solitary agent who can and must live the good life promised by capitalist culture. . . . It is about the fantasy of meritocracy, a fantasy of being deserving, and its relation to practices of intimacy, at home, at work, and in consumer worlds" (167). Despite the economic crises of global capitalism that have rendered these fantasies unachievable and turned normative aspirations for the good life into "cruel optimism," people maintain their attachments to the social-democratic promises of liberal capitalism. They have adjusted to economic catastrophes in a world where prevailing crisis has become ordinary, the new normal.

To a large extent, the psychological and subjective condition of freedom as the optimistic attachment to achieving the good life is what the United States sought to protect and disseminate against communism in the last century. But freedom as a state of mind in liberal democracy during the Cold War also implies, I suggest, the subjective achievement of the abstracted citizen whose "merit as a man" foretells the aspiration to be ordinarily American in a modern capitalist society. Freedom as a state of mind that indicates the normative subjectivity of the abstracted citizen can be understood as the psychological objective of the Asian immigrant's naturalization into the ordinary citizen. As Lisa Lowe argues, "Immigration can be understood as the most important historical and discursive site of Asian American formation through which the national and global economic, the cultural, and the legal spheres are modulated. . . . As the state legally transforms the Asian *alien* into the Asian American *citizen*, it institutionalizes the disavowal of the history of racialized labor exploitation and disenfranchisement through the promise of freedom in the political sphere" (*Immigrant Acts* 11–10, original italics). This promise of freedom in the political sphere both during and after the Cold War may be understood, furthermore, as the autonomy to imagine oneself in neoliberal America, despite its ongoing economic crises, as a self-sufficient individual who can and must live the good life promised by capitalism.

As Mae Ngai has shown, Cold War liberal nationalism was hegemonic discourse in America after World War II (245). In the advent of the Cold War during the late 1940s, "United States liberal capitalist democracy was defined as the 'good' of the world and its best hope against the 'evil' of Soviet Communism. . . . [Yet] Cold War liberalism diminished the cultural aspect of cultural pluralism. Pluralism was now less about ethnic identity (much less identity politics) than it was a means for ethnic participation in politics. Pluralism conceived of ethnicity as a legitimate 'interest' in a political world of interest groups. In this sense it was assimilationist, a strategy that recognized difference in order to efface it within the universality of liberal democratic politics" (234). Ngai here points out that Cold War liberals aspired to make America pluralist by reforming immigration policy to allow more immigration from Europe in order to address "discriminations faced by ethnic Euro-Americans who were racialized as white" (229). Thus the objective of Cold War liberalism was to create a modern society free of racial discrimination, but it was premised on maintaining the whiteness of Euro-Americans. The abstracted citizen (i.e., President Johnson's man of "merit") would emerge as the ideal American from having assimilated into the customs and norms of Euro-Americans. This liberal nationalist discourse of assimilation into Euro-American norms informed the 1965 Immigration Act's removal of national origins as the basis of America's new immigration policy. Its objective was to open the way for millions of new immigrants from Europe to come to America with its family reunification provisions, which allowed the spouses of US citizens, unmarried minor children, and parents of citizens to enter as nonquota immigrants without any limit.

In passing the law, to be sure, the United States wished to portray itself as the leader of the "Free World" by eliminating all racial discrimination both in domestic aspects of public life and in its immigration policy. Further, reforming immigration policy through passage of the act would uphold the ideals of liberal pluralism. Yet it was the culture of white Americans as the descendants of Europeans that liberals imagined would constitute most of this pluralism. As Ngai further explains, "The absence of non-European ethno-racial groups in the reform movement meant that liberals tended to view immigration policy for Asia, Mexico, and the Caribbean abstractly, disconnected from those immigrant communities in the United States and without the benefit of their experiences and perspectives" (246).

Advocates of the 1965 Immigration Act predicted there would be only a minor increase in Asian immigration because they thought there were too few citizens of Asian descent in the United States to make wide use of the family reunification provisions of the new law. Despite this expectation, the law quickly changed the pattern of migration of people from Asia to the United States. After the law went into effect in 1965, Asian immigration increased so steadily that Asians composed more than half of the total influx by the 1980s (Chan 145). The law's specified preferences for scientists, professionals, and skilled workers enabled a large number of highly trained professionals from Asia to immigrate. Many young Asian Americans born in the United States after 1965 come from parents who immigrated because of this law. Their attitudes about modern and mainstream America as a liberal pluralist society are the logical social and cultural consequences of Cold War liberalism's immigration and civil rights reforms (Song 35–37).

Liberal immigration reformers conceived the 1965 Immigration Act in conjunction with civil rights reforms, responding to rising political support for cultural pluralism and increasing demands among Americans to end racial discrimination. In the wake of the world war against fascism and in the midst of America's Cold War with the Soviet Union and its communist allies, liberal white elites found America's race policies falling short of its democratic principles. Racial discrimination throughout US society and in the nation's immigration laws contradicted the democratic image of America that Cold War liberals wanted to project to the world. This contradiction was a source of *national shame*. As early as 1948, for example, in the *Shelly v. Kramer* case, which involved a racially restrictive covenant in real estate, the federal government filed an amicus brief to support ending racial restrictions in housing that stated: "The United States has been *embarrassed* in the conduct of foreign relations by acts of [racial] discrimination in this country" (qtd. in Robert Lee, *Orientals* 157). Cold War liberals such as the social scientist Robert Amundson viewed race discrimination in immigration policy as an embarrassment. In a 1957 article that criticized racially restrictive immigration legislation, Amundson wrote: "Certainly most Americans must experience a sense of moral embarrassment when asked to justify our present immigration laws in light of the democratic concept of equal rights and justice for all" (qtd. in M. Ngai, 228). Cold War liberals who were embarrassed about racial discrimination throughout US society and in the nation's immigration policy thus articulated a collective politics of shame that underwrote immigration and civil rights reforms.

Here we might interpret Cold War liberalism's moral embarrassment in Sara Ahmed's terms of "national shame" that reveal a narrative of emotional reproduction for the nation's identity in the eyes of the world. A nation "may bring shame 'on itself,'" Ahmed explains, by failing to live up to national ideals (*Cultural Politics* 108). Shame can "become a form of identification in the very failure of an identity to embody an ideal" (108). By collectively recognizing and declaring the failure to embody national ideals, "*the nation can 'live up' to the ideals that secure its identity or being in the present*. In other words, our shame *means that we mean well*, and can work to reproduce the nation as an ideal" (109, italics in original). Following Ahmed, we might see that the professed embarrassment of liberal white elites for racism in America during the Cold War provoked national shame. Cold War liberalism's embarrassment articulated a collective politics of shame about the nation's failure to live up to the ideals of liberal pluralism. The sense of moral embarrassment that Amundson claims most Americans experience about racism in immigration policy is represented and recognized as national shame. By recognizing this racism and remedying it with civil rights legislation and immigration reforms, America allowed itself to be idealized and even celebrated during the Cold War. In this historical context, then, idealizing and celebrating America by overcoming national shame meant that America could show the world that its liberal capitalist system was the purveyor of universal freedom for the world, the best hope against the evil of Soviet communism.

Also in this historical context, we might understand that America's embarrassment about racial discrimination provoked its national shame in a hegemonic discourse of Cold War liberalism that structured its color-blind immigration and naturalization policy. This policy was premised on a philosophy of liberal individualism, which has conditioned today's aspirational norm among Asian immigrants to succeed and belong as ordinary Americans in neoliberalism. If feeling and being postracial is also a constitutive feature in achieving ordinary and normative American status, then we can see how an affective politics of race and assimilation in Cold War liberalism has influenced what is meant by freedom in US society today. This politics has structured postracial sensibility as the subjectivity of Euro-Americans, articulating freedom as an emotional commodity that the Asian immigrant must aspire to possess as an achievement of the American Dream. White racial ideals have been and continue to be central in producing discourses for norms, entitlements, and rights that uphold recognitions of personhood and citizenship through race in liberal democracy. Postracial sensibility thus encompasses racial feelings, in the context of racial liberalism, that articulate the US citizen's right to happiness through material acquisition in liberal democracy. Historically premised on Euro-American proprietary relations in possessive individualism, racial feelings both inform and articulate the contentment, security, and comfort that are the desired emotionality of normative American personhood.

Cold War liberalism's inadvertent identification of Asian Americans as model economic characters has paved the way for advocates of liberal multiculturalism to envision a color-blind society. In this sense, Asian America *is* a racial formation whose racialized perception by Euro-Americans as "integrated, modernized, and civilized" minorities exemplifies what Victor Bascara provocatively calls "model-minority imperialism" (5). Embodying postracial sensibility for a neoliberal politics of privatization, Asian Americans have been racialized as model minorities. Their racialization in this model minority context has allowed America to establish and manifest its capitalist system as an economic feature of its geopolitical discourse—a neoliberal politics largely having its basis in a series of colonial regimes and imperialist incursions throughout the Asia-Pacific. Racialized as a model minority of capitalist modernity, then, the Asian American as an exemplary agent of upward mobility and wealth accumulation has enabled America's capitalist system under neoliberalism to become a form of government shaped and defined by a culture of privatization and acquisitive individualism.

And yet, as the exploitive updating of yellow peril fears in contemporary US politics demonstrates, the Asian continues to embody the *impossibility* of assimilation into normative whiteness because—as the sign of an economically threatening and totalitarian Asia—the diasporic

Asian signifies the specter of racial fears that would imperil the very idea of "a free life" in America. Facing an abiding racial stereotype of Asians both as economic exemplars and as threats, how can Asian migrants in the narratives we will now explore feel anything but ambivalence about the American Dream?

## Feeling "Real American" in *Catfish and Mandala*

Andrew X. Pham was born in the town of Phan Thiet during the Vietnam War. In his memoir *Catfish and Mandala* (hereafter *Catfish*), Pham recounts his return to Vietnam after fleeing from the country as a refugee with his family in 1977. After the Viet Cong took over South Vietnam, Pham's father was sent to a prison and labor camp where he barely survived. When he reunited with his family he feared for their lives and immediately made arrangements for himself, his five children, his wife, and her sister to escape in a boat. In his memoir, Pham explains that for nearly twenty years he has lived in America feeling like an outsider even though he eventually became a naturalized citizen. In 1996 he goes on a solo bicycle journey traveling in Mexico, along the US Pacific Coast, in Japan, and finally around Vietnam. In between explaining his encounters while traveling, he tells the story of his family's harrowing escape from Vietnam, their lives of adjustment and assimilation in a newly adopted homeland, his experiences with racial prejudice in America, and his coming to terms with the suicide of his transsexual brother Chi, who ran away from home in response to ostracism from family and community.

One of Pham's greatest regrets is that he and his family "forgot" Chi in the years after his suicide when they moved to another town and his other siblings grew up to have families of their own. Chi's tragic death, the memory of his being forgotten, and the racism of Americans make Pham angry and ambivalent not only about belonging in America but also about his connection with Vietnam and other Vietnamese Americans. When he travels in Vietnam other Vietnamese refer to him disparagingly as a common *Viet Kieu* (an overseas Vietnamese), making him feel like an outsider. In America, he desires acceptance in mainstream society but feels no sense of belonging among Vietnamese Americans because he considers them to be psychologically damaged by the traumas of colonialism, war, and forced removal from the homeland. As Isabelle Thuy Pelaud points out, Pham "is attracted to mainstream America, but no matter how well he conforms, he is always regarded as the other"

(223); being perceived by whites as a foreigner fuels his ambivalence about belonging in America both as a Vietnamese in the diaspora and as a racialized Asian.

As a postcolonial narrative, *Catfish* may be understood to be a work of political and cultural diaspora that challenges normative expectations of development and progress (Bhabha 2). Pham exposes the actualization of the American Dream as a fantasy and its color-blind ideals of contentment, comfort, and belonging as the social norms of white privilege. Through his encounters and confrontations with other men, he reveals this dream's postracial sensibility for success and progress to be paradoxically based on the racialized perception of Asians as exemplars of economic success and social assimilation.

To the extent that Pham's anger articulates his ambivalence about belonging in America, he contests the white masculinity of Cold War liberalism's ideal American, an abstracted citizen whose "merit as a man" in a color-blind society defines his status as a real American. That Pham is both attracted to and repelled by the masculinity of white men suggests that he desires the racially abstracted real American as a normative expectation. Yet his conflicting feelings of attraction and repulsion, inclusion and exclusion, belonging and not belonging, reflect his own perception of existing "in-between" without a center as a diasporic Asian. His ambivalent attachments to the real and ideal American *and* this ideal's embedment in white male subjectivity critique the politics of normativity in a time of heightened Cold War liberal nationalist discourse.

## Normativity's Male Subjectivity

Pham sees himself as a man through the perspectives of other men, especially those of his father and white American men. When he bicycles through a desert in Mexico, for example, he meets Tyle, an American GI who appears as a prototype of the real American. "He is a giant," standing before Pham "bare-chested, barefoot, desert-baked golden" (5). He is also "charismatic, and shakes his head of long matty blond hair" (5), physically gesturing his manly rugged individualism. Admiring Pham's ability to maneuver his bicycle through the desert's rocky terrain, Tyle says, "'How you got here on that bike is *amazing*" (5). He recognizes Pham's inner strength and drive, and this pleases Pham because he wants his masculinity to be identical to that of white men.

But when Tyle asks Pham about his nationality and he replies, "I'm from Vietnam" (6), Tyle "grunts," turns his back to Pham, and heaves a mouthful of spit into a cactus forest. For Pham, a moment of recognition by an admirable and enviable white man turns into derogation and denial. He suddenly feels "small, crooked" (6) and remembers his sibling Chi: "I stand, a trespasser in his camp, hearing echoes—Chink, gook, Jap, Charlie, GO HOME, SLANT-EYES!—words that, I believe, must have razored my sister Chi down dark alleys, hounded her in the cold after she had fled home, a sixteen-year-old runaway, an illegal alien without a green card. What vicious clicking sounds did they make in her Vietnamese ears, wholly new to English? And, within their boundaries, which America did she find?" (6–7). In Pham's memory of his transsexual brother, Chi is an abject figure of racism and heteropatriarchal violence. When Chi runs away from home, fleeing from his father's rage and constant beatings because of his decision to live openly as a transgender man, he becomes an "illegal alien without a green card," dispossessed by his own family and community. Here it is significant that Pham repeats common anti-Asian utterances—"Chink, gook, Jap, Charlie"—by invoking Chi in relation to his own feelings of negative judgment by a white man. For his memory of Chi at an instant when he feels denied by Tyle attests to his own displacement and estrangement in America—feelings generated by his attraction to the masculinity of white men, as well as his own professed connection to Chi through abjection.

Pham realizes that Tyle has not, in fact, rejected him. Instead Tyle breaks down and cries, remorseful about atrocities he committed as a soldier in the war. He asks for forgiveness, thinking Pham represents the people of Vietnam. The ensuing silence leads Tyle to believe that he has been given "absolution," though Pham inwardly recognizes that absolution is not his to give: "And, in my fraudulence, I know I have embarked on something greater than myself" (9). Pham does not want to represent the people of Vietnam or act for fellow Vietnamese Americans because he is angry with them. He thinks they have accepted and replicated the American bigotries and racialized perceptions that caused Chi to run away and commit suicide.

Reflecting his own male subjectivity, which has been racialized by insistent identifications with whiteness, Pham pays extraordinary attention to the words and bodily gestures of Euro-American men. However, he is just as much repelled by these men as he is attracted to them. Because his father pressures him to succeed, Pham majors in engineering when he is an undergraduate at UCLA, but he realizes he is being pushed into a future work life whose rules of conduct and standards of professionalism are set and maintained by white men.

After graduation Pham lands "a cushy engineering post at a major airline" (25). During his interview, he meets his would-be boss, "a turtle-chinned, red-faced thirty-five-year-old-timer" named Paul, who, Pham further reveals, "waxed on about the company's expansion overseas and his getting an M.B.A. in international business to keep abreast of it all" (25). What most troubles Pham is that Paul perceives him as a model minority. He tells him on his first day at work: "I like you. . . . I like you people. Orientals are good workers. Good students, too. Great in math, the engineering stuff. . . . I think you'll do just fine here. We won't have any trouble at all" (25). Paul's perception of Asians as models of obedience and assimilation insults Pham. It also emasculates him and makes him hate being Vietnamese American.

Belittled and patronized by Paul's comments about "Orientals," which we may understand as an act of racial interpellation (Chong 34), Pham becomes enraged. His anger is, I further suggest, a forceful reaction to "racial naturalization," in Devon Carbado's formulation of this term (636). Racial naturalization is the nonwhite subject's affective experience of undergoing a naturalization process in which he is objectified and contained by an authority figure who both represents and is included in normative American identity. If "American identity" means the capacity "to be a representative body—figuratively and materially—for the nation" (Carbado 638), then Paul construes and identifies Pham through Orientalist tropes to exclude him from the representative body of normative American identity. Notwithstanding his legal status as a naturalized American, Pham experiences social identity displacement or a kind of "racial extraterritorialization" (638). When Paul tells him, "I like you," he understands this to mean he has been hired and included in the airline's engineering department because of the perception of Asians as "Orientals" who are "good workers."

Yet Paul's comment also registers Pham's being hired and included in liberal pluralist terms. Paul hires Pham and believes he will "do just fine here" because the company perceives itself as an equal opportunity employer, an advocate of color-blind ideals in liberal democratic capitalism. As the "boss," Paul has to represent the company's values of equality and opportunity that are ideally available to all regardless of racial and ethnic identifications.

As an authority figure, moreover, Paul has to represent the company's articulation of postracial sensibility. By this same perception, however, Pham is *excluded* from the racially gendered subjectivity that constitutes American identity. That is, Paul's perception of Pham as a model employee, his belief that he is a "good Oriental," is an instance of racial naturalization, but in *masculinist* terms. For Pham, then, Paul's perception of him as a model minority signals both his inclusion in America as a racialized laborer and his exclusion from the realm of normative male subjectivity, which is socially and culturally white.

This perception clearly denies Pham's belonging in America as a Vietnamese American male. Unable to recover from Paul's insults, which cause him to feel emasculation—what David Eng calls "the *avowal* of castration" (*Racial Castration* 150, italics in original)—Pham quits his job and exacts his revenge: "When I finally resigned, I was no longer a 'good Oriental.' I even left behind in my desk three files titled 'Stuff Paul Rejected Because He Doesn't Know Any Better,' 'Stuff Paul Rejected Because He Didn't Want to Jeopardize His Promotion,' and 'Stuff Paul Rejected Because They Didn't Originate from Engineers but from Mechanics Who Have More Practical Experience on the Subject'" (25). By quitting his job in this vengeful manner, Pham seems to challenge Paul's authority to deny him normative masculinity through racial naturalization. His resignation and vengeful actions of inscribing his rage onto the files imply his affirmation of self and his refusal of the model minority stereotype. To be sure, it appears that Pham is defining and claiming a space in which he can be an Asian American male on his own terms. But really he will be able to do this only when he can let go of his attachment to the masculinity of white men *and* when can he let go of his contempt for other Vietnamese Americans.

It does not help Pham to overcome his feelings of emasculation and disdain for the model minority stereotype when his father berates him for giving up his job. Pham recalls the tense exchange he had with his father when he told him about his resignation:

> Giving up this job and burning my bridges, my father believed, were the *undoing* of me, and nothing I had done since elicited a "Good" from him. "You don't do that. You do job best you can. You get promotion. You get new job. You say, 'Thank you very much, sir' and you go. Think about future. You are Asian man in America. All your bosses will be white. Learn to work."
>
> Yes, Father. Okay, Father. I will, Father.
>
> I can't be his Vietnamese American. (25, italics added)

By rearticulating his father's words in pidgin English, Pham expresses anger toward a Vietnamese authority figure, but one he sees as reinforcing white masculinity and the emasculation of Asian men. As Pelaud maintains, "His father's words are construed as requirements to be submissive and therefore as a demand to sacrifice his own romantic notions of manhood" (227). But how are we to construe Pham's anger about his father's words in relation to Chi's death? Are the father's words the same kind of authority that drove Chi to run away and commit suicide? How can a psychologically injured Pham, recovering from his own figurative castration, salve his conscience about Chi's suicide if his own father serves as a conduit for the perceived superiority of white men?

The father claims that not submitting to white male authority will be Pham's "undoing" in America. But, as Pham sees it, obedience to this authority and its hateful stereotyping of Asian men will lead to his own undoing. And because his father's authority led to Chi's banishment and death, Pham perceives his father's words to uphold a white male identity that maintains its normative subjectivity through violence.

Pham cannot obey his father's authority and continue to feel desirous of white masculinity because both are destructive. Yet what does Pham mean by saying that he cannot be his father's Vietnamese American? How are we to interpret his rejection of his father's words in relation to his antipathy for those Vietnamese Americans he considers submissive and "forever congenial" to white authority? Isn't Pham himself endorsing masculinist violence by holding in contempt those Vietnamese Americans whom he sees as having accepted Americans' racialized perceptions about who they are? Pham hates "their groveling humility" and "slitty-measuring eyes" (25), behaviors of acquiescence and accommodation he believes display infirmity. Yet such hatred, Pham should further understand, also serves as a conduit for the perceived superiority of white men.

Consequently, he cannot continue to see other Vietnamese Americans from a white man's perspective because this perspective—transmitted through the father and through himself—also led to Chi's tragedy. In realizing his predicament, Pham, like Chi, becomes alienated from his family. He is angry and ambivalent about his life in America. Therefore, he looks to Vietnam and the bicycle journey he's planned there to help him overcome his alienation, and possibly to give him resolution and transcendence.

## Consuming Authenticity

If Pham's objective in Vietnam is to overcome his alienation and reconnect with other Vietnamese, he will be able to do this only when he stops comparing himself with other Vietnamese in normatively masculine terms. But at the start of his trip in Vietnam, his anger and ambivalence remain unabated. He sees the Vietnamese as shameless beggars, a "wanting-wanting-wanting" people (102), in the same way that he looks down upon Vietnamese Americans as "groveling," too "accepting," and subservient. When he returns to Saigon (Ho Chi Minh City), the place where he spent his final childhood years before leaving for America, he refers to the city and all its citizens through a mother/whore dichotomy to define his own sense of self: "My Saigon was a whore. She sold her body to any taker, dreams of a better future, visions turned inward, eyes to the sky of the skyscrapers foreign to the land, away from the festering sores at her feet" (109). While in Vietnam, Pham construes himself as a masculine individual in opposition to an abject and a feminized Vietnamese people. Because the Vietnamese refer to him as a *Viet-Kieu*—a term for the millions of Vietnamese living outside Vietnam as foreigners after the communist takeover in 1975—he thinks his belonging with them is called into question. Called a *Viet-Kieu* repeatedly, Pham feels as if the Vietnamese perceive him as racially different, and this makes him ambivalent about having a place in his country of origin.

Yet he does find instances in which he readily asserts his own difference from the Vietnamese. For example, he tells a tour operator, Binh, about his plans to bicycle from South to North Vietnam. Binh warns him not to do it: "*You won't make it. Trust me, I've been around a long time. Vietnamese just don't have that sort of physical endurance and mental stamina. We are weak. Only Westerners can do it. They are stronger and better than us*" (77, italics in original). At this moment when he hears the first-person-plural "we" to include him as a fellow Vietnamese, Pham implicitly denies this inclusion, attempting to avow his strength as an American. He doesn't deny, in other words, Binh's allegation that the Vietnamese are "weak" and Westerners are "stronger." Rather, he denies this for *himself* as a Vietnamese American man. Binh's warning makes Pham want to tour Vietnam on his bicycle more than ever. He wants to challenge Vietnamese males such as Binh who perceive him as less masculine than Westerners. It is thus apparent that Pham is in Vietnam to recuperate his masculinity because he believes it has been wounded by his experiences with the racial stereotyping of Asian Americans as model minorities. In this sense, Vietnam indeed seems like "a battleground from which Pham wants to emerge as the first Vietnamese American man hero" (Pelaud 230).

In Vietnam, men demonstrate their individuality, vitality, and virility through food. As Pham explains, his male relatives challenge him to prove his manhood by joining them in a ritual of consuming offal and drinking alcohol. Women are excluded from this ritual; their only place in it is to serve the men. "We are dealing in men's business," the men tell the women and children who attempt to observe them. "Let us be" (84). Not wanting to appear weak and less capable, Pham joins them in a meal of goat stew and goat liquor, "two parts rice wine mixed with one part fresh goat's blood" (82). But Pham divulges that "halfway through the meal, my bowels heave and I sprint to the toilet" (82). When he returns to the table, the men are waiting for him to complete the final part: to drink "heart-liquor" made from a live snake. They order the bartender to make the concoction. He slits open the underside of a cobra, "plucks open the skin and shows the beating heart, the size of a chocolate chip. . . . He severs the arteries and transplants the heart into a shot glass half filled with rice wine. The heart pulses swirling red streamers of blood into the clear liquor" (83). When the glass is placed before him, Pham is reluctant to drink it. But the men pound the table: *Don't be such a wimp, drink up! . . . You said you want to be Vietnamese. You want to try everything we do. It doesn't get more Vietnamese than this*" (84, italics in original). Understanding their words as a challenge, Pham tosses the liquor into his mouth: "I feel the squishy live organ, tapioca-like, on my tongue. I double over and retch it onto the floor, alcohol up my nose, burning. . . . The audience hoots with laughter. That is how Vietnamese men bond" (84). By drinking the heart-liquor, Pham thinks he has passed the test of Vietnamese authenticity. He believes he's proven his worth as a man in the eyes of his relatives. He maintains that eating offal and drinking heart-liquor is for Vietnamese men an assertion of mastery over one's self.

What appears of greatest concern to Pham is, then, not to disabuse the Vietnamese of their perception that Westerners are their superiors. Rather, what concerns him is to define his own space of inclusion as a Vietnamese American man by construing himself within the realm of normative male subjectivity. And the ritual of eating offal and drinking liquor offers a way to determine this space. When he leaves his relatives to ride his bike north, he finds other Vietnamese men who want to challenge and test him through the food and alcohol ritual. For instance, when he boards a train bound for Hanoi he meets Tung, the train's cargo supervisor. According to Pham, Tung has "boiling-red drinker's eyes and withered smoker's teeth" (204); Pham thus dubs him "Redeyes." On the morning of Pham's second day onboard the train, Redeyes introduces him to his coworkers, who invite him to drink bottles of rice wine. While drinking and eating, they demand answers to questions about women and sex in America.

> They want to know about the West and about Western women. Sex before marriage, really? Sex on the first date, you serious? Sex in high school?! . . .
> With them shoving gizzards, intestines, livers, and hearts at me as though I've never seen such delicacies before, I succumb to the peer pressure and swallow. When we finish, Bugsy brings out another party platter, piled high with snails, goat testicles, fish heads, goat blood pudding, pig brain, and some sort of sausage the color of wet ash and old blood. After four bottles of wine, they doze off happily. I retch out the window. They wake, chortle, and curse me for wasting good liquor. I sit like a dead man, watching the land scroll forward and away. (209)

Again, Pham's ability to meet the challenge of eating offal and drinking liquor, despite having to vomit it all up "out the window," implies his assertion of male selfhood. He claims a sense of masculine *individualism* against others who attempt to deny him such individualism by calling his identity as a Vietnamese American man into question.

In the process, he wants to claim an "in-between" space, though this claiming is driven by his desire for inclusion in the heteronormative realms of manhood and patriarchy. This process, I contend, raises a host of questions. How, for instance, are we to interpret not only the exclusion of women from the determination of this space but also their *negation*? How are we to understand the formulation of this space as one that relies on *abjection*, indicated by the competitive eating and drinking that give Pham dysentery and, as he puts it, make his "innards faucet into the toilet" (219)? He further reveals: "It feels like a maniac is tenderizing my gut with an ice pick. I get on the toilet just in time as my gut empties itself. It keeps coming. *My insides turn inside out.* I'm being eviscerated. I look down and watch my heart emptying into the toilet bowl . . . Few things will put the fear of God into me as effectively as seeing blood gushing out where it shouldn't" (305). Does this space, defined in large part by these punishing rituals of eating offal and drinking alcohol, allow Pham to come to terms with Chi's death and the tragedy of his family's forgetting him?

We might understand Pham's self-induced illness—the fact that he purposely injures himself by repeatedly taking part in rituals of male bonding that make his "insides turn inside out"—as evidence of his self-reproach, a repentant and possibly masochistic desire to be forgiven for

Chi's death and the family's disremembering of him. By making him-self sick, Pham perhaps is punishing himself in memory of his sibling. He renders his own abjection in Vietnam to connect with Chi's pain when he was expelled from the family and into abjectness by the father's authority and, by implication, the violence of normative male subjectiv-ity and patriarchy.

Compelled to remember Chi, in conjunction with his own abjection in Vietnam and in America, Pham, I further contend, connects him-self to an Asian American history of exclusion and containment. His abjection through such remembering is to be, in the words of Rey Chow, "the inherited, *shared* condition of social stigmatization and abjection" (146, original italics). Julia Kristeva defined the abject as "the jettisoned object" that is "radically excluded" (qtd. in Chow 148). The abject, how-ever, is also "something rejected from which one does not part, from which one does not protect oneself as from an object. . . . It beckons to us and ends up engulfing us" (148). Chow perceptively reads this definition of the abject in Asian American autobiographical accounts of shame and self-reproach.

These narratives, Chow further explains, resonate with "feelings of neglect, dismissal, and humiliation" that reflect the Asian American sub-ject not only as an ethnic identity that is itself a form of abjection but also as a hybrid formation wrought by histories of anti-Asian stigmatization, rejection, and containment. Pham in his memoir, we can understand, makes himself ill in response to his melancholia as both a racialized and a diasporic subject. When the dysentery makes him feel that his insides have turned inside out, he implicitly realizes and remembers Chi's abjec-tion as "the jettisoned object" that has been "radically excluded." Illness is, therefore, his way to process the loss of his sibling as well as his own anger and ambivalence.

Pham thus attempts to create an "in-between" space for himself by partaking in male-bonding rituals that both hurt him *and* render his abjection. Such creation of space is perhaps a method through which to feel release and acquire a sense of belonging. If he can complete his journey in Vietnam, then he can possibly actualize reconciliation, abso-lution, and reconnection. Pham implies this when he explains, "Because I am angry, angry at the weakness of my body, angry at everything, I get on my bike and leave town. To hell with dysentery and fever. I am a survivor" (307). Claiming to be a survivor, Pham can accordingly assert a sense of self to remember Chi and to realize his own place, as well as Chi's, in a collective history of Vietnamese in the diaspora.

## Affirming Affiliation

Near the end of *Catfish*, Pham continues to feel ambivalent about belonging in both America and Vietnam. For example, he recalls a vexing conversation with a Vietnamese friend named Calvin, a successful businessman who has never left Vietnam. The conversation provokes Pham's memories of anti-Asian racism by white Americans that make him feel that he does not belong in the United States. Calvin asks Pham:

> *"America is like a dream, isn't it?"*
> After all I've seen, I agree. *"Sure."*
> We contemplate the beer in our glasses. I ask him, *"Do you want to go there?"* I don't know why I ask him this. Maybe, believing that he is my equivalent in Vietnam, I want him to say he really loves the country and that it is magical, wonderful in ways I have yet to imagine. More powerful, more potent than the West.
> Calvin sounds annoyed. *"Of course. Who wouldn't?"* He pauses, taking long, pensive drags on his cigarette. *"But perhaps only to visit. To see, understand-no?"*
> *"Why?"*
> *"Simple. Here . . . here, I am a king."* He leans over the table, shaking the cigarette at me. *"In America, I mean all you Viet-kieu, are guests. And guests don't have the same rights as hosts."* He sits back, legs crossed at the knees, and throws a proprietary arm over the city. *"At least, here I am king. I belong. I am better than most Vietnamese."*
> *"No, we're not guests. We're citizens. Permanent. Ideally we are all equal. Equal rights,"* I insert lamely, the words, recalled from elementary school history lessons, sounding hollow.
> *"Right, but do you FEEL like an American? Do you?"*
> *"Yes! Yes! Yes, I do. I really do, I want to shout it in his face."* Already, the urge leaves a bad taste in my mouth. *"Sometimes, I do. Sometimes, I feel like I am a real American."* (327)

That Pham cannot affirm feeling like a "real American" after living in the United States for twenty years reveals his ambivalent attachment to the American Dream's ethos of freedom and opportunity to achieve prosperity, security, and social equality. The American Dream is a liberal cultural norm, but also in modern America it is an ideal whose fulfillment for Asian Americans often requires *negating* origins and forgetting the past, especially for a Vietnamese in the diaspora such as Pham, who yearns to belong both in his adopted homeland and in his forsaken country of origin.

Pham's doubt about feeling like a "real American," moreover, registers his ambivalence toward the American Dream that many Asian diasporic writers articulate in their narratives about desiring to belong in an everyday life as ordinary Americans. Yet what encompasses, makes possible, and determines an everyday life as an ordinary American—what enables the diasporic Asian in the United States to feel like a "real American"—is aspiring to the American Dream. The intensity of aspiring to the opportunities available in America's liberal capitalist democracy underscores an optimistic attachment to this national ethos—a normative optimism to achieve the comforts of middle-class status and social belonging.

Pham's ambivalence has much to do with his desire to belong in America *unexceptionally*. He aspires, in other words, to the normative subjectivity of white Americans, but this requires overlooking his origins in the Vietnamese diaspora. "I wish I could tell [Calvin]," he further divulges.

> *I don't mind forgetting who I am*, but I know he wouldn't understand. I don't mind being looked at or treated just like another American, a white American. No, I don't mind at all. I want it. I like it. Yet every so often when I become really good at tricking myself, there is always that inevitable slap that shocks me out of my shell and prompts me to reassess everything.
>
> How could I tell him my shame? How could I tell him about the drive-bys where some red-faced white would stick his head out of his truck, giving me the finger and screaming, "Go home, Chink!" Could I tell Calvin about the time my Vietnamese friends and I dined in a posh restaurant in Laguna Beach in Southern California? A white man at the next table, glaring at us, grumbled to his wife, "They took over Santa Ana. And now they're here. This whole state is going to hell." (327–28, italics added)

Pham's "shame" that induces him "to reassess everything" may be understood to critique anti-Asian exclusion from normative American personhood: the subjective state of feeling like a "real American" that traditionally has been defined as "white" to preserve the whiteness of America's body politic. That it is "a white man" who feels comfortable to express anti-Asian racism publicly in a restaurant underscores how this racism is a form of *violence* that has maintained America both as a white nation and as a "violent body politic" (V. Nguyen 106). Insofar as shame "feels like an exposure" that makes the ashamed turn away from others who have caused or who witness this shame (Ahmed, *Cultural Politics* 103), Pham suffers his own shame as violence enacted on his body and his mind. He feels shame in reaction to the violence of anti-Asian racism, which he understands as his exclusion from the subjective realm of social belonging, a realm contingent upon defining the racial and cultural otherness of Asians.

If Pham's shame, generated by the racism of whites, jolts him out of his obliviousness and causes him to lose faith in the American Dream, his experience with racial prejudice impedes his aspiration to feel like an ordinary American. It weakens his optimistic attachment to the ideal of the abstracted citizen as President Johnson framed it nearly fifty years ago. For Pham, being subject-to-racialization causes him to feel a disabling and disorienting ambivalence about becoming American. His feelings of exclusion and alienation, because of racial stereotyping and his realization of how he's been represented and identified by this stereotype and continues to be subjected to the stereotype's persistence, painfully contradict his desire to achieve belonging.

Experiencing shame and ambivalence is intrinsic to the process of becoming Asian American, which involves being subject-to-racialization and entails the Asian subject's loss of "political naïveté (or the belief in the American Dream)" (Lye, "Literary Case" 257). The Asian subject becomes Asian American from having *lost* the political naïveté of being oblivious to racism, of not being acutely aware of racial interpellation through associations with Asiatic stereotypes. The process of becoming Asian American, as Pham consequently implies it, requires both experiencing and being conscious of racism, in turn causing the Asian American to refute the American Dream as an ideal. Pham's bitter memories of victimization by white racists and his demoralizing confrontations with anti-Asian hostility impress a tonal ambivalence throughout his narrative—an affective paradox of belonging that depicts his becoming an Asian American.

Near the end of *Catfish*, Pham indicates that he may have found respite from his anger and ambivalence. In finding such relief, he can let go of his hatred for Vietnamese Americans and claim a sense of belonging by becoming Asian American. At the conclusion of his journey in Vietnam, he relaxes at the beach and encounters an old Vietnamese woman, "splashing like a child, her white peasant shirt billowing in the water" (338). She tries to communicate with Pham, but he just smiles in return, not understanding her French. "I don't want to disappoint her with my commonality, to remind her of our shared history. So I let her interpret my half-truths. At this I am good, for I am a mover of betweens. I slip among classifications like water in cupped palms, leaving bits of myself behind. I am quick and deft, for there is no greater fear than the fear of being caught wanting to belong. I am a chameleon. And the best chameleon has no center, no truer sense of self than what he is in the instant" (338–39). Pham's claim of being "a mover of betweens" reflects his position as a Vietnamese in the diaspora in terms of denial and avoidance that confine him within borders of race and masculinity. Because he fears "being caught wanting to belong," he still positions himself in negation with other Vietnamese people. He continues to see them as embodied tropes of obedience and assimilation in model minority normativity. He thus does not avoid, I argue, being racially interpellated by white America's perception of Asians as exemplars of submission and accommodation. In fact, this perception contains him within a melancholic form of racialized subjectivity.

However, his conflicting feelings of living between two worlds simultaneously—the worlds of America and Vietnam, and the discourses of race and masculinity that encapsulate these worlds—poignantly articulate his attachment to a history of Vietnamese people. This is a history within the frame of Asian American collective experience. At his memoir's end, Pham is onboard a flight to America, and when it is about to land, a Vietnamese man sitting next to him asks: "*This is America?*" (342, original italics). Pham's reply, "*Yes, Brother. . . . Welcome home*" (342), is his narrative's final words. While his reply may not promise resolution and transcendence that come from finding a place of self-reclamation, it does attest to his getting there by affirming affiliation through a sense of "shared history" and also by his reconnecting with other Vietnamese in the diaspora.

## The Ambivalence of a Self-Sufficient Man in *A Free Life*

Affiliation with the history of Asian Americans as prompted by deep ambivalence about an idealized postracial America is the critical terrain of Ha Jin's *A Free Life*. Jin's novel is part of what scholars call the "post-Tiananmen literary diaspora," writings depicting the experiences of Chinese immigrants and exiles following the Tiananmen Square protests and massacre on June 4, 1989 (Kong). *A Free Life* chronicles the life of a man named Nan Wu who leaves China after Tiananmen to live in America with his wife and their six-year-old son. Having left a communist homeland that was beginning to industrialize through recognizably capitalist practices, Nan and his family are in America as diasporic immigrants, and they must adapt to their new homeland's modern capitalist society.

To raise his son and keep his family together, Nan works as a security guard in Massachusetts and then as a busser and waiter in New York City. At the novel's end in 1998, Nan clearly achieves success in America. With the help of his wife, Pingping, he owns and operates a profitable restaurant in Georgia. The money that he and Pingping earn from their business allows them to pay off the mortgage on their modest home in an Atlanta suburb. Nearly a decade after arriving in America, the Wu family live the good life of comfort, middle-class status, and job security. Such prosperity and happiness, Nan admits repeatedly, would never be allowed in China, a country he disclaims as his homeland because of its despotic government.

At the novel's beginning, Nan has been living in Boston attending graduate school in political science. Pingping eventually joins him in America after taking care of their son, Taotao, for some years. She leaves Taotao in the care of Nan's parents in China. Nan and Pingping have succeeded in obtaining a passport for Taotao just before the Tiananmen massacre. The grandparents put Taotao onboard a plane to San Francisco, where he will meet his parents. Nan is very anxious to meet Taotao because he hasn't seen him since he was an infant and fears that his son has forgotten him. Nonetheless, when Nan does meet Taotao at the airport, Taotao is eager to tell him "there was a big fight in Beijing, do you know? Hundred of uncles in the People's Liberation Army were killed" (9). Wanting to disabuse his son of China's government propaganda, Nan retorts: "It was soldiers who shot a great many civilians . . ." (9). Pingping also retorts: "Taotao, Dad is right. . . . The People's Army has changed and killed a lot of common people, people like us" (9). This scene of tense family reunion at the start of Jin's novel instantiates a familiar theme in Asian diasporic narratives: the aspiration to succeed and belong in America regardless of national origin, race, ethnicity and social class, and immigrant parents' sacrifice and hard work for the benefit of their children. Nan, for instance, waxes sentimental about the sacrifices that he and his wife will have to make to raise their son as an American:

> He was all the more convinced that they must live in this country to let their child grow into an American. He must make sure

that Taotao would stay out of the cycle of violence that had beset their native land for centuries. The boy must be spared the endless, gratuitous suffering to which the Chinese were as accustomed as if their whole existence depended on it. By any means, the boy must live a life different from his parents' and take this land to be his country! Nan felt sad and glad at the same time, touched by the self-sacrifice he believed he would be making for his child. (9)

Nan's anxious desire for a purposeful and gainful life that entails "self-sacrifice" in his newly adopted homeland articulates an ordinary affect typical to Asian diasporic literature. Aspiring to succeed and belong in America, especially through hard work to support his family, Nan yearns for his son to claim America for himself. And despite feeling some "uncertainty," he wants "to choose his own way and to make something of himself" because "a free life" is available to all in the United States (17), whereas in China such freedom is impossible because of the country's totalitarian rule. But what particularly makes Nan want to be in America is its national credo of individualism, which he wholeheartedly embraces both for his son and for himself. "I just want to be independent" (260), he repeatedly says, "standing on solid, independent ground" (189). Nan believes that operating his own business and purchasing a home for his family will prove his independence.

Achieving middle-class status and owning a business and a home are, however, not his only aspirations. Another is to rekindle romance with a woman named Beina. Nan fell in love with Beina while he was a student and lived with his family in Harbin, China. Although Beina spurned Nan's proposal of marriage because she was money oriented and she considered him incapable of offering her a life that would be filled with material comforts, he still desires her obsessively. He considers Beina a muse for artistic aspirations that uphold individualism in its most ideal and purest form. He yearns to acquire what he believes is the essential feature of genuine individualism: a poet's "free spirit," enabling him, he trusts, to become a self-possessing individual. In America, Nan wants to become a poet, to live as an artist and "produce literary work" (582). Jin portrays Nan's yearning to live and succeed as an artist as an ambition that is supposed to be consistent with America's national ethos of freedom and the pursuit of happiness. The novel upholds the American Dream as an aspiration whose accomplishment would register freedom and individualism as entirely realizable for a Chinese diasporic immigrant who dreams of becoming an artist. For Nan to achieve his dream by producing literature and living as a successful writer would affirm not only that he belongs in America but also that there is more to life in the country's modern capitalist society than striving for the material comforts of wealth and private property ownership.

More than anything, Nan wants to be, in his own words, "a self-sufficient man" (157). His desire to prosper and be his own self is an aspiration aptly reflecting President Johnson's liberal democratic "man," whose hard work and good behavior allow him to succeed and demonstrate his "merit" to belong in America. Both the Cold War's "man of merit" and Nan's romanticized "self-sufficient man" are abstractions devoid of historical context and grounding in race. They are premised on ideals conventional to the liberal political theory of individualism, whose notions of personhood and self-determination are realized through property acquisition.

Cold War liberals, as we have seen, articulated their ideal, derived from the European experience of modernity, of the American as a self-possessing "man". This abstracted experience shaped and determined nineteenth-century notions of the propertied individual that underwrote a narrative of citizenship as white and male under US liberal democracy. As an abstraction, individualism in modern America is a Euro-American cultural norm. Its historical basis in white male personhood and the preservation of this personhood through histories of exclusion and containment of women and nonwhite people remain unrecognized so as to uphold its idealization. In the beginning of the novel, before Nan moves his family to Georgia to start his own business, he thoroughly believes in the possibility of individualism as something "pure" according to liberal humanist principles, embodied by the free spirit of the poet. This individualism is readily available to him, he trusts, because of *and* despite the hard menial labor he performs to make money for his family.

However, when he leaves his family in Massachusetts to take a job as the managing editor of a Chinese-language poetry magazine in New York, he begins to realize that he may be at odds with individualism in America. Because his salary at the magazine does not pay him enough to live on, he looks for a second job and is interviewed for a position at a "Chinese cultural center" (106). After the interview, he wanders alone into the center's Museum of Chinese Immigrant Culture. He sees artwork that "had been created by a group of incarcerated illegal aliens, who had been seized by the Coast Guard when the boat smuggling them into America got stranded at Hawaii" (108). In this moment that attests to cultural expressions originating from experiences of denial and containment, Nan becomes aware of his own relation to other Chinese migrants in the diaspora. He then notices the museum's small collection of written works, "by contemporary authors such as Maxine Hong Kingston, Amy Tan, and Gish Jen. Near a tall window stood a trash can collecting water dripping from a leak in the ceiling. There wasn't another visitor in the poorly lighted room. The whole show was a letdown" (108). By juxtaposing works by Kingston, Tan, and Jen with "a trash can collecting dripping water," Jin is not disparaging Asian American women writers. Rather, he is making a point about the emergence of Asian American cultural expression from historical exclusion and restriction.

Alone at the "poorly lighted" exhibit, an evident sign of the museum's deficient funding, Nan begins to grasp his own place within Asian American history—a history of violence, hostility, and repression contradicting freedom and individualism in liberal democratic America. The museum's indication of alienation and pathos in the lives of early Chinese immigrants saddens him:

> Nan came out of the building with a sinking heart. Questions, one after another, were arising in his mind. Why do they call that place a cultural museum? Why are there so few exhibits that can be called artwork? How come there's no Picasso or Faulkner or Mozart that emerged from the immigrants? Does this mean the first Chinese here were less creative and less artistic? Maybe so, because the early immigrants were impoverished and many were illiterate, and because they all had to slave away to feed themselves and their families, and had to concentrate their energy on settling down in this unfamiliar discriminatory, fearsome land. Just uprooting themselves from native soil must have crippled their lives and drained their vitality, not to mention their creativity. How could it be possible for an unfettered genius to rise from a tribe of coolies who were frightened, exhausted, mistreated, wretched, and possessed by the instinct for survival? Without leisure, how can art survive?
>
> The more Nan thought, the more upset he became. (108–9)

For Nan, the realization of Chinese Americans ascending from "a tribe of coolies" and holding their own against a pantheon of great European and Euro-American artists is profoundly distressing. The disappointing exhibit signifies poverty and struggle both for the museum and for an early period of Asian American history. In effect, the "whole show" is a scene of ethnic abjection. The novel reflects this abjection by ascribing negative affects to the experiences of previous generations of Chinese immigrants in America: they were, Nan despairingly concludes, "frightened, exhausted, mistreated, wretched, and possessed by the instinct for survival."

We might understand Nan's distress about the exhibit and his framing of Asian American cultural expression within marginalization and "impoverishment" as a moment in which he is compelled to remember and hence become aware of Asian America's historical basis in exclusion and containment. This remembering is to be, again in the words of Rey Chow, "the inherited, *shared* condition of social stigmatization and abjection." In this sense, the exhibit's "handful of books"—the writings by Kingston, Tan, and Jen that are meant to showcase important works of Chinese American cultural expression—become objects of abjection for Nan. Their display next to a trash can collecting water from a leaking ceiling signifies the historical perception of Asians in America as aliens and others: objects for racialized labor exploitation, as we have seen in Kingston's *China Men*, that have enabled the proprietary subjectivity of white male personhood.

In this realm of ethnic abjection, Asian American works articulate racialized minority subjectivities that have been necessarily marginalized and disparaged as inferior in order for Euro-Americans to shape, define, and claim the realm of modern political-intellectual culture. The containment of Asian Americans as economic subjects—both as racialized laborers and as means for capital accumulation—is a form of ethnic abjection that, by extension, implies their containment within the economic form of capital and hence their inability to move freely into the experiential realm of *genuine* individualism because this realm is the affective possession and preserve of Euro-Americans.

As objects of ethnic abjection, the exhibit's meager display of Asian American writings suggests that works by artists and writers of Asian ancestry are marginalized, if not insignificant, within a vast terrain of canonical American literature that is almost entirely made up of Euro-American works—writings enabled, as an implication of ethnic abjection, by the perception of Asians as racialized others. This is a perception, Jin's novel implies, that renders inconceivable the inclusion and recognition of Asian Americans within the realm of genuine individualism inhabited by the free-spirited poet and artist. Nan flees from the museum upset by his awareness of an ethnic identity for Asian Americans that is grounded in histories of exclusion, containment, and abjection. And his awareness provokes his conflicting feelings. Nan becomes ambivalent about belonging in America with aspirations to pursue the individualism of the "ideal American"—the individualism of the "self-sufficient man"—by writing poetry and living as an artist. To be sure, he begins to see himself within the locus of racialized minority experience that characterizes ethnic identity and grounds this identity in history; he recognizes the way racialized perception would interpellate him, too, as a racialized other, effectively placing him within the space of disparaged ethnic identity. Yet simultaneously he is anxious about falling into his own place within the collective history of Asian Americans—an abjected ethnicity registering the confinement and immobilization of the racialized minority subject.

I have examined at length Nan's ambivalence in the museum because, for the purposes of my argument, this moment is one of the most important within the epic length of Jin's novel. It is a moment that sets up a pattern in which the narrative vacillates between valorizing the American Dream by depicting Nan's success through hard work and then criticizing it as empty and hollow because its logic ultimately requires making money and owning property as the means to actualize freedom and acquire happiness in the pursuit of individualism. After this moment, Nan's ambivalence about America's capitalist society and its effects on the artist intensifies. Jin wavers in his novel between depicting the American Dream as a praiseworthy social vision and criticizing the capitalist relations of making money that influence and determine all human activity in modern America, including writing poetry and creating art.

The pursuit of individualism is thus a contradictory tension articulated through Nan's ambivalence. As a force that informs "strategies of individuation and marginalization" (Bhabha 66), ambivalence in Jin's novel discursively signifies the diasporic immigrant's search for home and belonging in dialectical terms. Nan expresses attachment to the American Dream of property ownership as his realization of independence and self-worth. But he despairs when this attachment compels him to work fixatedly on making money, causing him to lose sight of his goal to write poetry and to contradict his belief in humanist ideals that inspire the artist's individualism. In this sense, questions arise for Nan. Does his ambivalence lead to redemption or resolution? Where do his conflicting feelings about art and individualism take him in America? In the end, is he able to claim individualism without negating his identity as a Chinese immigrant? For Nan, it seems, to shift from feeling ambivalence to realizing transcendence would require empathic attachment to an ethnic identity grounded in a history of Asian immigrant experience.

## The Happiness of Property Ownership

In *A Free Life*, the pursuit of individualism is inextricable from self-sufficiency. And to be self-sufficient is to attain a sense of belonging in America. For Nan and Pingping, the most obvious demonstration of self-sufficiency is to "become their own boss" by owning a business and a home (188). This is why they seize the opportunity to buy a restaurant from an elderly Chinese American couple in an Atlanta suburb. Nan goes to Georgia alone to bargain with the couple and "beat down the price by $3,000" (173). He succeeds and takes "great pride in the result, feeling like a real businessman" (173). After they arrive to start their new business, Nan and Pingping believe they must "own a house on a piece of land they could call their own" (218). They find a house they like near the restaurant and make a deal with the seller, John Wolfe. The three of them go to a lawyer named Mr. Shang to arrange a contract of sale. When Nan and Pingping sign the contract, John tells them: "A home is where you start to build your fortune" (219). Mr. Shang agrees, adding: "This is a major step toward realizing your American dream" (219). By applauding Nan and Pingping for buying a home, the two men uphold America's national credo of pursuing individualism through private ownership of capital. They maintain the American Dream's logic of making money as the means to actualize freedom and acquire happiness. To belong in America, they further convey, is to demonstrate independence by accumulating capital through owning property. Moreover, that Mr. Shang, a Chinese American attorney, praises Nan and Pingping for buying a home not only signifies formal recognition of their self-sufficiency but also communicates it in terms that affirm their place in the perception of Asian immigrants as exemplars of economic activity, as high achievers of the American Dream.

If the American Dream's logic involves making money so as to obtain and keep property, then it further implies a logic of hard work to demonstrate self-sufficiency and acquisitive happiness. Nan ponders this one day while observing Pingping and Taotao playing together in their new home's backyard: "He went on observing them, happy to see them in such buoyant spirits. . . . Though their mortgage was unpaid, he was on his way to becoming an independent man. His heart was filled with joy and gratitude. At long last he was hungry for making money, *a lot of money*, so that his family could live in peace and security" (227, italics added). While caught up in a reverie of his family's present happiness, Nan presumes that self-sufficiency means being able to provide comfort and safety for his family. As he observes his wife and child playing together, the novel reflects a logic of making money—"a lot of money"—and that of labor to suggest the realization of happiness for the self-sufficient man who is also a family man. That is, making money through hard work for the "peace and security" of one's family exemplifies a man's abilities and accomplishments in ideal masculine terms. It evidences his *worth* as a family man.

When the restaurant, the Gold Wok, yields a steady profit, the logic of property ownership and that of labor to delineate happiness becomes further clear, but it does so in ways that register contradiction. For example, a woman named Heidi Masefield, Nan and Pingping's former landlord and employer from Massachusetts, arrives at their home to pick up her daughter. Heidi's daughter has run away from home to be with Taotao, whom she befriended when the Wus were working for her mother and living in her home. Upon seeing the Wu's house, Heidi is amazed

> not only by the brick ranch but especially by the lake and the immense trees in the backyard. She turned to Pingping. "Now, tell me again, how many years have you been in the United States?"
>
> "Nan is here nine year, me seven and half years."
>
> "Wow, in less than a decade you already have your own business, a house, and two cars. I'm so happy for you, to see you doing so well. . . . This can only happen in America. I'm very moved by the fact that you and Nan have actualized your American dream so quickly. I'm proud of this country." (390)

Heidi's comments relay the importance of an affluent Euro-American's recognition and approval in the novel. Heidi, who "owns half a bank and an insurance company" and comes from "Old New England money" (41), acknowledges and identifies both Pingping and Nan as self-sufficient. Through her patriotic idiom—"I'm proud of this country"—she attributes their success to the principle of self-reliance within the American Dream. With regard to Nan's own ambition to become a self-sufficient man, Heidi's recognition—as relayed to Pingping, a wife and mother like Heidi—construes Nan's worth both as a family man and as a "man of merit" in liberal pluralist terms. Her recognition is an imprimatur for Nan's independence, which, by extension, has context in Cold War liberal pluralism. Her acknowledgment of Nan's success as an actualization of the American Dream should also be understood in relation to this dream's principle of freedom. It is a liberal democratic value from the Cold War signifying the "ideal American" as an abstracted citizen whose "merit as a man" foretells the aspiration to be ordinarily American in a modern capitalist society.

As conveyed by Heidi's recognition, moreover, both Nan and Ping-ping's demonstration of success through owning both a home and a business valorizes the American Dream as an ideal of postracial sensibility. Her comment "This can only happen in America" implies color-blind ideals that epitomize America's status at the forefront of capitalist modernity. That it is Heidi, furthermore, who lauds the Wus for their property ownership paradoxically registers their achievement both as evidence of the good life's availability to everyone in a color-blind society and as an indication of model minority status for Asian immigrants who realize the American Dream in proprietary terms. Her recognition and her praise, then, frame the Wus' success through language that suggests the perception of Asian immigrants as embodied tropes of aspirational normativity, exemplars of upward mobility, and that infers their actualization of the American Dream as an instance of model minority normativity.

Amid these praises from friends and neighbors for his hard work and accomplishments, however, Nan feels painful contradiction. The arduous labor it takes to operate the restaurant alienates and entraps him. When his father in China sends him a letter asking him to help an uncle, a painter, hold a show in America, Nan is furious: "*What is this? He thinks I'm a curator of a museum or a college president? I told him on the phone that I couldn't help Uncle Zhao hold a show here. I'm nobody*" (329, original italics). The father, a retired government official, represents paternal authority and China's communist system, which deny the freedom and individualism that Nan romanticizes. Although he claims to be "nobody" in the face of his father's and China's paternalism, he does so in recognition of his immigrant standing in America. Unlike other Chinese nationals, such as Nan's friend Manping Liu, who have been refused permission to return to China because of alleged anticommunist government activities, Nan is an immigrant, not an exile in America. According to Nan, Manping Liu is an exile whose life in America can "only exist in reference to the central power that had banished him from China" (356). He therefore is "noteworthy" to the people in his native land because of his "burdensome past" (356). In contrast, Nan is "nobody, nonexistent" to the people of China: "People of his kind, 'the weed people,' survived or perished like insects or grass and wouldn't matter at all to those living in their native land. . . . They were already counted as a loss" (356). Yet Nan's understanding of being perceived as a "nobody" in China also depicts his profound alienation as an immigrant in America. He feels like a cipher because he works hard every day to make money for paying off debts. He tells Pingping to write his father back: *"Tell him we're working like coolies every day and have nothing to do with the art world. Tell him he and my mother should know we're merely menial laborers at the bottom of America—we're useless to them"* (329–30, italics in original). Claiming that he and Pingping are "working like coolies every day," Nan expresses his alienation at work in terms that reflect his identification with a history of struggle and estrangement for early Chinese immigrants. His conflicting feelings about belonging are evident in his claim that he and Pingping are "at the bottom of America." And his ambivalent attachment to achieving and belonging in America, an attachment whose contradiction is alienation and entrapment in the struggle to make money, shifts to identification with the history of racialized Chinese migrant labor—a history of "coolies" and "menial laborers."

The most compelling instance of contradiction to the American Dream as an ideal of postracial sensibility comes at a moment of literal paradox in the novel, when a young couple who are Nan's friends want to buy a dilapidated house for sale in the Wus' neighborhood. The young couple, Shubo and his wife, Niyan, who works as a waitress in Nan's restaurant, are Chinese immigrants. Nan talks with a neighbor, Alan, about the possibility of having Shubo and Niyan join them in the community. Alan shocks Nan when he reveals that they would not be welcome because "'there's too many Chinese in this neighborhood already. We need diversity, don't we?'"

> Alan continued, "Mrs. Lodge, Fred, Terry, and Nate, we all talked about this. We don't want this subdivision to become a Chinatown."
> Nan was scandalized but didn't know how to argue with him. He managed to say, "All right, I will tell Shubo what you said. You want to keep Chinese as minority here, but don't you sink our neighborhood should be a melting pot?" (411)

If owning a house allows one to actualize the American Dream and also to realize belonging in America, then denying home ownership for Shubo and his wife because they are Chinese discloses the racialized terms of belonging that are now shockingly evident to Nan. The attempt by Alan and other white neighbors to make sure the neighborhood has "diversity" as a white majority reflects the history of Euro-American proprietary relations in possessive individualism. In this particular instance of contradiction for Nan, the opposition of Alan and other white homeowners to Shubo and Niyan's living in *their* neighborhood shows that the contentment, security, and comfort of property owner-ship have been and continue to be the desired emotionality of normative American personhood.

Nan's realization of this further indicates his awareness of an ongoing racialized perception of Asians as perpetual outsiders in America. To many white homeowners in the neighborhood Nan and his family will always be strangers: "The thought flashed through Nan's mind that some people in the neighborhood had taken his family to be interlopers all along and probably would continue to do so whether they were natural-ized or not. When he passed Alan's words on to Shubo, his friend was so outraged that his eyes turned rhomboidal and his face nearly purple. The opposition made Shubo all the more determined to bid for the house, even though he was uncertain how to renovate it" (411). As a "thought" that "flashed through Nan's mind," the recognition of white Americans who continue to perceive Asians as foreigners invading America is a moment of instant awareness that resembles the experience of abruptly remembering an emotionally intense event. Nan's sudden realization that "some people in the neighborhood had taken his family to be inter-lopers all along" is like a flashbulb memory in the novel: a penetrating emotional experience provoking a "distinctly vivid, precise, concrete, long-lasting" memory of an event (Misztal 81). The flash of Nan's acute awareness of how he and his family are perceived as intruders returns us to an earlier moment when Nan was at the Museum of Chinese Immigrant Culture and became conscious of America's history of anti-Chinese exclusion and containment. His realization of this history was an especially distressing event because it signaled his own relation to the ethnic abjection of past and present Chinese immigrants, a relation that made him feel ambivalent about belonging and that strained his attach-ment to the ideal of the abstracted (postracial) citizen, whose hard work and home ownership are supposed to demonstrate his ability both as a self-sufficient man and as an ordinary American.

This moment of Nan's consciousness about the way he and all Chinese immigrants are perceived as trespassers by many white Americans is a memory device in the novel that *obliges* us to place Nan's and his friends' experiences with racism in the historical context of anti-Chinese exclu-sion. His communication of this racism to Shubo not only provokes his friend's outrage, as well as his determination to possess the house as pro-test against racism, but also makes us understand that the emotionally intense moment of Nan's awareness of abjection involves a collectively shared recollection of this moment with other Chinese immigrants. In this sense, Nan's communication of the neighbors' anti-Chinese racism to Shubo is an interpersonal rehearsal of his own memories about becoming critically aware of ethnic abjection, which "plays an important role in maintaining and consolidating such memories" (Misztal 81).

Shubo and Niyan are demoralized when a real estate broker outbids them on the house and then sells it to a Euro-American woman. They complain to Nan and Pingping about the racism that has thwarted their attempt to buy their first home: "Shubo kept shaking his round chin and said, 'Without money you can't fight racism in America.' 'Just as you have to be rich enough to love your country,' added Nan" (413). Nan's cynical comment acknowledges Shubo's claim that one has to have a lot of money and hence political representation in an economically elite class to protect oneself against injustice and prejudice. His pessimism expresses his view that the American Dream's logic of making money and owning property as the means to belong as an ideal and ordinary American is paradoxical. It also articulates his awareness that the logic of property ownership and that of labor to delineate the pursuit of individualism in financial terms is contradictory for nonwhite immigrants in America.

## The Poet, the Individual, and the Logic of Making Money

But does Nan's pessimism about making money and owning property as the means to achieve belonging in America extend to his belief in humanist ideals that inspire the artist's genuine individualism? If Nan can acquire happiness for his family by giving them comfort and safety, can he find such happiness for himself writing poetry? Nearly every friend that Nan makes in his restaurant affirms the logic of making money and of labor to delineate independence and individualism. Yet this logic does not extend to artistic production until Dick Harrison, a poet Nan met while working in New York, walks into the restaurant one day. Nan is delighted to see Dick and become reacquainted with him. Dick tells Nan that he's just moved to the area to begin working as a creative writing instructor at Emory University. He asks about Nan's family and life in Georgia. When Nan replies that he owns a house and the restaurant, Dick says: "This is impressive. I can see that you're becoming an American capitalist. . . . You're on your way to realizing your American dream, aren't you?" (260); Nan directly responds: "I just want to be independent" (260). Here Dick's compliment may not be as backhanded as it seems, for it dawns on Nan that wealth and art are not incompatible and that in fact making money shapes and defines artistic production, especially writing poetry.

The logic of working hard to make a lot of money that indexes one's worth both as a self-sufficient man and as a family man therefore *includes* writing poetry. This becomes evident to Nan when Dick invites him to the Emory campus to attend a reading by Edward Neary, "a famous poet" from Canada who has written highly acclaimed love poetry. At the reading Dick introduces Neary, "enumerating the awards and grants the poet had garnered and calling him a 'major poetic voice of our time'" (300). When Neary reads one of his poems about a young woman mourning her husband who is killed in a plane crash, Nan is moved by its cadence, "supple and tender, in keeping with the pathos" (300). During the reading, it is clear that Neary reflects the poet's free-spirited individualism Nan yearns to attain. Afterwards, however, when Nan accompanies Dick with Neary and a group of women students at a nearby bar, he's perplexed to witness the poet's egotism while bragging about his accomplishments to the students:

> Mr. Neary said to them again, "Feel free to send me your work. I'm a maker and breaker of poets. I'm a powerful man, you know. . . . I'm also a rich man, you know," Mr. Neary went on. "Imagine, a poet paid sixty thousand dollars for federal tax last year. This is indeed a great country where even a poet can become a millionaire."
>
> "Amazing," Emily mumbled, lowering her eyes.
>
> Anita put in, "So Canada is no longer your homeland?"
>
> "No. I'm an American."
>
> Dick winked at Nan, who was bemused, knowing Neary had been born in Ontario and had come to the United States in his early thirties. He wondered why the poet would talk so much about power and money. How did those bear on his poetry? Why was he acting more like a business magnate? (303–4)

Nan's questions here, again, register his ambivalence about belonging in America with aspirations to pursue the individualism of the "ideal American" by writing poetry and living as an artist. The questions reflect his awareness about the inextricable linkage between artistic production and the totalizing relations of commodity capitalism. He spends the next few days mulling over "what Neary had meant by being 'a maker and breaker of poets'" (305). When Dick comes by the restaurant Nan asks him about this and learns that Neary is the editor of a major poetry anthology. By deciding whose work to include and exclude in his anthology, Neary has the authority to decide the fates of poets. For reasons of egotism and vengeance, Neary purposely rejects the work of aspiring young poets and destroys their careers. Poets have allies and enemies, Dick reveals. "Nan was surprised that poets could be so vindictive and malevolent" (305). To survive, most poets live in cliques, Dick further informs Nan: "The network is essential" (306). But what most bothers Nan about Dick's reply is to learn that the poetry world is "a rough and tumble territory" thoroughly in the grip of money and power. "To some extent Nan was disillusioned by what Dick said. To him the poetry world should be relatively pure, and genuine poets free spirits, passionate but disinterested. Yet according to Dick, many of them were territorial and xenophobic. Could someone like himself ever belong to a coterie? Unlikely. He couldn't imagine being accepted by any clique. Besides, above all what he wanted was to become a self-sufficient individual" (306). As Nan now realizes, a poet's work and individualism are just as much shaped and defined by capital accumulation as a self-sufficient man's worth and independence are determined by property acquisition. The spheres of writing poetry and operating a business, which Nan had thought were fundamentally and ideally separate, turn out to be entirely contained within capitalism's economics.

When Dick returns to the restaurant another time to show Nan the "mock cover of his new book" (404), Nan further realizes that an artist creates not with the purpose to represent and teach humanist ideals but to commodify a product and make money. Dick explains that his book's red cover is "eye-catching and will help it sell better" (405). For the same reason that Nan once "added steamed dumplings and several kinds of noodles" to his restaurant's menu to help fetch more customers (229), Dick selects a cover for his book to make it look more attractive for consumers. Art, like food, transforms into a potential commodity in America. For Nan, commodification denies the ideals that are supposed to inspire a writer to create poems. These ideals are synonymous with true artistic passion, which, as we have seen previously, Marx realized in his conclusion that true artists are influenced by ethics that allow them to create art and poetry as "spiritual production" (Marx and Engels, *On Literature* 141). Yet capitalism is antagonistic to these values. Capitalism's emotional productions of self-interest and greed are hostile to other "branches of spiritual production, for example, art and poetry," which express the humanist principles that motivate genuine artists (141). The capitalist's apparently "innocuous interest in acquiring wealth," in Albert Hirschman's terms (x), contrasts with the ethical perspectives and values of genuine artists. Further, as Marx and Engels put forth in the *Manifesto*, the capitalist "has stripped of its halo every occupation hitherto honoured and looked up to with reverent awe. It has converted the physician, the lawyer, the priest, the poet, the man of science, into his paid wage-labourers" (476).

To be sure, the notion of the artist's humanist ideals conflicting with the capitalist's self-interested aim of making money at first appears less clear, if not unintelligible, in the midst of Nan's denunciations of China as a country whose repressive government has "bridled" the "individual tastes and natural appetites" of the Chinese people (132). For example, earlier in the novel he tells coworkers at a New York restaurant that because of China's repressive communist government "we have lost the child in ourselves" (132). However, now that Dick has exposed the poetry world's enmeshment with capitalist profit motives—the rivalries of poets competing for acclaim and economic success—Nan can no longer uphold the creation of art in America as the pursuit of genuine individualism. Disabused of his belief in the ideals of writing poetry by Dick's assertions of self-interest, Nan realizes "he had to keep his mind alert and clear and find his way" (426).

Even though he understands that narcissism and personal advantage motivate poets in America, Nan still yearns to have the artist's free spirit. He believes that writing poetry will prove that his life has purpose and meaning. Although his business and home demonstrate his worth as a self-sufficient man, his happiness about these accomplishments is short lived.

> The struggle had ended so soon that he felt as though the whole notion of the American dream was shoddy, a hoax. In his mind he wrestled with the bewilderment that had begun to enervate him and made him work less hard than before. He tried to convince himself that the house was really theirs, and so were the van and the restaurant, that the realized dream wasn't merely an empty promise. . . . He was baffled, wondering what was wrong with him. Why couldn't he be as happy as his wife? Why couldn't he enjoy the fruits of their hard labor? He should feel successful. But somehow the success didn't mean as much to him as it should. (418)

Nan's doubt about his own life having purpose and meaning through making money reveals his achievement of the American Dream as a

Pyrrhic victory. Although he reasons that "freedom" for him is "not owing anybody a penny and having no fear of being fired" (418), he also realizes that such freedom has merely meant the freedom to work—to sell his labor—in order to buy and pay off debts. For Nan, the American Dream feels like "a hoax," less because the "struggle had ended so soon" than because as entirely a matter of capital it is hollow, "an empty promise" contradicting the deeper freedom to be found in the artist's "spiritual production."

Although Nan has worked hard to maintain the Gold Wok and has used the profits to pay off his mortgage, the years of toil have prevented him from writing poetry. In the midst of his ambivalence about realizing the American Dream, Nan "remembered the credo he had repeated to [his friend] Danning six years before: Do something moneyed people cannot do. The memory occasioned a sudden pang in his heart. It seemed he had forgotten his goal and gotten lost in making money. Why hadn't he devoted himself to writing poetry? Instead, all these years he had been working like a brainless machine" (419). Actualizing the American Dream to make money and own a home has accordingly *alienated* Nan from his greater dream to create art. That he is unable to "feel successful" and "enjoy the fruits" of his hard labor indicates his disaffection not only from his work but from the affective needs of satisfaction and contentment that are to be experienced in fulfilling work.

This moment in Jin's novel is thus a forceful depiction of the worker's alienation that Carlos Bulosan's writings depict. For years, Nan admits, "he had been working like a brainless machine" (419), disclosing his self-estrangement by the hard labor he does at his restaurant. The meals he prepares are commodities largely foreign to him. And the alienation of these commodities triggers his alienation from creativity. Laboring to cover the high costs of living in America has restricted his creative drive; he ponders, "Only after you were fed and sheltered could you mull over ideas and enjoy the leisure needed for creating arts" (419). Nan further admits, "His disappointment wouldn't abate, its heaviness weighing down his mind" (419), implying that his ambitions to make as much money as possible to pay off loans and sustain his business have reduced him to feeling that his sole purpose in life is to toil for basic human needs. In this telling moment, Nan's anguish intensely contradicts the American Dream's acquisitive happiness of property ownership and likewise deepens his ambivalence about belonging in America. His alienation wrought by hard labor to make money and prove himself a "self-sufficient man" not only reflects profound contradiction with the ideals that inspire the artist's creativity but also again registers his awareness of his place in a collective Asian American history that largely encompasses the racialized labor and exploitation of Chinese immigrants. Nan is implicitly becoming ever more aware of his place in this history.

The logic of making money and working hard to obtain happiness and comfort applies equally to the poet. Dick brings up this capitalist logic in relation to his own situation in the tenure process at Emory. He tells Nan that he will get tenure only if he publishes a successful book: "If Emory doesn't give me tenure, I don't know where I'll go. Look, you have your wife and kid and you have a home. That's already a success. I have nothing but myself. . . . Whatever happens to you, your family will be with you and love you. To top it all, you have your own home and business, a solid base" (424). As Nan is forced to realize, Dick writes poetry for reasons of self-interest and to affirm his own individualism, as well as his worth as a man, in *economic* terms. Dick further tells him: "'I'm not fragile. But I have to assert myself, even to pat myself on the back. A lot of poets just write dreck, but still they have everything—fame, money, and women. . . . Poets are not saints. We have to make our way in the world too" (426). Although Nan finds Dick's reasons of personal advantage for writing poetry objectionable, he sees his point that he has nobody but himself and therefore deserves recognition for accomplishments that would define him as a "man of merit." With this realization also in mind, Nan takes stock in his family as a means to feel happiness and belonging in America. Family is, he once more fathoms, the American Dream.

Nearly every event in Nan's life is translatable within the frame of the American Dream, including having another child and losing it. Pingping becomes pregnant but then suffers a miscarriage. Had the baby been born it would have been their daughter. Nan mourns this loss in reference to his alienation in America: "Having her would have made his life more bearable and lessened his misery and loneliness in this place" (472). Had the baby been born alive and healthy, "she could have become his American dream" (472). Nan grieves the miscarriage as another indication of his failure to actualize his one true passion of writing poetry. "He must resume working on his poetry," he realizes while mourning his wife's miscarriage. Only in writing poetry will he be able to follow "his own heart" (472). Only in poetry will he find his own way, Nan further suggests, to achieving a sense of belonging.

Near the end of *A Free Life*, Nan's awareness of the limitations he faces to write poetry and attain recognition as an artist further registers the dialectic of individualism. The pursuit of individualism by others who lead economically successful lives as artists both inspires and confuses Nan, making his feelings about his own abilities and prospects to produce art even more conflicted. Dick arrives at the restaurant another time, for example, to announce that his book of poems has won the National Book Critics Circle Award. While Dick's accomplishment inspires Nan's awe, he realizes again the direct relation between succeeding as an artist and making money in America, as well as the implications of this relation for him as a Chinese immigrant whose first language is not English. "'Now my task is how to manage success,' said Dick":

> "How do you mean?" Nan was puzzled, unable to see how success was something to be managed.
> "I must capitalize on the opportunity to promote myself and my work, also to raise my fee."
> "What fee?"
> "The fee for my readings and talks."
> "Oh, you'll rake in zer kind of mahney like Edward Neary?"
> "You bet."
> That surprised Nan, because Dick was talking like a businessman. (505–6)

This dialogue is astonishing for the way it reveals the interplay between the forms of capital in Bourdieu's terms. It reflects the way individualism in artistic pursuit transmutes readily into the possessive individualism of capitalist enterprise. Nan comprehends Dick's aspiration to "capitalize on the opportunity to promote [himself]" as an ambition to convert the award's symbolic capital into the economic form. While the honor and prestige of the award are capital that thoroughly demonstrates the genuine individualism of the artist, its conversion into profit, as Dick so baldly and concisely puts it, is not. But there are further implications of this award and the freedom it enables for the awardee: the freedom to play between the symbolic and economic forms of capital. Dick, a Euro-American whose first language is English, is in the comfortable position of having representation and status in America's dominant white culture. There's no question about *his* inclusion in the modern political-intellectual culture of Euro-Americans, as well as the recognition of his abilities to create poetry and literature, and hence to *produce* cultural capital that allows him to achieve symbolic capital. Yet Nan's inability to achieve his dream of writing and publishing poetry allegorizes the Asian immigrant's experience of entrapment and alienation within economic capital, a containment that implies the Asian immigrant's inability to convert finance capital into symbolic capital. As a Chinese immigrant whose first language is not English, Nan realizes he will never be able to obtain the symbolic capital that Dick has acquired and that is achievable for Euro-American artists. He can earn and accumulate economic capital through the restaurant, but his inability to convert it into the honor and prestige that come with producing art effectively contains him within this form of capital.

In the midst of his pessimism about property ownership and his disillusionment over the "power and money" of capitalism governing the poetry world, Nan's ambivalence further strains his attachment to an idealized and abstracted individualism. He endures more struggles, disappointments, and losses that dishearten him. When he returns to China to visit his parents for the first time in nearly ten years, they sadden and depress him by their constant demands for money. "Both of you are greedy," he wants to tell them, after they try to make him feel guilty about not being filial to his family. They flippantly dismiss his explanations about the "fear and misery" that he and Pingping "had gone through in America" (560). They show no compassion for his wife when he tells them about her miscarriage: "How lonely he felt in his parents' home, as though he hadn't grown up in the very apartment building. Perhaps he shouldn't have come back in the first place" (560). When he returns to America, he visits Dick, who has relocated to the University of Iowa to be a full professor in the university's prestigious writing program. Nan tells Dick that after returning from China he desires more than ever to become a poet. Dick replies that he believes Nan has talent but also declares that he will have to give up his family and business to become a "professional poet": "If you want to be a poet, you may not have perfection of both the work and the life. It all depends on how much you're willing to sacrifice. . . . You need to give up a lot in order to develop your talent" (582).

Dick's sobering advice further dispirits Nan. He tries to relieve his depression by finding and visiting Beina, who has moved to America and lives in Illinois. Beina is still vain and manipulative, Nan clearly sees upon meeting her. He tells her that Pingping loves him and "is always ready to suffer" with him. She laughs derisively, replying that he really doesn't love his wife and predicts he will come to see her again. "Well, you think you still have your hooks in me?" Nan asks (589). "Try to get them out," she says (589). Nan once considered Beina his muse for writing poetry, but now she evidently represents the corruption, avarice, and totalitarianism of his native land: "Deep down, he knew this trip was a mistake—all the years' longing and anguish had been caused by a mere illusion and all his pain and sighs had been groundless, wasted for the wrong person. What an idiot he had been!" (590). When he returns home and tries to write poetry, he can't make any progress: "As he had failed in his search for an ideal woman, his project on a bunch of love poems had come to a halt" (604). While reading an advice book about writing, he stops at a quotation by Faulkner: "The writer must teach himself that the basest of all things is to be afraid; and, teaching himself that, forget it forever, leaving no room in his workshop for anything but the old verities and truths of the heart" (604). Nan interprets the Faulkner quote to mean that he has let fear mislead and obstruct him: the fear of appearing substandard, less than self-sufficient, "of becoming a joke in others' eyes . . . of writing poetry in English" (604–5), and especially the fear of not working hard enough to make profits. The relentless drive to earn and accumulate money has entrapped and contained him. He's forsaken his aspirations to create art because of his attachment to a hollow and empty American Dream:

> Tears were rolling down his cheeks. How he hated himself! He had wasted so many years and avoided what he really desired to do, inventing all kinds of excuses—his sacrifice for his son, his effort to pay off the mortgage, his pursuit of the American dream. . . . The more he thought about his true situation, the more he loathed himself, especially for his devotion to making money, which had consumed so many of his prime years and dissolved his will to follow his own heart. A paroxysm of aversion seized him, and he turned to the cash register, took all the banknotes out of the tray, and went to the alcove occupied by the God of Wealth, for whom they had always made weekly offerings. With a swipe he sent flying the wine cups, the joss sticks, and the bowls of fruit and almond cookies. . . . He thrust a five-dollar bill on the flame of a candle and instantly the cash curled ablaze. . . .
>
> "I hate this mahney, this 'dirty acre'!" he yelled in a voice verging on a sob. . . . Nan had meant to say "filthy lucre," but in the throes of frenzy he got the idiom wrong. (605–6)

Pingping rushes to stop Nan as he sets aflame "a whole sheaf of banknotes" (605). She yells, *"Don't burn our sweat money!"* (605, original italics). The "sweat" of money in this scene, as Pingping's exclamation asserts, not only registers the pains of sacrifice for home and business ownership wrought by the drudgery of everyday hard labor but also, as "filthy lucre" in Nan's view, signifies the psychological costs of alienation in the fantasy of actualizing the American Dream. Nan's enraged self-reproach is a classic case of what David Eng calls "internalized self-loathing and a subjectivity that is radically split" (*Racial Castration* 72). The "true situation" of Nan's struggle to make money and own property as the means to achieve belonging in America is, as it is for Andrew Pham, the attempt to grasp an American identity that is socially and culturally white. His effort to pay off the mortgage in pursuit of the American Dream has all been done to prove himself in the eyes of others who maintain this materialist ethos as the measure of his worth as a man and as an individual through white norms of property ownership and personhood. All these years Nan has worked hard to make money in order to have others recognize him as both an ideal and a normative American. However, for these others, he's also been living by their perception of Asian immigrants as exemplars of actualizing the American Dream. He has strived to conform to their view of the Asian's ability to succeed without regard to historical matters of racial oppression, and therefore, by working hard to make "a lot of money" he takes his place in a realm of model minority normativity. Nan's incessant efforts to prove himself as a self-sufficient man in accordance with racialized perception has thus induced within him "psychic self-splitting" (Eng, *Racial Castration* 73). The "paroxysm of aversion that seized him" indicates the melancholic form of his divided and racialized subjectivity—underscored by his hostility, disaffection, and self-loathing.

Angry and unapologetic, Nan turns into his laboring and alienated self again "and without a word set about cutting a basket of eggplants. . . . For the rest of the day he was very quiet and did everything he was supposed to do" (607). His unhappiness is mirrored by a low level of trust in the future of his business. He persuades Pingping to sell their restaurant because they are not making enough to cover medical expenses. By working full time elsewhere, Nan reasons, he can take advantage of health insurance available to employees. He finds work as a motel desk clerk. Although he makes much less money and "a third of his wages went to health insurance" (618), Nan is satisfied with his job because it allows him to write poetry.

In Jin's solemn novel about a Chinese immigrant family's adaptation to the American way of life, art and the ambivalence of a "self-sufficient man" are reconciled. Nan gives up "the illusion of success in order to accept his diminished state as a new immigrant and as a learner of this alphabet" (619). By creating art, he is "willing to face failure" (619) but understands as well that the American Dream's attainment is entirely imaginary; he knows "such a dream was not something to be realized but something to be pursued only" (619). Nan does want to publish his poems, however, to find success in the poetry world. He publishes two poems but receives denial and harsh criticism from Gail Upchurch, the editor of a poetry journal *Arrows*: "You may be able to write prose in English eventually, but poetry is impossible. So don't waste your time anymore. Do something you can do. For instance, write a memoir about the Cultural Revolution, which I'm sure will be marketable" (626). The editor accuses Nan of improperly using the English language; she says, "the way you use the language is too clumsy. For a native speaker like myself, it almost amounts to an insult" (626).

Yet Nan's poetry is clearly Asian American cultural expression, insofar as it depicts his experiences of exclusion, rejection, and containment. His poems register the condition of becoming Asian/American by reflecting ambivalence about belonging, denial, and abjection, "becoming a joke in others' eyes." They speak about the diasporic subjectivities of Chinese immigrants—feelings of rootlessness, displacement, alienation, and the projection of otherness, as in these lines from his poem "Homeland":

> You packed a pouch of earth into your baggage
> as a bit of your homeland. You told your friend:
> "In a few years I'll be back like a lion.
> There's no other place I can call home
> and wherever I go I'll carry our country with me.
> . . . . . . . . . . . . . . . . . . . . . . . . . . . . . . . . . . . . . . . .
> You won't be able to go back.
> Look, the door has closed behind you.
> Like others, you too are expendable to
> a country never short of citizens.
> You will toss in sleepless nights,
> confused, homesick, and weeping in silence.
> . . . . . . . . . . . . . . . . . . . . . . . . . . . . . . . . . . . . . . . .
> Eventually you will learn:
> your county is where you raise your children,
> your homeland is where you build your home. (635)

So resonant with the challenges of exile and loneliness in a newly adopted homeland, Nan's poems convey characteristic features of Asian diasporic narrative. In the poem, the immigrant is "confused, homesick, and weeping in silence": these affects of separation and estrangement inform us of the constant sense of "unhomeliness" for the diasporic subject (Bhabha 12). And the poem expresses longing for a home, as well as the conflicting feelings of living in two worlds simultaneously.

Nan's poems reflect, we might further see, his attachment to a collective history of Asian diaspora in the Western world because they represent his "in-between" position as a diasporic immigrant who is "inside the nation formally but between nations culturally" (Koshy, "Minority Cosmopolitanism" 601). In *A Free Life*, the poetry of an Asian/American individual as a "self-sufficient man" thus portrays a hybridized rendering of subjectivity through language that avows the experience of double (even plural) identifications, another distinctive feature of diaspora's signification in Asian American cultural expression. Nan's poetry discursively registers history, ethnic identity, and diasporic subjectivity. In this sense, he *is* truly finding his own way and following his heart in America.

Andrew Pham and Ha Jin articulate the deep ambivalence that ethnic and cultural minorities experience in relation to the *feeling* of being American. In their narratives, they express this particular type of feeling as an affect of social belonging mobilized within late capitalist culture: the American Dream emerges as a feeling that would be produced through economic uplift and prosperity, and also through historically contingent modes of consumption and wealth accumulation. Pham and Jin give shape to the ambivalent attachments felt with regard to an American Dream that is at once promised and placed out of reach, contrasting emotions of belonging to the experience of exclusion and alienation. Asian diasporic narratives, such as *Catfish* and *A Free Life*, show us that experiences of racial abjection and interpellation for Asians in modern America do indeed exist. For these writings attest to an ethnic identification that both accommodates, questions, and resists today's conditions of Asian American racialization.

**4 /**   Feeling Ancestral: Memory and Postracial
          Sensibility in Mixed-Race Asian American
          Literature

In recent Asian American writings, there has been an upsurge of interest in mixed-heritage people and particularly multiracial persons. Ruth Ozeki's *All over Creation,* Kip Fulbeck's *Paper Bullets* and *Part Asian, 100 Percent Hapa,* Paisley Rekdal's *The Night My Mother Met Bruce Lee,* Jessica Hagedorn's *Dogeaters* and *The Gangster of Love,* Nora Okja Keller's *Comfort Woman* and *Fox Girl,* Heinz Insu Fenkl's *Memories of My Ghost Brother,* Kien Nguyen's *The Unwanted,* Brian Ascalon Roley's *American Son,* and Don Lee's *Country of Origin* are just some of many works that feature the experiences of mixed-heritage and multiracial Asian Americans.[1] These writings are particularly compelling in the ways they ascribe a consciousness about mixed race to their characters that not only reveals the harshness of human life in our modern capitalist system but critiques a politics of color blindness legitimizing this system under neoliberalism.

The very concept of multiracial consciousness—in representations of interracial relations and characterizations of mixed-heritage people—expresses anxieties about life in a time of war, neoimperialist incursions in the Asia-Pacific, environmental crisis, and the global expansion of capitalism. These anxieties express, in turn, a critical structure of feeling that utterly contradicts neoliberalism's politics of color blindness underpinning our modern capitalist system. The negative affects that express the multiracial consciousness of Asian Americans, I argue, refute the postracial sensibility that disavows histories of racial oppression in the name of freedom and progress. This refutation is apparent in the expression of negative emotions (i.e., affects of shame, melancholia, psychic pain, and bodily suffering) in recent mixed-race Asian American literature. These affects are negative precisely in the way they *affirm* the social relevance of race in an era of transnational capital—an era in which race supposedly no longer matters, according to the neoliberal logic of personal responsibility and privatization (Lipsitz 26).

This literature shows, furthermore, how racially mixed people mediate the emotions of multiracial consciousness to affirm and identify with disparaged ancestral origins. Race matters in this literature. It matters through the emotions of mixed race, which articulate the experience of history and cultural memory and reveal ties to immigrant ancestors and ethnic forebears. I call this experiential process *feeling ancestral*.[2] To be mixed heritage or multiracial and Asian American in these writings is to experience feeling ancestral amid the political, social, and economic upheavals in a time of postracial sensibility. *Feeling ancestral* describes, on one hand, the dialectical tension between a politics of color blindness in neoliberalism and, on the other, cultural memory in the empathic and often painful identification with heritage and genealogy.

Mixed-race Asian American literature thus *revives* the memory of ethnic origins. It depicts the social remembering important to the complex search for self-placement in history—a history intimately tied to the human consequences of modern capitalism. Memory of origins evokes the Asian American subject's ambivalent attachments to the American Dream and this dream's aspirations to live the good life and to belong as an ordinary person in a color-blind society. In signaling the Asian American subject's containment in the economic form of capital, implied by the inability to produce as well as assimilate into the symbolic form of capital, ambivalence articulates criticism of the racialized perception that construes Asian Americans as exemplars of economic activity and of assimilation into neoliberalism.

This chapter further explores ambivalence by examining it as a critical structure of feeling in novels by Chang-rae Lee and Ruth Ozeki. These authors show how mixed-heritage or multiracial Asians try to accommodate a postracial sensibility that neoliberal discourses of privatization idealize and commodify. Lee's *Native Speaker* and Ozeki's *My Year of Meats* depict a dialectical tension between neoliberalism's politics of color blindness and literature's memory of immigrant history, a memory affirming identification with Asian heritage and genealogy. In this sense, to be mixed heritage or multiracial in these novels is to experience and feel *ethnic remembering*: emotions of affiliation and identification with immigrant ancestors that articulate remembering the psychological pains of transnational Asian movement and dislocation. Ethnic remembering not only describes the historical displacement felt and remembered by mixed-heritage and multiracial Asians but also articulates current anxieties about immigration and border crossing under economic processes of globalization.

## Postethnic Melancholia and Memory's Responsibility in *Native Speaker*

Chang-rae Lee's *Native Speaker* is a novel about desire and remembering origins, though its memory of origins is in profound contradiction with the desire to lose connection, disavow history, and refuse inheritance. In Lee's novel, to remember is to accept the responsibility of reaffirming the history of ancestors in the diaspora, no matter how disagreeable it is. In his critique of discourses that celebrate capitalism's globalization as the termination of history and, therefore, the end of accountability to effect the progressive transformation of society, Jacques Derrida argued: "Inheritance is never a given, it is always a task" (67). For Derrida, the inheritance of responsibility to create a just and an equitable world is as inescapable as it is indeterminate and enigmatic. Yet pronouncements about capitalism's planetary triumph rationalize the end of such accountability and thus structure inheritance as mourning. To mourn the death of responsibility to those seeking justice and fairness in the future is to keep *alive* the work of consciousness that counteracts social oppression and inequality. It is also to realize that global capitalism's end of history and cessation of responsibility is deeply melancholic.

Henry Park, the Korean American protagonist in Lee's novel, is in mourning. He grieves the loss of his relationship with a white woman whose love he believed would help him attain belonging in America. He mourns the death of their son, who was tragically killed while playing a game with other neighborhood children. Because his child was half white, Henry not only looked to him as his own flesh-and-blood sign of perfect assimilation into white America but also considered the child an embodied achievement of the transcendence of race, ethnicity, and history. "I knew our son would never learn the old language," Henry admits in his mourning, "this was never in question, and my hope was that he could grow up with a singular sense of this world, a life univocal, which might have offered him the authority and confidence that his broad half-yellow face could not. Of course, this is assimilist sentiment, part of my own ugly and half-blind romance with the land" (267). Henry saw in his son a reason to look to the future as a time and place for letting go of his connection to an immigrant history of struggle, exclusion, and ethnic abjection. Yet it *is* his responsibility to inherit this history from his father as well as from all Korean immigrants in the diaspora. Henry mourns the death of his son as the loss of refusing his own cultural inheritance, as the melancholic *end* of assimilation into an imaginary postethnic America.

In *Native Speaker*, Henry narrates his story of growing up in New York as the American-born child of Korean immigrants. In contradiction to the arduous working-class life of a grocer that his father led, Henry secures employment as a spy for a private intelligence agency that investigates immigrants and ethnic groups. The organization's employees are of various ethnic and racial backgrounds, making up a transnational-like firm that privileges multiculturalism for the exploitation and eventual ruin of the immigrants it targets. "We casually spoke of ourselves as business people," Henry explains.

> Domestic travelers. We went wherever there was a need. The urgency of that need, like much of everything else, was determined by some calculus of power and money. Political force, the fluid motion of capital. . . . These basics drove our livelihood. . . . We pledged allegiance to no government. We weren't ourselves political creatures. We weren't patriots. Even less, heroes. . . . Our clients were multinational corporations, bureaus of foreign governments, individuals of resource and connection. We provided them with information about people working against their vested interests. . . . Typically the subject was a well-to-do immigrant supporting some potential insurgency in his old land, or else funding a fledging trade union or radical student organization. Sometimes he was simply an agitator. Maybe a writer of conscience. An expatriate artist. (17–18)

Masao Miyoshi remarks on the way transnational corporations mandate a code of multiculturalism not only to assure the loyalty of their multiracial work force but also to cultivate a postethnic climate for seamless communication. "In that sense," Miyoshi avers, "transnational corporations are at least officially and superficially trained to be color-blind and multicultural" (90). While Henry's firm requires its multiracial work-force to pay no allegiance to government, it simultaneously commands its agents to repudiate their own ethnic and family backgrounds and histories. "Our mode at the firm," Henry divulges, "was always to resist history, at least our own" (25).

Reflecting neoliberal discourses of color blindness and multiculturalism, Henry's work manifests his desire for a life that escapes hardship and the painful material conditions of working-class immigrants such as his father. As the firm sublates and represses the material histories of both its immigrant targets and its own multiracial workforce, Henry can believe he occupies a privileged and normative position in mainstream America, a process of assimilation whereby he seeks integration into dominant white culture. His intentions for such assimilation are implied in his marriage to a white woman, Leila. She and her family "would help me make my way in the land" (53), he explains; and the birth of his biracial son further signals his desire for a whiteness that would erase the material history of his immigrant heritage.

Despite Henry's requirement to spy on immigrant subjects and eventually bring them to ruin, he cannot help but empathize with the Asian men he is assigned to investigate, especially those men who remind Henry of his own father. For instance, he sabotages an early assignment to investigate a Filipino psychoanalyst, Emile Luzan. Working undercover as Luzan's patient, he cannot resist bonding empathically with the doctor during therapy sessions, confiding in him the most private matters of his life: "Dr. Luzan kept delving further into my psyche," he explains: "plumbing the depths. . . . I was looping it through the core, freely talking about my life, suddenly breaching the confidences of my father and my mother and my wife. . . . I was becoming dangerously frank, inconsistently schizophrenic. . . . When I was in the chair across the desk from Luzan I completely lost myself. I was becoming a dependent, a friend" (22). That Henry feels empathic identification with Luzan while remaining loyal to the firm is a contradiction he expresses in feeling "schizophrenic." Here, I suggest, are the psychic pains in the Asian American subject's racialized split subjectivity. As David Eng argues in his reading of Freudian mourning and melancholia, racialized minority subjects "are all coerced to relinquish and yet to identify with socially disparaged objects on their psychic paths to subjectivity" ("Melancholia" 1278). Henry experiences an ambivalence like the "melancholic's psychic ambivalence toward the lost object" ("Melancholia" 1278) in vacillating between his feelings for Luzan and his allegiance to his firm. Henry must deny (i.e., relinquish) the doctor's Asian immigrant ethnicity and the associated material conditions that would give historical context to such ethnicity. But Henry cannot deny Luzan because he reminds Henry of the disparaged lost object that is his own father.

Failing to investigate and therefore ruin Luzan, Henry is offered a chance to redeem himself at the firm. His next assignment is to spy on John Kwang, a Korean American immigrant who has made millions from his dry-cleaning business and now pursues political ambitions as a city councilman making a bid in the race for mayor of New York. What characterizes Kwang's politics is its opaque but insurgent interests in forming cross-racial alliances, a multiracial network based on remembering and recognizing the material conditions and histories of immigrants and people of color. In a rousing speech to quell tensions between Korean American shop owners and their African American customers, Kwang emphasizes the historical similarities of economic violence committed against blacks and immigrants:

> Know that the blacks who spend money in your store and help put food on your table and send your children to college cannot open their own stores. Why? Why can't they? Why don't they even try? Because banks will not lend to them because they are black. Because these neighborhoods are troubled, high risk. Because if they did open stores, no one would insure them. And if they do not have the same strong community you enjoy, the one you brought with you from Korea, which can pool money and efforts for its members—it is because this community has been broken and dissolved through history.
>
> We Koreans know something of this tragedy. Recall the days over fifty years ago, when Koreans were made servants and slaves in their own country by the Imperial Japanese Army. How our mothers and sisters were made the concubines of the very soldiers who enslaved us. I am speaking of histories that all of us should know. (152–53)

To affirm "speaking of histories that all of us should know," Kwang acts on his cross-racial political vision by setting up an underground economy to help financially struggling immigrants, African Americans, Latinos, and other racialized minorities. He models this program on the *ggeh*: "A Korean money club in which members contributed to a pool that was given out on a rotating basis. Each week you gave the specified amount; and then one week in the cycle, all the money was yours" (50). The premise of the *ggeh* pivots on a traditional concept of familial piety and relations, which Kwang redefines as an affiliative association in order to include all people who need financial help in the borough over which he presides.

As Kwang rises to fame espousing a multiracial platform, the political machinery of the media and of his own organization contradict the insurgent interests of his politics. Working undercover as a member in the organization's media team, Henry cynically observes the consumer marketing techniques of election politics. The team's commercialization of Kwang's image has the ironic effect of downplaying his serious political objectives. "They passed out flyers, pamphlets—A Message from City Councilman John Kwang—buttons, ballpoint pens, keychains, lapel pins, every last piece of it stamped with his perfectly angled script, simply signed, John" (83). Henry travels with the team throughout the city's boroughs, helping to set up the locales of Kwang's campaign speeches. The team's leader, Janice, uses Henry as a stand-in for Kwang while she choreographs the ideal campaign stop. Janice arranges "the positions of the preachers, the crowd, Kwang, paletting their various skin tones into an ambient mix for the media. She asked that I remind her to bring along a young blonde who temped at the office to be in the throng the next day. 'It's like flower arranging,' she said to me. 'You've got to be careful. Too much color and it begins to look crass'" (93). That Janice likens her campaign work to "flower arranging" is a telling reminder of the way consumerism and corporate advertising have become ingrained in the culture of political election campaigns. Here the "various skin tones" of Kwang's supporters blend into an image befitting consumer multiculturalism. Stylized multiculturalism as the commodity production of diversity is what Lee's novel implies about consumerism and political campaigning in modern America. Moreover, the duality between the insurgent interests of Kwang's multiracial politics and the commodification of his image in slick marketing techniques reflects an ambivalent tone in the narrative, an ambivalence that underscores the contradiction between Kwang's political emphasis on the material histories of oppression, segregation, and economic violence and the corporate management and stylization of multiculturalism for a media that markets politicians as consumer items.

The split between leftist cross-racial politics and neoliberal consumer multiculturalism mirrors Henry's conflicting feelings for Kwang. For Kwang uses the media to align himself with neoliberal ideology to garner wide public support for his campaign. Henry observes Kwang's manipulation of the media with a cynicism and ambivalence that register the Janus-faced affair that is Kwang's politics. At the same time, he can't help bonding with Kwang empathically as he did with Luzan. He empathizes with Kwang not only because of their similarity as Korean Americans but also because Kwang reminds Henry of his father, and by extension, the immigrants and diasporic workers who, like Henry's father, struggle to make a living in New York's boroughs.

Equally important, Kwang reminds Henry of his regret for the "abject shame" he once felt as a child not only about his father's daily life (53) but also about his mother, whose decorum and modesty he disparaged and loathed; he remembers "thinking of her, *What's she afraid of,* what could be so bad that we had to be that careful of what people thought of us, as if we ought to mince delicately about in pained feet through our immaculate neighborhood . . . as if everything with us were always all right, in our great sham of propriety" (52, italics in original). The shame Henry felt for his family's "great sham of propriety" he blamed on his mother, not realizing at the time that she felt alienated as a Korean immigrant woman with limited English proficiency in a neighborhood that was almost entirely populated by Euro-Americans. Henry was only ten years old when his mother suddenly died from liver cancer. As she was dying he "*practiced* for her the deepest sense of duty and honor" (58, italics added), indicating his suppression of grief and his attempt to mimic his father's "steely" reserve (59). He claims that he never observed in his father "a devotion" he "could call love" (58), but he implies remorse for realizing the same thing about himself while his mother was alive.

Henry's regret extends to the Korean immigrant woman called Ahjuhma (meaning Aunt) who came to take care of him after his mother's death. From the moment Ahjuhma arrived, Henry could relate to her only through stereotype. "She smelled strongly of fried fish and sesame oil and garlic. . . . My friends called her 'Aunt Scallion,' and made faces behind her back. . . . Sometimes I thought she was some kind of zombie. . . . It seemed to me as if she only partly possessed her own body, and preferred it that way" (65). As a woman who had always been a "mystery" to Henry (72), Ahjuhma personifies the American perception of Asians as racialized others and unassimilable foreigners. One day in the summer before he left for college, Henry further recalls, he and a friend followed Ahjuhma as she walked into town on her day off. "She went into Rocky's Corner newsstand and bought a glossy teen magazine and a red Popsicle. She flipped through the pages, obviously looking only at the pictures. She ate the Popsicle like it was a hot dog in three large bites. 'She's a total alien,' my friend said. 'She's completely bizarre'" (78). Henry's perception of Ahjuhma as a racial alien is the same as that of his friends. How is he to understand himself as Korean in any affirmative way if he takes the same racially pejorative views as his friends? Ahjuhma dies suddenly of pneumonia when Henry is an adult with a family of his own. And as with his repressed anguish for his mother's death and his guilt about not realizing her alienation in America, Henry can comprehend feeling grief for Ahjuhma only through his father. He laments not recognizing Ahjuhma's estrangement in America; he regrets not mourning her death on his own terms.

Henry's familial-like affection for Kwang invokes his memory of Korean diasporic history and origins, as well as his melancholic bond with Korean immigrant alienation and abjection. His affection articulates *feeling ancestral*: the experience of an acute emotional attachment to an ancestral figure that links him to a genealogy of diasporic predecessors and immigrant forebears. What I am suggesting here is the possibility of reading empathy and compassion as affects wrought from the pain of experiencing inequality and economic struggle, pain that is intimately and specifically tied to ethnic identity and community. Henry's empathic connection with Kwang—and figuratively, with Asian immigrant workers of the past and the present—expresses his feeling ancestral: memory and emotion that reflect material histories of inequality in the economic and political domains, histories forgotten and unresolved in the conditions of consumer multiculturalism and neoliberalism.

To argue for ethnicizing affective bonds between an American-born generation of Asian Americans and their immigrant forebears is to tell a historically grounded narrative of Asian American identity that resists the neoliberal erasure of class struggle. As the overlapping histories of oppression and exclusion for African Americans and Korean immigrants in Lee's novel suggests, a critical emphasis on ethnicizing bonds that register the material realities of working-class immigration argues for "coalitions of Asian American and other racial/ethnic minorities within the United States" (Wong, "Denationalization" 18). Ethnic and affective bonding expresses an identity for Henry that is tempered by his melancholic connection to political alliances between oppressed minorities and his grounding in a collective history of racialized immigrant labor. His ethnic identity, in this regard, contests disparities and contradictions in neoliberalism that fracture racialized minority communities and split his racialized subjectivity.

Kwang, a non-native speaker of English, reminds Henry of his own father because of his way of speaking and his ethnically specific Korean gestures:

> He was how I imagined a Korean would be, at least one living in any renown. He would stride the daises and the stages with his voice strong and clear, unafraid to speak the language like a Puritan and like a Chinaman and like every boat person in between.

I found him most moving and beautiful in those moments. And whenever I hear the strains of a different English, I will still shatter a little inside. Within every echo from a city storefront window, I can hear the old laments of my mother and my father, and mine as a confused schoolboy. (304)

The Korean-inflected signs of Kwang's language inspire in Henry a wistful remembrance of his family's working-class background. That he "will still shatter a little inside" when he hears the non-native speaker's voice suggests the vacillating dichotomy between his underlying desire for the cultural inheritance of his immigrant Korean upbringing and the neoliberal flattening or forgetting of his family's painful history, a history that is intrinsic to his inheritance. As much as Henry wants to reject his inheritance, through his compliance with the firm's postracial sensibility, the cultural objects that shape and provide depth to his subjectivity—objects he willfully tries to lose—appear as haunting reminders of his past.

Try as he may, Henry cannot deny these objects. The melancholic tone of his remembrance—"every echo from a city storefront window," "the old laments of my mother and my father"—intimates the psychic pains he experienced as a child. He feels these pains as an adult when remembering his shame about having looked upon the daily life of his mother in abject shame; he feels these pains when recalling his part in the estrangement of Ahjuhma, and in his subsequent efforts to forget these two disparaged women. Henry's attempt to mediate emotions dialectically in his split subjectivity is especially poignant here, insofar as he expresses an empathic bond with Kwang that contradicts his desire to perform his job as a spy, destroy Kwang, and remain loyal to the firm.

Yet Henry's bond with Kwang cannot last. Kwang's defeat and tragic downfall are swift. His political opponents plant a spy in the organization, and Kwang responds by having the spy assassinated. His crime drives Henry to betray him. Kwang's ensuing arrest leads to the annihilation of his underground economy and the deportation of dozens of undocumented immigrants who received help from him. To his dismay, Henry learns that the Immigration and Naturalization Service commissioned the firm to hire him to investigate Kwang's underground economy. He later confesses his complicity in the arrest and deportation of the immigrants. In making this confession, Henry tells us about his accountability to those who seek justice and fairness in America. But he has failed this responsibility for the sake of his own "daily survival," like the survival that his father "came to endure, the need to adapt, assume an advantageous shape" in America (319). His betrayal of Kwang and, by extension, of the immigrants who are arrested and deported is his "ugly immigrant's truth" (319); he further confesses, "I have exploited my own, and those others who can be exploited. This forever is my burden to bear" (319–20). Any empathic connection that Henry has to family, ancestors, and community is now haunted by the shame he feels for having inadvertently betrayed immigrants.

Henry's shame is an inheritance he shares with his father, a "poor cabbage farmer's son" (262) who profited from exploiting Korean immigrants in his own grocery stores. This painful fact Henry cannot deny because he knows that his Ivy League education and the upper-middle-class status he now enjoys have been purchased at the expense of the workers his father exploited: "And although I knew he gave them a $100 bonus every now and then I never let on that I felt he was anything but cruel to his workers. I still imagine Mr. Kim's and Mr. Yoon's children, lonely for their fathers, gratefully eating whatever was brought to them, our overripe and almost rotten mangoes, our papayas, kiwis, pineapples, these exotic tastes of their wondrous new country, this joyous fruit now too soft and too sweet for those who knew better, us near natives, us earlier Americans" (54–55). A melancholic memory arousing shame in the metaphor of the workers' impoverished children eating "too soft and too sweet [fruit]" expresses the psychic pains of Henry's postethnic melancholia. For in realizing the way he, like his own father, is guilty of exploiting immigrants and ethnic groups, Henry feels that his complicity in this exploitation not only contradicts his empathic bond with immigrant father-figures such as Luzan and Kwang but also underscores the disparaged object of his inheritance—his "ugly immigrant's truth"—which he yearns to refuse because it so clearly registers his shame in betraying his own kind. Between Kwang's defeat and the firm's and the INS's triumph, Henry thus remains as cynical and ambivalent as ever. Implicitly, he recognizes the way his desire for assimilation into dominant white culture has led to Kwang's ruin, as well as destroying the possibility of effecting real change in the lives of the people over which Kwang presided. Henry cannot even hope for white assimilation in the futures of his marriage and of his "perfect" and "beautifully speaking" son. In the upper-middle-class suburb of Westchester, neighborhood boys crush his son to death while playing a ball game on his birthday, and soon after this tragedy, Henry and his wife separate.

*Native Speaker* concludes with Henry's ambivalence and the dialectic of material history and postethnic melancholia intact. As David Palumbo-Liu contends, a "nonpathologized, fluent and happy mixedness is thus not for the world at present" in Lee's novel (*Asian/American* 320). Yet what solution does the novel offer for resolving the conflict between ties to family and community *and* a neoliberal postracial sensibility that fragments and severs such ties? Is there a multiraciality that doesn't require the suppression of remembering origins and the refusal of cultural inheritance? Yes, there is such a multiraciality. It exists as a critical structure of feeling, a complex arrangement of emotions and affects that are tempered and mediated by a melancholic bond with immigrant community and history. It exists as the multiracial consciousness of racially mixed protagonists who are intimately connected to the struggles and material conditions of immigrants and ethnic forebears.

As this chapter shows in its next section, Ruth Ozeki's *My Year of Meats* is a late twentieth-century novel in which a discourse of neoliberal color blindness produces a postracial sensibility in tension with the author's attempt to critique the commercialization of human feeling. The protagonist of this mixed-race narrative, as in Lee's novel, expresses a split subjectivity: she dialectically mediates desire for the postracial sensibility of neoliberal consumerism and the poignant emotions of historical memory that manifest ethnic affiliation and community.

## Ethnic Remembering and the Commodification of Human Feeling in *My Year of Meats*

One of the most memorable scenes in Ruth Ozeki's *My Year of Meats* reflects the experience of feeling ancestral, the agency of identifying a sense of belonging within a history of those who have been racially defined by colonial, gender, and class oppressions. This scene occurs when the narrator, Jane Takagi-Little, a racially mixed person from Minnesota, tells us about the time she first began to realize she was not white. She reveals that she "didn't feel racial yet" until she became aware of sex (148). In her teenage years Jane thought about having children with men of other races; for she was the child of a Japanese immigrant mother and an Anglo-American father. She went to a public library in her hometown to do some research and looked up "'The Races of Men' in an old Frye's geography book" (149). The book's descriptions of people in Africa, South America, and Asia disturbed her because they were racist. They referred to South America as "the hot belt of the New World" in which are "found millions of savages" who "resemble the black savages of middle Africa" (150). "They wear little clothing," the book declared, "and use about the same kinds of weapons. They hunt and fish, and lead a lazy, shiftless life" (150). This scene in Ozeki's novel is a striking example of ethnic remembering's power to shape and define racial identity, even if it is not directly about one's actual origins and ancestry, as is the case for Jane. That Jane remembers when she first became aware of racism through the book's racial interpellation of others effectively grounds her in an ethnic identity that links her to the collective history of Asian Americans. By recalling a moment of initial awareness about racial difference, she tells us that remembering is important to her awareness of the racialization process. Through remembering the racial interpellation of others as represented in the geography book, she realizes her own connection to other racialized people in the past, an interpellation that enabled the Western world to define itself in terms of domination and patriarchal authority. But this instance of ethnic remembering's power to ground race in history is in tension with the novel's implication to get over race—to affirm postracial sensibility—in its story about narrator Jane's racially mixed identity, an identity she claims is "evidence" for the end of race.

In the beginning of the novel, Jane explains that she is on a mission to expose the truth about corrupt forces in her work as a media publicist for a TV production company in Japan. She also reveals that she is recently divorced, unemployed, broke, and overdue with the rent for her tenement apartment in New York's East Village. When the production company calls to ask for help with a new television show called *My American Wife!* she jumps at the opportunity for work that will lift her from poverty. The show is sponsored by a Texas-based meat industry lobby organization called BEEF-EX, which seeks big profits from increased beef consumption in Japan. Each weekly episode of the show presents a midwestern housewife cooking a featured meat in her home. Through the program's midwestern wives, "Japanese housewives will feel the hearty sense of warmth, of comfort, of hearth and home—the traditional family values symbolized by red meat in rural America" (8). For Jane, however, the problem with the program is not that it uses wives to commodify the warmth and comforts of "hearth and home" for BEEF-EX's profits. Rather, the problem is cultural representation and the limited geographic locations of the Euro-American wives whose "wholesomeness" the program wants to commercialize in its transnational scheme to advertise and sell American-made beef to Japanese consumers (11).

As a job requirement, Jane is responsible for globalizing America's "heartland" as an essential place of whiteness and Euro-American authenticity, a place apparently free of "deformities" such as race (57). *My American Wife!* is a provocative example of "emotional capitalism" (Illouz 5) because it is a television show that produces and markets emotions as commodities for consumption—affects that express and represent normative values of the traditional white American family. In her job as an assistant and eventually as the director of the program, Jane tries to be loyal to the show's ideals to market American "wholesomeness," "attractiveness," and authenticity (11–12). However, her ambition to "educate" Americans about diversity—what she calls the "Larger Truth" of culture and race (27)—through her work not only gets in the way but nearly gets her fired. Yet Jane does succeed in her ambition to educate. When she becomes the director, she includes as stars of the show a Mexican immigrant family, a disabled young woman in a wheelchair, and an interracial lesbian vegetarian couple from Northampton, Massachusetts. Through network television, she is able to inform all of America and Japan that multiculturalism and diversity are "an integral component" of the American Dream (126).

But how does Jane's success in marketing multiculturalism and diversity prove her declaration that race is over in America? In the beginning of her story, Jane claims that "being racially half" is evidence that race "will become relic" in America (15). "Eventually we're all going to be brown," she says. "Some days, when I'm feeling grand, I feel brand-new—like a prototype" (15). How can Jane claim to embody a postracial sensibility while concurrently using race to commercialize multiculturalism as an aspirational norm of the American Dream? Perhaps there is no getting over race, Ozeki's novel tells us, just as there is no place outside the totalizing grip of global corporatism. And possibly Jane's postracial sensibility and the happy multiculturalism she commercializes end up being the same thing.

To the extent that Ozeki's novel is optimistic in its affirmation of the American Dream for nonwhite immigrants, lesbians and gays, and people with disabilities, it is simultaneously ambivalent, if not restrained, in giving us an alternative to global corporate domination. The novel provokes us to ask, what resistance is there to corporate control of American life and that of the world? We have arrived, then, at our argument about Ozeki's fascinating novel: *My Year of Meats* is *ambivalent* about the end of race because, as an underlying mechanism of corporate globalization, race is essential to produce the emotions that get people to buy and consume commodities.

Whether it is using white housewives to commodify wholesomeness or presenting a Mexican immigrant family to market the idea of the American Dream as multiculturalism, the bottom line is that race is necessary to commodify human feeling and generate consumer subjectivities.

But, again, does *My Year of Meats* suggest any contradiction to this commercialization of feeling? If Ozeki implies resistance and contradiction in her novel, it would have to be through ethnic remembering and the emotions that such remembering evokes. Identifying a sense of belonging through ethnic remembering—the empathic experience of feeling ancestral—is a form of resistance that becomes evident when Jane tells us about her bodily pain and injury. Her physical suffering reflects her mother's own pain and injury from having taken DES while pregnant with Jane. DES has damaged Jane's uterus. Not only has it made her susceptible to developing cervical cancer, but she likely will never be able to bear children of her own because of the drug. "I know what happened. The bludgeoning my uterus received occurred when I was still only a little shrimp, floating in the warm embryonic fluid of Ma. I can imagine the whole thing. Ma, frightened, pregnant, not speaking a word of English, sitting in the doctor's office. . . . I sat in a doctor's office today. *I know how scary it is*" (156, italics added). By way of her imaginary and empathic memory of her mother's fear while pregnant, Jane thus indicates that she receives from her an inheritance of affects—"I know how scary it is," she envisions telling her mother—that not only affirms bonds of kinship and filial love between them but registers her origins in Japanese immigrant history and implies her responsibility to remember this history.

The empathic connection that memory evokes and that affirms a realm of common humanity *within* globalization is also evident when Jane tells the story of her friendship with Akiko, a young woman in Japan whose husband forces her to watch *My American Wife!* The husband, Joichi Ueno, is the Tokyo-based producer of the program. He commands Akiko to rate each show for its "Authenticity, Wholesomeness, Availability of Ingredients, and Deliciousness of Meat" (21). He also instructs her to prepare each show's featured meals to "put some meat on her bones" so that she can become pregnant and bear him a son (20). When Ueno disagrees with her ratings and she prepares a meal not to his liking, he abuses her verbally and physically. He beats her when he finds out she's been avoiding meat to block her menstrual cycle and not get pregnant. When he catches her sending faxes to Jane in which she tells Jane about the assaults and her desire to leave her husband and move to America, he rapes her brutally, sending her to the hospital. Ueno leaves Akiko at the hospital to recover on her own while he's away in America to work for the show. While improving at the hospital Akiko realizes she's become pregnant. She makes plans to escape to America and find Jane, whom she trusts will help her, so that then she can "have a happy life" like the interracial lesbian couple she has seen on the show (233).

For Jane, we must realize, receiving Akiko and offering help further confirm her ambition to educate America and Japan about the Larger Truth of culture and race. But also these ethical actions suggest her realization of international humanist ideals to recognize and help others in need who are different from her and who may live in another part of the world. In effect, Jane's actions to help Akiko uphold the transnational humanist project to strive for a better world in which justice, egalitarianism, and fairness, rather than global corporate profits, are aspirational norms.

To be sure, Jane does commercialize human feeling for the procurement of corporate profit by filming American families for the television show. That she commercializes America's heartland as the sign of traditional family values and white "all-American" wholesomeness implicates her in the perpetuation of corporate domination and the norms of race, gender, and nationalism that are consistent with the ideology of American commerce. As Monica Chiu argues in her reading of Ozeki's novel: "The invisible (read: multicultural) ideology that the novel creates reconstitutes the very localized, national framework that it initially attempts to subvert" (108). Yet it is not so much the people that Jane finds and tapes for the show that most attract her. Rather, what most appeals to her are the politics and the ideas she believes these people embody: the liberal pluralist ideology of multiculturalism, as Chiu points out. In this respect, it is not "the novel" itself that creates multicultural ideology to reconstruct an American nationalist vision. It is Jane. Ozeki depicts Jane's commodification of multiculturalism as the primary way in which she attempts to re-represent the heartland and thus to subvert its image as the essential place of whiteness and Euro-American authenticity. "After four months," Jane explains, "the BEEF-EX injunction on the demographics of our wives was still in effect, and we continued to shoot primarily middle-class white American women with two or three children" (58). However, when she finds the Martinez family, a Mexican immigrant household in Texas, she eagerly tapes them because she claims they "would obviously break this mold" of whiteness in the show:

> The boy, whose name was Bobby, lived there with his parents, Alberto and Catalina Martinez. Alberto, or Bert, as he now

preferred to be called, was a farmworker. He'd lost his left hand
to a hay baler in Abilene seven years earlier, a few months after
he and Catalina (Cathy) had emigrated from Mexico, just in time
for Bobby to be born an American citizen. That had been Cathy's
dream, to have an American son, and Bert had paid for her dream
with his hand. Since then he had worked hard in the fields to support the family, and Cathy had worked too, in factory jobs, and
finally their efforts had paid off. They had scraped up the money to
buy the little white farmhouse and a few acres of surrounding land,
and the way I figured it, Alberto, Catalina, and little Bobby were on
their way to becoming a real American success story. (58)

The actualization of Cathy's dream to raise Bobby, her American-born
son, in the "little white farmhouse" and "few acres of surrounding land"
that she and her husband own effectively counters the perception of the
Midwest as the heart and spirit of America's white culture. Cathy's fulfilled dream narrativizes the pursuit of happiness as an American social
vision. But the fact that she is Mexican redefines this vision to include
multicultural ideals. And because her husband, Bert, "had paid for her
dream with his hand," the Martinez family's pursuit of happiness in Texas
is a story about suffering and sacrifice entirely conventional to European
immigrant stories of hardship and endurance in the heartland. Hence,
the Martinez's "real American success story" is, as Jane wants us to see
it, about race and multiculturalism as social phenomena that are both
indispensable and normative to the American Dream.

Jane's objective is to depict the Martinez family as a personification
of America's nationalist ethos. She packages the family's success story
as racialized sentiment—as affective multicultural capital—in order
to celebrate the American Dream as the actualization of diversity and
identity politics in the US capitalist system. But isn't Jane's celebration of
the American Dream for the Martinez family an instance of "cruel optimism," as Berlant would put it, an emotionally exploitative mechanism
that gets people to believe they can and must live the good life promised by capitalism? Moreover, how is it possible to fit Jane's multicultural
vision of the American Dream within the novel's critical objective to
disclose capitalism as a totality of social relations? Undoubtedly Jane's
taping of the Martinez family as the stars of the show aestheticizes multiculturalism as the American Dream, which, as I noted in chapter 1,
is a stylization of diversity that promotes neoliberal business ideologies
of color blindness and emotional commodification. Ultimately, for the

purposes of my argument, I suggest that we interpret Jane's sentimental depiction of the Martinez family as part of the novel's dialectic of postracial sensibility and ethnic remembering. The story of the Martinez family advances a complex *tension* in the novel between Jane's declarations about the end of race (i.e., her contention that "race will become relic") and her implicit attempts to remember immigrant history, a social remembering that invokes feeling ancestral and affirms ethnic identification with Asian heritage and genealogy.

The novel's most obvious instance of emotional commodification, one for which Jane proudly takes credit, concerns the disabled young woman in the wheelchair, Christina Bukowsky. While riding her bicycle Christina is hit by a Wal-Mart truck. The injury paralyzes her and puts her in a coma. Wal-Mart refuses to take any responsibility, and the parents, who are working class and have no health insurance, have to take their daughter out of the hospital and care for her alone in their home. Townspeople and sympathizers from all around come to visit and show their support. They bring food and gifts to offer empathy and comfort: "You had to bring the Thing in Life That You Love Best, to share with Christina" (134). This outpouring of kindness works: seven months later Christina awakens from her coma, and the mother, Jane says, attributes her daughter's recovery to "Compassion: 'com' (with, together, in conjunction with) plus 'passion'" (134).

The collective act of compassion leads to another happy outcome: "The media got hold of the story and pumped it for all it was worth from every angle, including the exploitation of small-town America by the corporate retail giants. Wal-Mart did the right thing, paid a handsome settlement, and the family used the money to transform the Living Room into a Deluxe Physical Training Center" (135). The townspeople's compassion thus generates a global corporation's compassion, as indicated by the "handsome settlement." It becomes evident to the whole town that money—a lot of it—can be made from compassion: "The town of Quarry had discovered a new natural resource—compassion—and they were mining it and marketing it to America. . . . Quarry became Hope, and Mr. Bukowsky was elected mayor. . . . The townspeople found jobs with the Center or started their own businesses as affiliated service providers. . . . The Mayor and Mrs. Bukowsky starred in a promotional videotape, 'Welcome to Our Living Room: the Bukowsky Method of Compassion and Renewal,' and published a best-selling book by the same name" (135). One meaningful way to understand Jane's optimistic take on the marketing of compassion here is to contrast it with her comments about America as a "grisly nation" (89).

While traveling across the country, Jane explains, the production team's Japanese nationals were "astonished at how deeply violence is embedded in our culture" (89). In light of these comments, it is clear that the marketing of sympathy as a "new natural resource" opposes the ubiquitous commodification of violence in America. Her optimism about the "mining" of compassion contradicts the capitalist's pessimistic expectation that there's more money to be made by peddling hatred and aggression than by cultivating kindness and fellow feeling. Compassion, as Jane also seems to imply, can cause people to think of others as being more universally alike. Across the Pacific in Tokyo, for instance, Akiko watches the story of Christina and experiences a transformative moment of self-realization. Although her realization is negative, it has the intended effect to elicit our compassion for her: "Akiko wondered what it would be like to be incapacitated like that. After she fell into the china cabinet, her stomach hurt so badly she couldn't get out of bed, and all she wanted was to slip into a coma and not move, not speak, not eat. There were no townspeople. Nobody came" (141). Akiko "fell into the china cabinet" because Ueno beat her and pushed her into it. The compassion that Christina's story transmits to Akiko underscores her desperate alienation and heartbreak about her husband's abuse. Moreover, it signals the potential of Jane's work as a media maker to effect and affirm a realm of common humanity within globalization.

The tension between Jane's ambitions to reveal the Larger Truth of the ongoing matter of race in America and her own aspiration, as a racially mixed person, to embody postracial sensibility is further evident in the story of Dyann and Lara, the interracial lesbian vegetarian couple, whom Jane perceives as opponents of everyday white culture. The couple's respectability challenges the normativity of whiteness. "There was nothing unwholesome about their lifestyle," Jane informs us, describing Lara and Dyann in model minority terms. "The women were pillars of their community: one was a district attorney, the other a well-published author; their tiny children were unusually smart and cute; and they were exemplary mothers, both of them" (173). After she tapes the couple with their children, Jane further explains a compelling moment when she was in the editing room, "finishing the Lesbian Show," and she appreciated her achievement. "The program was uplifting, a powerful affirmation of difference, of race and gender and the many faces of motherhood, and I was filled with a moral certitude" (177). In this particular moment, when Jane remembers pondering her accomplishment in the editing room, her narration comes closest to reflecting what I contend is the novel's dialectic of postracial sensibility and ethnic remembering. It might appear she does not care about all of the show's wives, Jane says:

> But the fact is, I did care, and at the same time I couldn't afford to care, and these two contrary states *lived side by side* like twins, wrapped in a numbing cocoon that enabled me to get the work done. Psychiatrists call this "doubling." . . . I realized that truth was like race and could be measured only in ever-diminishing approximations. . . . Halved as I am, I was born doubled. By the time I wrote the pitch for *My American Wife!* my talent for speaking out of both sides of my mouth was already honed. On one hand I really did believe that you could use wives to sell meat in the service of a greater Truth. On the other hand, I was broke after my divorce and desperate for a job. (175–76, italics added)

In the beginning of the novel, Jane embraces her "racially half" identity as a sign for the end of race in America, but here she says her biraciality— "Halved as I am"—is the reason for any double standards we may have noticed thus far in her story. We should not doubt her sincerity. True, she has only been using "wives to sell meat in the service of a greater Truth" about race and culture in America. And her only recourse to publicize this "Truth" has been through the mechanisms of her employment at a global corporation. There's been no alternative, Jane avows. Her abysmal economic situation has compelled her to accept a job offer through BEEF-EX. For she was "broke" and "desperate for a job" after her divorce, and if the only work available to her involved the shameless packaging and selling of sentimentality, then so be it. In this moment, when Jane remembers and discloses her growing awareness of capitalist totality and her contradiction with the totalizing relations of global corporatism, we might see how her awareness reflects the racial diegesis in the novel. For in these moments when Jane remembers and reveals her awareness of BEEF-EX's production and exploitation of emotions, she's also telling us about being racially conscious in her narration. Even though she claims "truth was like race and could be measured only in ever-diminishing approximations," the fact that she strives to represent this truth and assert her belief "in it wholeheartedly" attests to her consciousness about race as something more than a means for commercializing emotion and generating corporate profits. Race matters, Jane suggests. It matters as a material condition and force of history.

The novel's tension between Jane's declarations about getting over race (i.e., the end of race in multicultural America) and the corporate use of race to commercialize sentimentality (i.e., BEEF-EX's use of white housewives to market wholesomeness) reaches a climax when Jane exposes the hormonal poisoning of cattle in the beef industry. In this part the novel, Jane tells us about her greatest opportunity to work in the service of a greater Truth, and thus she gets to act as the investigative documentarian she's always wanted to be. The reprinting of fax messages, office memos, journal entries, paragraphs from science texts, and passages from Sei Shonagon's tenth-century *Pillow Book* throughout the novel's pages leads up to this climactic moment in which Jane uncovers a big story about corruption and fraud in the global meat industry.

While taping a show in a cattle ranch in Colorado she finds evidence of the ranch using hormonal growth promoters for its livestock. The Dunn & Son feedlot uses drugs to fatten up its cattle. Cows are given growth hormones to control their reproduction. In one of the feedlot's dumpsters Jane sees piles of empty bottles. She reaches in and grabs one to read its contents. The bottle contained Lutalyse, "the hormone used to synchronize the estrus of a herd for easier artificial insemination" (261–62). She asks the ranch owner's son, Gale, if the feedlot is using Lutalyse to breed cattle. "Now, ain't that something?" he replies. "That's just another example of modern science comin' up with a way to kill two birds with one stone. We ain't breedin' here, but we use that same Lutalyse to abort our heifers when they get accidental bred, you know?" (262–63). But the proof of hormonal growth promoters at the ranch is everywhere. Jane wanders into a feedlot and witnesses a horrifying sight: "In the dust lay a slimy, half-dried puddle containing a misshapen tangle of glistening calf-like parts—some hooves, a couple of bent and spindly shins. It was an aborted fetus, almost fully grown, with matted fur, a delicate skull, and grotesquely bulging eyes" (267).

After taping a segment with Gale holding Rosie, the five-year old child from his father's second marriage to a woman named Bunny, Jane is further horrified to witness sexual abuse. In the video she sees Gale fondling his half sister. And she also sees that Rosie is suffering from estrogen poisoning because she has breasts. Jane confronts Bunny to tell her about her daughter, and it is noteworthy that she links her own condition as a DES-exposed daughter to Rosie's illness: "I think she's received some sort of hormone poisoning, probably from the drugs around the feedlot, and that's why she's got breasts. There's a name for it. It's called premature thelarche. . . . I had a kind of estrogen poisoning too. Different—I got it from my mother—but, well, it screwed me up inside. I had a growth, like a cancer, on my cervix. And my uterus is deformed. These things are

dangerous, Bunny" (274–75). The link between Jane and Rosie that registers their illness from hormone poisoning—implied consequences of
their victimization by patriarchal authority and masculine violence—is
extended to Jane's injury at the slaughterhouse. After telling Bunny about
Rosie's illness, Jane and the production team enter the slaughterhouse to
finish taping the show. Jane describes a scene of sheer horror: "Blood was
everywhere: bright red, brick red, shades of brown and black; flowing,
splattering, encrusting the walls, the men. . . . The place was caked with
a deep, rotting filth. And thick with flies" (281). The running blood of
butchered cows here reflects an earlier scene when Ueno rapes Akiko,
making her bleed profusely from her rectum. Two days after her rape,
"her rectum was still bleeding. . . . As she watched, a trickle of bright-red
blood oozed from the center. Like a bleeding eye, she thought" (251). The
gruesome scene in the slaughterhouse is further connected to Akiko's
rape when Jane sees a cow about to be killed: "The cow balked, minced,
then slammed her bulk against the sides of the pen. She had just watched
the cow before her being killed . . . *and she was terrified.* Her eyes rolled
back into her head and a frothy white foam poured from her mouth as
the steel door slammed down on her hindquarters, forcing her all the
way in" (283, italics added). In Jane's narration the suffering cow is not a
slab of meat but a living being with the capacity to feel pain, express fear,
and communicate pleas for help. These negative emotions of fear and ter-
ror have the effect of not only tying Akiko's misery to the cow's suffering
but also provoking our compassion and compelling us to feel empathy by
imagining *ourselves* in relation to their pain and trauma. This identifica-
tory relation through compassion and empathy has its intended effect
on Jane, moreover, in her narration as a trauma victim in the slaughterhouse; for she is next to experience agonizing pain: "I must have caught
the meat just as it swung around a corner at the peak of its centrifugal
arc. It slammed me, lifting me right off my feet. . . . On the way back
down I hit the base of my skull against the edge of the knocking pen,
which, appropriately, knocked me right out" (284). Our empathic attachment to Jane in this moment at the slaughterhouse is all the more intense
because we can imagine her agony in relation to Akiko's misery and the
inhumane butchering of cows.

In contradiction with her work to globalize heartland whiteness for
corporate profits is the trauma Jane suffers from the accident while filming in the slaughterhouse. Her trauma is powerfully conveyed through
the loss of her pregnancy. Jane miscarries not necessarily from getting injured at the slaughterhouse or from handling an empty bottle of

Lutalyse. Rather, she miscarries because of the deformation in her uterus caused by her mother's ingestion of DES. In any case, the bodily trauma she endures from her injury ties her to her mother in Minnesota. After she recovers, Jane visits her mother to tell her about her miscarriage and her body's deformation from her mother's ingestion of DES. "'The pills damaged my uterus and my cervix. . . . They never developed properly. Do you remember the tumor I had operated on in Japan? That was part of it. I had *cancer* . . . . When I'm in my forties the risk increases again. I could still *die* of this, Ma'" (312, original italics). Provoked by her daughter's anguish, the mother responds by telling Jane about her own trauma when giving birth to her: "I am sorry for taking bad medicine that hurt you. . . . But you are wrong for blaming me. . . . I not blaming you for being too big baby that break me to pieces inside when you come out. Doc say I almost die. And bleeding and bleeding, so he take out my inside woman parts. No more chance for babies. All gone" (312). It is important to note that all of these instances of female suffering in the novel are the result of men who traumatize women directly by raping and abusing them or implicitly by objectifying their bodies in science and medicine.

The mixed-race daughter in Ozeki's novel thus shares bonds of trauma with her heartland immigrant mother. By *bonds of trauma* I mean they share affects of pain and suffering that figuratively ground them in a history of Japanese immigrant displacement and exclusion. Such pain not only opposes the conventional immigrant story of melting-pot assimilation commonly accepted in US liberal-pluralist discourse but also contradicts the heartland as a global sign of American whiteness. The trauma of Jane and that of her mother further reflect the suffering of Akiko, who at this point in the novel has fled to America to find Jane. When the two women meet in New York they bond by telling each other about their personal experiences with pain and trauma. "Over the next three days," Jane says, "she told me the whole sordid story of her marriage and her struggle with fertility. And I told her mine" (330). The bonds between Jane, Akiko, and Jane's mother are wrought by shared experiences of trauma caused directly or implicitly by men and the problem of global corporate greed. In this context of empathically formed bonds of trauma between Asian immigrant and mixed-heritage women, the novel powerfully demonstrates its critique of global corporate violence. To be sure, these bonds might be understood as the exploitation or manipulation of sentimentality, as David Palumbo-Liu points out in his reading of affect and ethical content in *My Year of Meats* ("Rational and Irrational Choices" 65). Yet as he further explains, these bonds may also constitute a "circle of affect" encompassing Jane, Akiko, and Jane's mother that validates their humanity within an affective public community (59). When Akiko writes to Jane telling her about the abuse she suffers from her husband, Jane finally *understands* the transnational effect of her television show to structure a sense of human commonality with other women: "Maybe it was because my shows were broadcast in Japan, on the other side of the globe, but up until now I'd never really imagined my audience before. She was an abstract concept: at most, a stereotypical housewife, limited in experience but eager to learn. . . . Now it hit me: what an arrogant and chauvinistic attitude this was. While I'd been worried about the well-being of the American women I filmed as subjects, suddenly here was the audience, embodied in Akiko, with a name and a vulnerable identity" (231). In this epiphanic moment of realizing a sense of commonality, Ozeki portrays the dialectical relationship between Jane's multiracial consciousness of another woman's humanity "on the other side of the globe" and humanity's emergence as an affective contradiction to clichés of multicultural harmony—clichés predicated on the heartland as all-American wholesomeness and whiteness. Therefore Jane's awareness of Akiko's humanity, tied to her remembering her immigrant mother's displacement and pain in America, is in the final analysis her feeling ancestral as an emotional contradiction to corporate processes that use race to commercialize human feeling and extract profit. Her consciousness of Akiko's trauma and the help she gives her in the wake of her own injury, suffering, and loss occasioned by men at the slaughterhouse counteract the acquisitive happiness of possessive individualism. In this contradiction, likewise, the novel articulates a critical structure of feeling to envision being receptive to others in the world and to feel ourselves, in Palumbo-Liu's words, "in the world with others" (67).

The multiracial consciousness that Ozeki represents in *My Year of Meats* hence allows us to place her novel alongside Kingston's *China Men*, Bulosan's *America*, Pham's *Catfish*, and Jin's *A Free Life*—narratives this book has examined as literary testaments to Asian American historical experience. Kingston, Bulosan, Pham, and Jin have shown us in their works how the Asian American in the US cultural imaginary has historically occupied a place of containment as a racialized subject who threatens the happiness of normative American personhood. This happiness is the subjective domain of white male individualism, which, as Victor Bascara maintains, "inherently invoked the various unfree, nonwhite ones against whom the enfranchised defined themselves" (12). The articulation of this history in these works reveals Asian America's importance in the making of a capitalist culture of happiness, insofar as this culture has been shaped and defined as the preserve of white Americans by the racialized otherness of Asians.

Ozeki's complex and multiform novel also articulates this history by invoking recent histories of anti-Asian racism and violence in America. One of these is the case of Yoshihiro Hattori, the Japanese exchange student residing in Baton Rouge, Louisiana, who was shot and killed by Rodney Peairs, a supermarket butcher and affiliate of the Ku Klux Klan. On the evening of October 17, 1992, Hattori was on his way to a Halloween party and went to the wrong house by accident. Peairs, the property owner, thought Hattori was trespassing with criminal intent and shot Hattori point blank in the chest, killing him instantly. The state court of Louisiana acquitted Peairs of the homicide, which ignited international outcry. The "accidental" killing of Hattori is one of America's most controversial instances of violence against a foreign exchange student. "Hattori was killed," Jane explains, "because Peairs had a gun, and because Hattori looked different. Peairs had a gun because here in America we fancy that ours is still a frontier culture, where our homes must be defended by deadly force from people who look different. And while I'm not saying that Peairs pulled the trigger because he was a butcher, his occupation didn't surprise me. Guns, race, meat, and Manifest Destiny all collided in a single explosion of violent, dehumanized activity" (89). That Ozeki specifically refers to the case of Hattori in order to critique America's culture of anti-immigrant violence suggests how Asian Americans have been at odds with a national credo of possessive individualism traditionally reserved for white men. Jane's mentioning of Hattori in her narration recounts a recent history of anti-Asian violence important to understanding Asian America as a racial formation continually in process. Hattori's murder, as explained by Jane, further asserts ethnic remembering's power to shape and determine racial identity. By telling us not to forget Hattori's murder, Jane puts the novel in contradiction with global capitalism's false claims about the end of accountability to those seeking justice in the future. Her ethnic remembering critically opposes neoliberalism's postracial sensibility: its lie about the end of race in twenty-first century America.

Chang-rae Lee and Ruth Ozeki are two of many contemporary Asian American writers whose portrayal of multiraciality goes against the grain of neoliberal color blindness. Asian American writings express the pain of racial subject formation within a materialist framework of hybridity. The emotions of mixed race render visible, in the words of Lisa

Lowe, "the histories of forced labor migrations, racial segregation, economic displacement, and internment [that] are left in the material traces of 'hybrid' cultural identities" (*Immigrant Acts* 82). As Lowe further notes, "These hybridities are always in the process of, on the one hand, being appropriated and commodified by commercial culture and, on the other, of being rearticulated for the creation of oppositional 'resistance' cultures" (82). It is within this materialist conception of hybridity that mixed-race Asian American literature resists the violence of historical amnesia and color blindness. Feeling ancestral and the negative affects of shame, melancholia, psychic pain, and bodily suffering become, in the end, an empathic way for mixed-heritage and multiracial Asians to claim both filial and affiliative origins.

# 5 / Happiness, Optimism, Anxiety, and Fear: Asiatic Racial Sentiments in Twenty-First-Century America

In June 2012, the Pew Research Center released its report "The Rise of Asian Americans" proclaiming Asian Americans to be the most successful race group in the United States. The report asserted that Asian Americans are the "best-educated, highest-income, fastest-growing race group in the country" (1). It lauded the six largest Asian American ethnic groups (Chinese Americans, Filipino Americans, Indian Americans, Vietnamese Americans, Korean Americans, and Japanese Americans) for having achieved "milestones of economic success and social assimilation" that have enabled them to be "more satisfied than the general public with their lives, finances, and the direction of the country" (1). The report's most striking conclusion, expressed in its Overview, is that because Asian Americans are the most successful race group in terms of income and social assimilation, they are therefore the *happiest* ("more satisfied") minority population in the United States. In the context of being the most economically efficient of racial minorities, and therefore a people who epitomize the pursuit of happiness intrinsic to the proverbial American Dream, Asian Americans constitute, the report deduced, a race group whose achievements may be seen as reasons to be optimistic for America's renewed growth in the global economy. By upholding educational attainment and higher earnings as the main criteria for success, the report accordingly characterized Asian Americans as subjects of happiness for assimilation into economic processes of globalization.

Yet days after the report's release various Asian American organizations accused the Pew Research Center of making generalizations that upheld stereotypes about Asian people as model minorities and threats. For example, the Asian American and Pacific Islander Policy Research Consortium (AAPIPRC), a national organization of university-based Asian American research centers, wrote a letter criticizing the report for providing "highly biased" information about the income earnings of Asian immigrants ("Letter"). The report's aggregate-data information conceals, the AAPIPRC maintained, the more crucial matters of other ethnic immigrant groups and threatens alliances with these groups ("Letter").[1]

Of particular note is the response from the Association for Asian American Studies (AAAS), which sent to all of its members a letter that accused the Pew Research Center of perpetuating the "sentiment" felt by Americans that Asians in the United States are exemplary minorities of economic achievement. According to the AAAS, the report also implicitly validates the racialized perception of Asians as foreigners who threaten to invade America. By claiming that Asian Americans are the most successful minority in the United States, the Pew Research Center highlights only the "positive accomplishments of Asian Americans" and ignores the "significant body of our community who are not happy, educated, or high-income earners." There will be dangerous repercussions because of the report, warns the AAAS: "What is even more alarming is the message that the report permeates to those who feel that Asian Americans have an unfair advantage, that they are taking over, and that perhaps they are going to take over our society. The framing from the media is likely to flame the fires of anti-Asian sentiments in an economically challenged United States." Just by entitling their report "The Rise of Asian Americans," the Pew Research Center suggests that Asian Americans have achieved "success" and managed to escape the prevailing economic anxieties felt by most Americans. Moreover, the Pew Research Center implicitly endorses the perception of Asian Americans as threats because their success, according to the report, derives from an overly aggressive and disciplinary work ethic such as that of the "tiger mother,"[2] implying cultural differences for Asians that are alien and alarming to most Americans.

In a current time of widespread anxiety and uncertainty amid the ongoing catastrophes and crises of the capitalist world system, the Pew Research Center's characterization of Asian Americans as exemplary minorities who epitomize satisfaction and happiness with the global economy is indeed troublesome. Despite the report's intention to represent Asian Americans objectively according to such criteria as economic mobility and social assimilation, its characterization of Asian Americans as the most successful race group invokes past resentments and perceptions of them as "Orientals" who embody the logics of economic exchange for American businessmen.

## Anti-Asian Sentiment: An Emotional Aesthetic of Race

American resentment toward Asia's growing economic power, which gets conflated with the "success" of Asian Americans, is real and ongoing. Popular culture and media have portrayed Asian Americans as conspiratorial agents of an Asian tiger economy that portends an Oriental control and conquest of the capitalist system. In these popular depictions of Asians as figures of global domination, anti-Asian sentiment is an *emotional aesthetic of race* that gives a corporeal texture and form to anxieties about economic processes of globalization. If economic globalization can be defined simply as the integration of capitalist activities across national borders through markets, then its planetary impact and incessant transnational expansion would characterize it, in Jameson's terms, as a global capitalist totality that defies perception (*Geopolitical Aesthetic* 4–5). For Jameson, in his reading of conspiracy-thriller films as allegories for the oppressive facelessness of "the present multinational stage of monopoly capitalism" (*Signatures* 50), the capitalist world system is a totality "so vast that it cannot be encompassed by the natural and historically developed categories of perception with which human beings normally orient themselves" (*Geopolitical Aesthetic* 2). According to the political scientist Dominique Moïsi, the very fact that economic globalization is a totality which cannot be perceived means it is an omnipresent yet invisible force causing insecurity and raising "the question of identity" (i.e., how to identify one's self, community, and nation in relation to an imperceptible global force that changes day-to-day life rapidly and irrevocably everywhere in the world) (12).

As a totality, global capitalism eludes visualization and representation, despite generating so much anxiety. Since economic globalization has in the American context radically transformed everyday life, thereby generating immense inequalities and rendering uncertain not only America's future but also the world's, it does seem that globalization's resistance to concrete representation would create the demand for it to be visually representable as a perceivable object or material thing through popular media. Advertising, film, television, and visual media have both in the past and in the present graphically depicted the Asiatic as a figuration for an impalpable capitalist totality. American media and popular culture have harnessed the insecurity and anxiety produced by globalization and transmuted them into a perceptible racial figure of fear. By signifying capitalist totality as an Asiatic threat, the media and popular culture engender fear as "the emotional response to the perception, real or exaggerated, of an impending danger" felt by Americans in the midst of economic globalization (Moïsi 92).

The media's portrayal of Asian Americans as agents of finance capital thus provides something *personified* to be perceived as an identifiable figure of capitalism's transnational expansion. This figure is a corporeal racial form characterized by decidedly negative affects in globalization that have spatial and temporal dimensions. As a racialized body of evidence for what generates "all the anxieties that rush to fill our current vacuum" in an anonymous and alienating global totality (Jameson, *Geopolitical Aesthetic* 4), the Asiatic as the sign of globalization is, I argue, an archetypal category of perception through which Americans have historically attempted to apprehend the root cause of their economic anxieties. In this context of the need to perceive a representable form of totality, the modernization and growing economic power of Asia are sensational material for the media to allegorize pervasive unease and suspicion among Americans about economic processes of globalization. The media thus depict the Asian American as the face of Asiatic threat in order to cognitively map American anxieties about living alienated, lost, or "left out" in the capitalist world system.

By transmuting these economic anxieties into a distinguishable racial form, the media clearly demonstrate "the logic of anxiety and that of projection," as Sianne Ngai conceptualizes it in her argument that anxiety has its own "special temporality: the future-orientedness that makes it belong to Ernst Bloch's category of 'expectation emotions'" (215). Ngai further explains that "anxiety has a spatial dimension as well. In psychological discourse, for example, anxiety is invoked not only as an affective response to an anticipated or projected event, but also as something 'projected' onto others in the sense of an outward propulsion or displacement—that is, as a quality or feeling the subject refused to recognize in himself and attempts to locate in another person or thing (usually as a form of naïve or unconscious defense)" (210). If, as Ngai argues, "The logic of anxiety and that of projection, as a form of spatial displacement, converge in the production of a distinct kind of knowledge-seeking subject" (215), then we may consider how anxiety's logic of projection here produces a normative American personhood by rendering the Asian an object or a thing either to be used as a means for the pursuit of happiness or to be excluded and expelled from the terrain reserved for actualizing personhood. Anti-Asian sentiment is, I suggest, born from the logic of anxiety and that of projection as generated by an emotional culture in capitalism. The media transmute nervousness about life in capitalist modernity into fears about Asia as an economic threat. Anxiety and fear thus make up the Asiatic threat. If perception takes an unrepresentable "something" and materializes it into a recognizable and commonly understood form, then we can see how Asiatic threat and anti-Asian sentiment are the negative affects of an Asiatic racial form that represents, as an identifiable configuration of race for Asian Americans, a seemingly invisible and imperceptible global capitalist totality.

Take, for example, the 2012 political campaigns and elections, whose advertisements, particularly for Republican candidates, were salient for featuring anti-Asian sentiments that expressed fears about Asia as an economic threat. Campaign ads exploited anxieties about economic distress and job loss amid the new Cold War between China and the United States. In the months before the Super Tuesday Election, Mitt Romney's campaign released its "Stand Up to China" ad, which criticized the Obama administration for not labeling China a currency manipulator and for allowing the Chinese to steal "American ideas and technology—everything from computers to fighter jets," and ostensibly costing the United States over two million jobs.[3] People of Asian descent were popular in TV ads produced by right-wing organizations that sought political capital by stigmatizing politicians for endorsing government spending, which they claimed fed an Asian economic predator threatening to overtake the United States in financial productivity and development. Citizens Against Government Waste (CAGW), an advocacy group for fiscally conservative causes, launched an ad called "Chinese Professor" that first aired on television in the fall of 2010 for the midterm elections. The ad begins with the sound and image of a man's approaching footsteps. The man stands before an auditorium of students in Beijing in the year 2030. The students listen to him lecture in Mandarin that the United States has fallen and China has succeeded because of America's reckless borrowing and spending. Ominous music plays while the man screens iconic images of government buildings and memorials in Washington, D.C. English subtitles translate his lecture: "America tried to spend and tax itself out of a great recession.... Of course, we owned most of their debt. So now they work for us" (see Figure 5.1). The ad ends with the man staring menacingly into the camera and the students snickering arrogantly in agreement with him.

*so now they work for us.*

FIGURE 5.1. The aesthetic of yellow peril fear in Citizens Against Government Waste TV ad, "Chinese Professor," 2010.

The "Chinese Professor" ad is a telling example of how anti-Asian sentiment has been used in the visual media as an emotional aesthetic of racial stereotyping to manipulate anxieties about the global economy. These anxieties are visually transmuted into fear by taking the form of "race" through the faces and bodies of Asian Americans as personifications of Asiatic threat. Asian American cultural critics have roundly criticized CAGW's ad for using Asian American actors.[4] In his Internet blog *Angry Asian Man*, Phil Yu reports that the actors had signed up to be extras in the *Transformers 3* movie, but when they arrived at the set the production team told them they were performing in the ad because the *Transformers 3* shoot was full. One of the actors explained in an interview: "It was filmed at a community college (NOVA in Alexandria, VA) and when we got there, the production team did tell us about the ad, but in a misconstrued kind of way. I know that the ad was about the US deficit and they did tell us the premise of the ad (taking place in the future, and we all were supposed to be 'Chinese' students in a lecture). I saw the commercial and it's pretty intense and one thing I did not know that the commercial would do, is put this almost red-scare type of fear in the eyes of Americans" ("Extra"). Aiming to foment anti-Chinese xenophobia as "red-scare fear" during the 2012 elections, CAGW aired its notorious ad again in October 2012 to help Mitt Romney defeat Barack Obama. The "Chinese Professor" ad therefore joined other racially offensive political ads on television that fall, making the 2012 election season memorable for its prevalent manipulation of American hostilities to immigrants and ethnic minorities.

The popular imaging of anti-Asian sentiment as an emotional aesthetic to provoke fear in American politics was particularly striking in a campaign ad for Michigan Senate candidate Pete Hoekstra that aired during the Super Bowl in February 2012. Hoekstra, a Republican congressman, approved and used the ad to attack his chief rival, incumbent Democratic senator Debbie Stabenow. The half-minute ad begins with a young Asian woman riding a bicycle along a dirt path beside rice paddies. She wears a yellow shirt and white pants. A conical Asian hat hangs behind her head. Stereotypical Oriental music with gongs, tick-tocking strings, and drums plays in the background. The woman stops her bike and smiles, saying in broken English: "Thank you Michigan Senator Debbie Spend It Now. Debbie spends so much American money. You borrow more and more from us. Your economy get very weak. Ours get very good. We take your jobs" (see Figure 5.2). A smirking Hoekstra then appears and says: "I think this race for US Senate is between Debbie Spend It Now and Pete Spend It Not. I'm Pete Spend-It-Not Hoekstra, and I approve this message." In merely thirty seconds, Hoekstra in his ad exploits every pervasive fear about Asians as threats to US jobs, wealth, comfort, and security. In the context of Asia's modernization and growing economic power since the late nineteenth century, this fear is not new. Generated in large part by the media's representation of the Asiatic as the sign of globalization, this fear registers the ways in which the Asia-Pacific has been racially identified as exploitable terrain for capital accumulation. At the same time, however, the Asiatic can readily become perilous, depending on the existing political discourses that articulate US relations with Asia as either ally or adversary.

As I noted in the Introduction, the identification of the Asiatic as the sign of globalization that manifests both positive and troubling outlooks for US capital emerges from a long history of Asian stereotyping, beginning with America's ambitions for constructing and controlling the modern capitalist system. Today's perceptions of Asians as figures of economic gain or peril emerged from over a century of US discourses about Asia as a territory for conquest and control. The emergence of the physical, material, and visual manifestation of the Asiatic racial form—an economic trope for capital's unbridled globalization—has its origins in the late nineteenth century, when industrialization in the United States proceeded alongside its imperialist expansion beyond the nation's continental frontier, primarily in its relations with China and

FIGURE 5.2. Michigan Senate candidate Pete Hoekstra's campaign TV ad, 2012.

Japan (Lye, *America's Asia* 10). American Orientalist discourse has produced a particular racial form for Asian Americans that gets rearticulated as anti-Asian sentiment in contemporary US politics. It is through this affectively charged Asiatic racial form, moreover, that Americans continue to perceive the Asia-Pacific and people of Asian descent in paradoxical terms: *optimistically* as opportunities for economic profit and *fearfully* as hazards to US social order and the American liberal democratic way of life.

The fear-based identification of the Asiatic as the sign of globalization also emerges from American anxieties about the rise of successful capitalist states in Asia since the mid-twentieth century. As Lisa Lowe maintains, "Since World War II, Asia has emerged as a particularly complicated double front of threat and encroachment: on the one hand, Asian states have become prominent as external rivals in overseas war and in the global economy; on the other hand, Asian immigrants are still a necessary racialized labor force within the domestic national economy" ("International" 81). To remain a leader in a postwar global order, the United States has restructured its domestic national economy to be compatible with an expanding economic internationalism in which newly industrializing countries in Asia emerged as competitive and successful players in the growth of global capitalism. To increase capital in a worldwide economy that is greatly influenced by successful capitalist states in Asia, the United States has deregulated its domestic economy to allow a greater flow of immigrant workers across its borders in an effort to increase the role of the private sector, which now greatly determines and controls state power. By decreasing the size of the public sector to befit the global economy's pressures to privatize through neoliberalism, the United States has retracted its liberal democratic promise to provide opportunities for citizens to achieve upward mobility, job security, and social and political equality. Anxieties born from an expanding economic internationalism that has compelled the state to cooperate with the private sector and fulfill its expectations are the affective responses of Americans who must adjust to life in a neoliberal capitalist regime.

Yet politicians such as Pete Hoekstra exploit these anxieties by representing Asia and people of Asian descent as threats to America's liberal democratic way of life. Although Hoekstra's supposed target is China with an economy that gets "very good" at the expense of America's diminishing middle class, he notably makes no mention of China in his ad. It's apparent that his aim is to incite resentment toward his political opponent by associating her with an Asiatic communist threat proliferating in US society and haunting Americans. To be sure, Hoekstra's ad invokes the specter of the Vietnam War by using a rice paddy backdrop to suggest Southeast Asian battlefields where American troops fought against the Viet Cong. But the ad engages, moreover, in race-baiting and fearmongering by using a Chinese American named Lisa Chan to perform the role of "yellowgirl."[5] The ad's script, available in Hoekstra's campaign website, identified Chan in html code as "yellowgirl" (Stone). A statement released by Hoekstra's campaign explained that the html code was mistakenly shortened from "yellowshirtgirl" (Catanese). In any case, by naming Chan's character "yellowgirl," the ad's script clearly deploys yellow peril fear. Furthermore, Hoekstra's hiring of Chan, an actress and student from UC Berkeley, to perform an overseas Asian attests to his exploiting the anti-Asian xenophobic logic in the "Chinese Professor" ad. This logic conflates Asian Americans with stereotypically fearsome Asian communists from the Cold War and deems all Asians invasive Orientals in a yellow peril scenario from the early twentieth century.

In the present time of capitalist privatization as an adaptive world system, fears of Asiatic threat among Americans from over a century ago have been updated in contemporary visual media as an ideological response to the neoliberal economic policies that have accelerated the dismantling of the welfare state and erupted into ongoing financial crises. In response to recent global economic decline, today's representation of yellow peril fears in the visual media exploits the anxieties of Americans about the demise of liberal democracy's promises of upward mobility, social and political equality, and job security. With the widespread perception of China, Japan, India, and South Korea all strengthening as global economic powers and the United States weakening as a deindustrializing nation, contemporary popular culture and media revive yellow peril fears in an objectification process that deploys recession anxieties about America's immense economic debt through visual depictions of Asians as figures of fear and crisis. Through a restored yellow perilism, then, Asian Americans are once again identified "as the agents of Orientalized capitalism responsible for America's economic ruin" (Robert Lee, "Foreword" xiii).

In this sense, we might understand the anti-Asian xenophobic logic in the 2012 political ads to express fears about the Orientalization of global capital in the aftermath of America's economic collapse during the Great Recession of 2007–9. Ads such as CAGW's "Chinese Professor" and Hoekstra's "Yellow Girl" blame Asians and Asian finance capital for America's declining home-based industries and shrinking middle class. They attempt to Orientalize global capital as a new yellow peril to address an emotional condition in neoliberalism in which the demise of the public sector through economic deregulation and privatization has exacerbated experiences of displacement, alienation, and disillusionment among Americans. These distressing emotions, transmuted into new yellow peril fears by media depictions of Orientalized capital, express the immense consequences of a global laissez-faire economy. Increasing class stratification, poverty, social injustice, and especially the diasporic spread of people searching for work and survival the world over are some of these *human* consequences (Bauman 117).

## The Yellow Peril Aesthetic in *Crash* and *Contagion*

If American visual media identify Asia and people of Asian descent as emotionally charged signs of globalization, nowhere is this more obvious than in recent Hollywood films that represent Asians as metaphors for crisis in global capitalism. As can be seen in ads for the 2012 election campaigns, popular visual culture exploits a racial politics of anxiety that registers today's culture of anti-Asian sentiment and underscores how the Asiatic, for Americans, continues to be identified as the sign of globalization. By rendering the global economy an Asiatic threat to suggest that Asian Americans are agents of Orientalized capitalism and are responsible for America's economic decline, the ads reify anxieties about globalization and transform them into distress about something readily identifiable: the Asiatic foreigner and alien who is always ready to infiltrate US borders and threaten America's liberal democratic way of life.

As an especially popular visual cultural production, the 2004 Academy Award–winning film *Crash* represents Asians as economic figures of trouble and anxiety. In its representation of the Asiatic as threat, *Crash* stylizes and updates past Orientalist fears of an invasive and threatening Asia as a yellow peril aesthetic that fits our current era of economic crisis and calamity. *Crash* is an ensemble film whose plot revolves around racial tensions in Los Angeles. It tracks the daily lives of several characters whose stories interweave during two days in the city. Its primary stories concern a black detective estranged from his mother; his criminal younger brother and his gang associate who carjack the SUV of a white district attorney and his ill-tempered wife; a racist white police officer whose outspoken bigotry against blacks repels his more principled younger partner; a black Hollywood film director and his wife who are stopped arbitrarily in their SUV and harassed by the racist police officer; a disillusioned Iranian immigrant shop owner who is distrustful of Americans and orders his daughter to buy him a gun; and a Mexican American locksmith who works hard to support his family and yearns to move them out of their crime-ridden neighborhood. These are *Crash*'s main stories making up its interacting plot lines. That they involve protagonists who are white, Hispanic, Iranian, and black would indicate the film's ability to provide a fairly accurate vision of Los Angeles as a racially and ethnically heterogeneous global city.

If the global city in America is understood to be created, facilitated, and enacted by "processes of economic globalization" that largely maintain the accumulation of profit for a wealthy white elite (Brenner and Keil 6)—wealth that is enabled by an unrepresented mass of poor immigrants, racial minorities, and women who labor in low-paid, menial, and unstable service-sector jobs (Sassen 85)—then this understanding of the global city would clearly characterize Los Angeles in *Crash*. But one racial group that is not so present in the film, a group whose place and position in Los Angeles appear to be both unrepresented and repressed, is that of Asian Americans. The one story in *Crash* about Asians seems on the surface quite marginal. It concerns a Korean immigrant couple, a man called Choi and his wife Kim Lee. They make only a few brief appearances: at the beginning Kim Lee is involved in the film's eponymous multiple-vehicle collision; in the middle Choi is standing in the street while trying to unlock the driver's door of his van and gets run over by the criminal younger brother and his gang associate in the stolen SUV; and near the end Kim Lee arrives at a hospital frantically looking for her husband. Although this one story about a Korean immigrant couple seems marginal to *Crash*'s multiple plot lines and their highly tense interaction, their minor part turns out to be quite significant in terms of the film's tone of fear and conspiracy. Throughout its 112 minutes *Crash* is suffused with agitation and distress that comes, I argue, from its anxiety-driven attempt to allegorize something impalpably troubling Los Angeles, an omnipresent yet invisible force worrying this global city, causing its inhabitants such as the district attorney's incessantly irritated wife and the weary Iranian immigrant to become *paranoid*.

It turns out that Choi and his wife are involved in human trafficking. When Kim Lee finds her horribly injured husband in his room at the hospital, he orders her to get his wallet from his pants and retrieve the money they have made from smuggling undocumented Asian immigrants. Through this disclosure of a Korean immigrant couple's involvement in the illicit trade of human beings, the Asiatic in *Crash* personifies the seemingly imperceptible danger felt everywhere in Los Angeles. In the affectively charged racial form of the Asiatic, a yellow peril threat, the film at its end identifies and thus aestheticizes the intangible yet pervasive force that has been menacing the global city.

*Crash* represents the Asiatic for racial consumption as a spectacle of catastrophe: the sight of Asians together either as a family unit or as a mass population to be contained and destroyed is a racial aestheticization of threat and horror for audiences to consume as a cathartic experience. In this respect, the threatening Asiatic figure is synonymous with globalized capital, a reflection and a device of abstractions that many Americans have come to fear in a rapidly globalizing world. In this sense, too, it is a yellow peril aesthetic in an emotional popular culture because of the way in which American visual media Orientalize distress and disquiet about the grave and disturbing developments of an ongoing global economic crisis. As a trope, capitalism in *Crash* is a symbolic yet invisible language for visualizing the physical and psychic violence that comes with the passage of a neoliberal order and the transnational movement of Asian people to and from North America. The film both generates and exploits fears about an external other permeating and transgressing urban spaces that have been subjected to neoliberal privatization.

The real culprit in *Crash* causing fear and anxiety, what Jameson would describe as the film's reference to "an impalpable but omnipresent culture of paranoia" (*Geopolitical Aesthetic* 17), are the forces of capitalist totality. Yet these forces of violence, exclusion, and exploitation in the film remain visually foreclosed and unutterable against an invasive other embodied by Asian immigrants. Asians therefore appear in *Crash* not just as minor characters to advance the plot but as highly visual and memorable figures on which the film's anxieties and other negative affects about neoliberal privatization and globalization revolve. Jameson's argument that conspiracy-thriller films allegorize the omnipresent and oppressive forces of global capitalism clearly applies to *Crash*'s aesthetic of updated yellow perilism. In its depiction of characters attempting to grasp global capitalism's social totality, then, the film exploits xenophobic fears in our current time of economic instability.

In the present era of worldwide fiscal crisis, negative emotions such as anxiety and fear are produced by globalized capital while simultaneously playing an important role in shaping identities and subjectivities in ways that reconcile them to the uncertainties and structural inequalities of economic globalization. Capitalism as universal consumerism produces social division and exclusion instead of equality. Consumerism attempts to create an ideal of equivalence, but instead it produces differentiation and contradiction. Assimilating into consumerism is an uneven process, yet consumer capitalism has restructured human life to accommodate perpetual fluctuation and volatility. Feelings such as alienation and cynicism are, for instance, both generated by and instrumental to the perpetuation of the contemporary workplace and its unpredictable changes (Virno 12–13). Critical theorists have examined how global businesses turn these negative affects into professional ideals of flexibility and adaptation for a contemporary working environment in which sudden and unpredictable changes are the norm and in which the corporate culture that fully administers the world remains invisibly omnipresent (S. Ngai 4–5).

My argument about emotions in *Crash* focuses on this affective dimension of capitalism's omnipresence and its invisibility. The film provokes emotions that are instrumental to capitalism's invisible omnipresence but also incites those affects that render capitalism visible by expressing contradiction, as well as the "uneven and contested process" of trying to accommodate and assimilate into a neoliberal globalized world (Hong 68). As Slavoj Zizek has argued, the social form of capitalism today in the form of neoliberal ideology has become a universal world system (46). It is a given that no space on earth remains untouched by the planetary reach of capitalism. "It bears witness," Zizek contends, "to the unprecedented homogenization of the contemporary world. It is effectively as if, since the horizon of social imagination no longer allows us to entertain the idea of an eventual demise of capitalism—since, as we might put it, everybody silently accepts that capitalism is here to stay—critical energy has found a substitute outlet in fighting for cultural differences which leave the basic homogeneity of the capitalist world-system intact" (46).

Here Zizek's objective is to critique multiculturalism as identity politics in the logic of homogenizing consumer capitalism. He wants to expose and interrogate multiculturalism as a symptom of an unalterable world of capitalist exchange relations (the commodity fetish) that distracts critical attention from the harsh underside of economic globalization. My concern is not to rehearse this same objective, but I do want make clear the distinction between a *critical* multiculturalism produced by critical thought that calls for radical social change, including the redistribution of wealth, and the sensation and affect of commodified and consumer multiculturalism, which really seems to be the target of Zizek's critique. A paradigm shift of immense proportions, economic globalization as an unprecedented universalization of the capitalist system has achieved omnipresence through the regulation, appropriation, and neutralization of critical thought—conceptualized in Zizek's terms as "critical energy."

As the structuring ideology of economic globalization, neoliberalism within the logic of state privatization is, to a large extent, about desiring the sensation and affect of acquisitive individualism and the possessive and propertied subject. This privatization of affects works through capitalist discourse and culture to prohibit the critical dissent and resistance that would render capitalism visible as a world system (again in Zizek's terms). To be sure, these affects of critical thought engage in dialectical tension with the social forces of capitalism: commodifying processes that appropriate, fragment, and neutralize political community and citizenship. Yet these forces *mask* their global systematicity by making hypervisible the human consequences—the victim subjects—that embody the harsh underside of capitalism. These human consequences, such as the undocumented Asian immigrants in *Crash*, get constructed and articulated as the source or cause of social disorder and breakdown.

In *Crash*'s stereotypical depiction of Asians, anxieties about race and immigrant populations in a time of neoliberal globalization collide and explode within this film's ensemble narrative. The film exploits various meanings of violence against Asians, especially as they pertain to fears and unease about poor migrants transgressing racialized class lines and the privatization of space in the global city. In his study of urban space and anxiety, Liam Kennedy argues that Los Angeles "is very much an imperial city, economically and culturally formed by the dynamics of American empire building" (33). In the twenty-first century, Los Angeles "has taken on a leading international role as a hub of the global flows of late capitalism and a point of focus for the United States' technocratic contributions to the New World Order. Imperial relations are evident in the high levels of immigrant populations from Mexico and Central America and South East Asia that have increased dramatically in the last [thirty-five] years" (33). Mike Davis has also described Los Angeles as a city "in which economic and cultural formations are rigidly stratified along racial and class lines" (qtd. in Kennedy 33). Davis identifies a "paranoid spatiality" in Los Angeles, associating it with the city's "underlying relations of repression, surveillance and exclusion" and claiming that it has been "strikingly reproduced" in recent Hollywood movies (33). In these films, Los Angeles "has long functioned to focus the psychic processes of paranoia, hysteria and repression" (33). These are the predominant affects that Hollywood cinema depicts to exploit apprehensions about racial and class lines in the highly insular and privatized space of the American global city.

That said, two scenes in *Crash* are important instances in which Asians appear not just as characters to advance the plot but also as highly visual and therefore memorable figures on which the film's anxieties about an external other invading and menacing Los Angeles pivot. Although I mentioned both scenes earlier, *Crash*'s screenplay by Paul Haggis and Bobby Moresco describes them with details that further register the film's dramatization of something indiscernibly troubling Los Angeles, an omnipresent yet invisible force upsetting this global city. The first scene is when Choi gets run over by the criminal younger brother named Peter and his gang associate, Anthony, in the stolen SUV. Anthony is driving the SUV while explaining to Peter his argument about white racism against blacks. When Peter turns on the radio to listen to a hip-hop song that has racially derogatory lyrics, Anthony becomes angry and tells Peter his theory about the FBI's involvement in producing hip-hop music that degrades and oppresses black people. He does not see Choi step out from in front of his van into the street. Anthony hits Choi and skids to a stop, trapping Choi under the SUV. He and Peter hop out of the SUV and talk excitedly when they find Choi horribly injured but alive. They exclaim the following to one another:

ANTHONY: Where the hell did he come from?

PETER: Fuckin' China! What do you mean where'd he come from?

ANTHONY: He was standing in the street?

PETER: No, I think he comes with the truck, Anthony! It's an option now, for people who don't want to go through all the trouble of running over their own fucking Buddhahead!

ANTHONY: What the hell he do, leap out in front of the truck?

PETER: I don't know, maybe the FBI planted him under there to make car-jacking black people look bad in the eyes of the larger community. You got a theory about that, too? (Haggis and Moresco 25)

This scene as described in the screenplay is particularly noteworthy for dialogue not included in the film. Peter's reply ("I don't know, maybe the FBI planted him under there!") to Anthony's question ("What the hell he do, leap out in front of the truck?!") is not in the film, but it clearly is meant to mock Anthony's previous comments about white racism. When Peter teases Anthony for his antiblack conspiracy theories, the film thus suggests that Anthony's critical perspective, which blames white racism for every social ill, is wrongheaded.

In other words, there is something else invasive and threatening that can be blamed for the anxiety and fear circulating throughout Los Angeles. The Asian man who Anthony assumes has leaped out in front of the SUV from seemingly nowhere embodies a paranoid spatiality in the city, according to the logic of *Crash*—and he embodies this negative affect not as a victim subject but as a signification of cause and culprit. An invisible yet omnipresent Asiatic threat hence constitutes the feeling of tension and distress running throughout the entire film. *Crash* further suggests this logic in the scene with Choi's wife, Kim Lee, yelling in a hospital as she frantically tries to find her husband. She finds him conscious and coherent in his hospital bed, but he's horribly disfigured from injuries. Choi carefully instructs his wife to cash a check inside his wallet. He has made this money by smuggling undocumented Asian immigrants who sit chained inside the van that he was going to drive when Anthony ran him over. Choi is exploiting other Asians to make money; thus we can deduce that he represents the Asian immigrant as a metonym for *illicit capital*.

In *Crash*, capitalism as the actual culprit for anxiety and paranoid spatiality remains unrecognizably articulated, suggested by the film's ending in L.A.'s Chinatown. In this last part, Anthony is driving Choi's van that he and Peter took after running him over.[6] Anthony pulls the van over, parks, and opens its doors to free the Asians inside. They are frightened and hesitate to exit. Anthony says, "Come on—come on—come on. This is America, time is money" (112). For the purposes of my argument, it is important to quote the rest of the scene in the screenplay.

ANTHONY (cont'd): Chop-chop, let's go.
And from there, two-dozen wide-eyed Illegals step out into the street and get their first real look at America. They weave off through traffic, and down the crowded sidewalk.
ONE stops at a fruit and vegetable stand, marveling at the variety of produce—pokes something strange.
ANOTHER TWO step out of the van and find the fish market—they laugh and finger the fish on ice.
THE MARKET OWNER rushes out of his store YELLING in CHINESE and shooing them away.
ANOTHER COUPLE stop at the store displaying bins of CD's—and push a stack back and forth like dominoes.
A FRIGHTENED MAN squats on the sidewalk, his back to a shop wall, watches the passing faces, nodding hellos to strangers who ignore him.
A WOMAN walks, stunned and awed by the signs above her, being jostled and bumped by the stern-faced pedestrians.
BACK AT THE VAN: An impatient driver behind the van lays on the horn. The last few Illegals climb out of the van. Anthony stuffs a couple twenties in one man's hand.
ANTHONY (cont'd): You split that up. Buy everybody chop-suey, you understand?
The man walks off into the street.
ANTHONY (cont'd): Dopey fucking Chinamen. (112–13)

The violence of neoliberal privatization may appear ineffable in *Crash* because global capitalism's omnipresence and dominion are so thoroughly accommodated and rationalized that it is rendered invisible. But this violence is evident not only in the film's misguided depiction of the Asian immigrant as a metonym for illicit capital but also in its stereotyping of poor migrants as alien others and as the cause of social disorders structuring the discomfort of watching this film. Anxiety, fear, and paranoia, in other words, as the affective symptoms of capitalist totality—a yellow peril aesthetic in a time of neoliberalism—get located, personified, and racialized, according to *Crash*'s screenplay, in the bodies of "dopey fucking Chinamen."

Steven Soderbergh's medical-thriller disaster film *Contagion* is another recent Hollywood film that exploits America's anxieties about the consequences and contradictions of neoliberal privatization. *Contagion* depicts a virus's rapid spread around the world. Scott Z. Burns, the film's screenwriter, was inspired by various pandemics such as the 2003 severe acute respiratory syndrome (SARS) epidemic and the 2009 influenza pandemic. He consulted with medical experts and representatives of the World Health Organization to devise *Contagion*'s accurate depiction of a pandemic event. In *Contagion*, it is the body of a Euro-American executive named Beth Emhoff (played by Gwyneth Paltrow) who is the "patient zero" spreading a plague and sowing unprecedented misery for people all over the world. While representing her employer, a multinational mining company, on a business trip in China, Beth gets contaminated by an airborne virus that she brings home to Minneapolis. After taking Beth's life, the virus infects two billion people and kills nearly two hundred million in a most gruesome manner; it causes profuse foaming at the mouth and seizures that wrack every muscle of an infected person's body. A pivotal scene in the film shows Beth in a casino blowing on the hands of a Japanese businessman for luck before he rolls dice onto a craps table. In this scene, Beth infects the businessman with the virus because an hour or so earlier she became infected by shaking the hands of a chef who contracted the virus after butchering a piglet and preparing it for roasting in his kitchen; the night before the piglet was butchered, it ate a piece of banana dropped by a bat that was eating this same banana while clinging to the ceiling of a pigpen. This sequence of events revealing the virus's genesis and its chain of rapid mutation and infection consequently registers Asia as the disease-ridden origin of *Contagion*'s global pandemic.

But if we consider the bilious yellow graphics that suffuse *Contagion*'s movie poster, it becomes apparent that the film portrays Asia not only as the source of deadly planetary illnesses but also as capitalism's totality in formal or representational terms—visceral terms that indicate the aesthetic of yellow peril threat and fear. This is evident at the end of *Contagion*, when we learn that a rapidly industrializing China has become a container, so to speak, for the ecocidal profit-driven objectives of global corporate capitalism. It turns out that the bat that begat the virus was eating and infecting a banana in a pigpen because its natural habitat, a rainforest, was destroyed by the American mining company that employed Beth Emhoff. *Contagion* thus deploys a yellow peril aesthetic to signify anxieties and fears of corporate globalization's environmentally destructive reach everywhere in the world, a totality the film implies through China as the container for unregulated capitalist profit extraction under neoliberal schemes of privatization. Following Jameson, who has noted the ways in which Hollywood blockbuster movies such as *The Godfather* and *Jaws* allegorize corporate capitalism as "organized conspiracy against the public" (*Signatures* 31), Soderbergh's hit movie may be understood to exploit yellow perilism to signify the transnational stage of capitalism as a totality reaching into every corner of our daily lives. *Contagion* therefore registers Asia as the source of deadly planetary illnesses in order to allegorize the way neoliberalism "in its most systematized and computerized, dehumanized, 'multinational' and corporate form" has infected "our political structures to exercise a wanton ecocidal and genocidal violence at the behest of distant decision-makers and in the name of an abstract conception of profit" (31).

In the end, both *Crash* and *Contagion* leave us with questions about their updating of yellow perilism through their decidedly problematic depiction of Asians as agents of illicit capital and destructive corporate globalization. If the Asian American subject is a particular medium of contemporary power relations, how might the affective world of Asian Americans in their cultural works *diagnose* economic crisis in a time of neoliberalism? Instead of representing a threat that suggests containment in a present historical moment of capitalist totality, might Asian American cultural works offer a view onto the conditions of *possibility* for the future?

## Accommodation and Resistance in Asian American Cultural Works

As forms of literary realism and minority discourse, Asian American cultural works call into question the identification of Asians as signifiers of globalization. In doing so, they diagnose belonging in our current era of neoliberalism. The desire to belong and feel like a normal person has long been an aspiration for immigrants in the United States. The spirit of being American is a central part of the experience of citizenship in which US national culture powerfully models not only who ideal and normative citizens are but also how they feel, what they remember, and what they aspire for in life. Yet just as the normative American citizen and his subjectivity are an abstraction from Euro-American experiences of modernity, so too is the concept of "feeling American" abstracted from historical forces of oppression and conquest. For the Asian immigrant who aspires to become a normal person in the United States by acquiring the subjectivity of possessive individualism that both constitutes and signals normative personhood, to feel like a naturalized and an assimilated American requires the accommodation of possessive individualism's abstracted racial feeling. Feeling American, in other words, necessitates disavowing and forgetting the imperialism, colonization, genocide, racism, and oppression from which the normative American has been constituted.

With keen insight, Lisa Lowe explains that the terrain of US national culture politically forms an individual subject into a citizen and promotes to immigrants "the promises of salvation, prosperity, and progress" that constitute "the American feeling, the style of life, and the ethos and spirit of being" (*Immigrant Acts* 2). But for Asian immigrants, this access to the promises of "American feeling" through naturalized citizenship and its property rights has been historically problematic. If American feeling is the subjectivity of US citizenship premised on the origins of white freedom and personhood in a contractarian liberalism that is racially exclusionary, then this feeling derives from white racial feeling insofar as it expresses the subjectivity of Euro-American individualism that is the privileged domain of racial liberalism. The US Congress made whiteness a prerequisite for naturalization in 1790, granting "all 'free whites' the right to claim citizenship, and barred all nonwhites until after the Civil War in 1870, when the statute was enlarged to include freemen of African nativity or descent" (*Immigrant Acts* 19). Yet for Asian immigrants, the racial bar to naturalization remained in place and was reconfirmed for over a century by immigration exclusion laws that "restricted and regulated the possibilities of Asian American settlement and cultural expression" (7). From the mid-nineteenth to the mid-twentieth century, and also with the passage of the 1965 Immigration Act, "The American citizen has been defined over against the Asian *immigrant*, legally, economically, and culturally" (4, italics in original). It is for these reasons of historical exclusion and the violent denial of rights to citizenship that the naturalization process of becoming and feeling American is particularly vexatious for Asian Americans.

For Asian Americans both immigrant and US born, the disavowal and forgetting of this history required to accommodate the abstracted citizen and its normative ethos and spirit of being continually give rise to contradiction. Critical race theorists have shown how the experience of "Americanization" or the naturalization process of becoming American for Asians has been contradictory because of ongoing articulations of racial ideology by the state and in popular media that ascribe race and racial difference to Asian Americans. Popular depictions of Asians that objectify them as racially different and other, and hence as objects of racialized consumption for the preservation of an exclusionary American identity and subjectivity, strain and antagonize the Asian American's naturalization process of becoming and feeling American.

For Asian Americans, experiencing racial discrimination or witnessing and thus being subjected to anti-Asian stereotyping evince an affective naturalization process that involves the experience of being racially identified, interpellated, and naturalized outside the category of normative American identity. By *affective naturalization*, I mean "what it feels like" to undergo racial naturalization: the nonwhite subject's subjective experience of being excluded from normative American identity despite being included in citizenship as legal status. The feeling of belonging in America only as a racial other for exclusion in order to maintain an American identity that is socially and culturally "white" has long been the experience of Asians in the United States. As Devon Carbado contends, Asian Americans have "experienced a kind of national identity displacement or racial extraterritorialization" (638). This entails their "inclusive exclusion," whereby they are "included in the category of formal citizenship" while simultaneously perceived to be foreigners or citizen aliens (638). Racial difference has disqualified Asian Americans from inclusion in an American identity whose social norms and cultural values are defined by white subjectivities and experiences. To maintain the whiteness of American identity as normative and the attainment of this identity's American feeling as an aspirational norm, the nonwhite in America necessarily experiences racial estrangement, while disavowing and forgetting histories of racism.

"To racially belong to America as a nonwhite is to experience racial inequality," Carbado further contends. "To become an American citizen is often to cross the border into, not outside of, this racial inequality" (639). Here, Carbado's broadening of Giorgio Agamben's notion of "bare life" to include race may be understood as an affective naturalization process for Asian Americans, insofar as their experience of inclusive exclusion or racially belonging in America only as foreigners and citizen aliens requires their having to accommodate anti-Asian antipathy—a history of anti-Asian sentiment that is born from the acquisitive happiness of white personhood and individualism but that must be disavowed and forgotten if one is to secure an abstracted white citizenship.[7] The experience of inclusive exclusion expresses "what it feels like" for people of Asian descent to undergo Americanization in which they are conscious of their presence in US society as economic subjects, aware of their containment within the economic form of capital. Limited to being agents of economic opportunity and commercial advantage, they are essentially excluded from the culture-making norms and ideals of a traditionally white US society. This affective naturalization process of the Asian American subject's restriction to finance capital necessitates exclusion from the production of political and symbolic forms of capital.

In this chapter's next part, I examine racial feelings in three recent novels by Asian Americans: Karen Tei Yamashita's *Tropic of Orange*, Don Lee's *The Collective*, and Han Ong's *Fixer Chao*. In my analysis, I maintain that racial feelings are the effect of a capitalist culture of emotion, an affective system of reproduction shaping and determining racialized perception as an emotional precondition of Asian American racialization. Yamashita, Lee, and Ong critique the racial naturalization process that a capitalist emotional culture maintains through Orientalist representations of Asian people. In their novels, they show how these representations are an aspirational norm, even among Asian Americans themselves, for people of Asian descent to accommodate and perform in the United States. They critically evaluate the Asiatic racial sentiments that America's liberal capitalist society has historically produced and continues to generate in the twenty-first century.

## Against Happiness in *Tropic of Orange*

A funny moment in Karen Tei Yamashita's novel *Tropic of Orange* demonstrates this book's argument that capitalism produces an emotional commodity culture in which Asians are economic subjects of happiness and optimism for the global economy. In Yamashita's novel, a Japanese American TV news producer named Emi embarrasses her Chicano boyfriend in a Los Angeles sushi bar when she volubly declares, "Cultural diversity is bullshit" (128). She asks, "Do you know what cultural diversity really is? . . . It's a white guy wearing a Nirvana T-shirt and dreads. That's cultural diversity" (128). Emi then turns to the sushi chef across from her and says, "Don't you hate being multicultural? . . . You're invisible. I'm invisible. We're all invisible. It's just tea, ginger, raw fish, and a credit card" (128). As Emi cynically sees it, to be Japanese American in an international city such as Los Angeles is to be an appetizing commodity for those who celebrate multiculturalism. In the United States, multiculturalism has become a consumer phenomenon in which everyone is supposed to feel optimistic about diversity, most especially because of Asians, whose presence in this "diversity" signifies something positive about American capitalism in economic processes of globalization.

Today's multicultural consumer in America has "supplanted" the citizen-subject by being what "we might call the abstract citizen-consumer, defined as inhabiting a site for export market expansion" (Bascara 11). But the consumer representation of Japanese Americans angers Emi because it makes her feel that the history of Japanese immigrants in America is "invisible." In this sense, the unappetizing underside of American capitalism is institutionalized racism and discriminatory laws, which caused the racial exclusion, internment, and alienation of Japanese Americans during the first half of the twentieth century. Yet the perception of Asians as optimistic signs for global capital conceals this ugly history of racism in the United States. The perception of Asians as subjects of Orientalist optimism for American capitalism, Emi asserts in her outburst against "being multicultural," fetishizes them as commodities for consumption. As fetishized objects of optimism for capitalism, Asians and their past struggles against racism in the United States become forgotten. Optimism, in this context of liberal multiculturalism and consumer capitalism, entails forgetting a truly unpalatable history.

In his critique of capitalism's political economy, Marx argued that the fetishism of commodities mystifies relationships between people when these human relations are transformed into objects for consumption and mediated by market trade. Commodity fetishism makes consumers *forget* that commodities are the products of human labor. In *Capital*, Marx explained that the commodity is "a very queer thing" because it appears "mysterious" to people who cannot perceive the physical labor of workers that produced the commodity (47). "There is a physical relation between physical things. But it is different with commodities. There, the existence of the things quâ commodities, and the value relation between the products of labour which stamps them as commodities, have absolutely no connection with their physical properties and with the material relations arising therefrom" (47). However, what people do perceive about a commodity is their desire to possess and consume it. "This is the reason why the products of labour become commodities, social things whose qualities are at the same time perceptible and imperceptible *by the senses*" (47, italics added). What's intriguing here is Marx's emphasis on perception, an awareness by means of "the senses" that we may understand for consumers as their recognition of their own desires to possess and consume commodities. When people consume a commodity, they perceive it and recognize their own feelings for it as a palatable object. Their perception, which is also their responsiveness to their own affective attachment to the commodity, becomes itself objectified with the commodity's representation in advertising.

As Raymond Williams claimed, advertising is the "magic" of transforming commodities into alluring signs for personal meaning and self-worth ("Advertising" 335). A commodity gains added value to signify and enhance *personhood* by virtue of its aesthetic representation in advertising. But when the fetishized commodity is Asian Americans, a minority whose formation as a race group emerges from histories of anti-Asian violence, exclusion, and legalized discriminatory practices, then there is the problem of how commodification causes blindness to history. In other words, the commercialization of race and ethnicity for the sole purpose of profit extraction converts racial differences into alluring signifiers for the accumulation of economic and social forms of capital, making us forget the history of racial oppression for people of color in the United States.

As both a fetishized object and an aestheticized product in consumer packaging, the advertised commodity as something that signals personhood is about the consumer's feelings of self-worth. It is not about wanting to recall anything unpleasant that undermines feeling good about one's self. If, for example, consumers were to perceive traces of labor exploitation in the commodity they wanted to consume, it would intrude on their happiness for the commodity as an object to incorporate into their own self. As Jameson muses in his sardonic assessment of how reification or the fetishism of commodities effaces traces of labor production:

> This sees the matter from the standpoint of the consumer: it suggests the kind of guilt people are freed from if they are able *not to remember* the work that went into their toys and furnishings. . . . You don't want to have to think about Third World women every time you pull yourself up to your word processor, or all the lower-class people with their lower-class lives when you decide to use or consume your other luxury products: it would be like having voices inside your head; indeed, it "violates" the intimate space of your privacy and your extended body. (*Postmodernism* 314–15, italics added)

Here we may infer, following Jameson's attempt to put the guilt back into consumerism by compelling us to perceive the exploited labor necessary to produce a commodity in the Third World, why Emi in Yamashita's novel is such a killjoy, why her irritability and cynicism are "ugly feel-ings," to refer to Sianne Ngai's term for a "minor, low-intensity affect" (26). Her declaration in the sushi bar that "cultural diversity is bullshit" provokes, for instance, a white woman sitting next to her. "'I happen to adore the Japanese culture,' this woman tells Emi. "What can I say? I adore different cultures. I've traveled all over the world. I love living in L.A. because I can find anything in the world to eat, right here. It's such a meeting place for all sorts of people. A true celebration of an inter-national world. It just makes me sick to hear people speak so cynically about something so *positive* and to make assumptions about people based on their color. Really, I'm sorry. I can't understand your attitude at all'" (128, italics added). What reason could there possibly be for Emi to be so cynical, this woman seems to ask, when the good life promised by liberal multiculturalism in the global economy is available to all, if everyone would just to do their part to work hard and look ahead to the future? Yet Emi will have none of it. She turns to face her antagonist and notices her wearing "two ornately-lacquered chopsticks" to hold up her hair (128). She grabs two forks and asks, "Would you consider using these in your hair? Or would you consider that . . . unsanitary?" (128). The woman blanches, and it is clear that she can no longer swallow her sushi rolls without feeling the sting of shame provoked by Emi's rude questioning. Although this woman claims that she cannot understand Emi's "attitude at all," she is in fact now aware of something not quite savory about liberal multiculturalism.

Emi's sarcastic remarks about cultural diversity threaten the woman's naive perception of Japanese people and presumably other Asians as figures of commodity happiness. Like Jameson's sardonic observations, which incite our collective guilt by making us aware that the luxury products we consume are made by exploited Third World laborers, Emi's comments provoke the diversity-adoring woman to realize something unpalatable about the global economy. This realization, which intrudes on the woman's consciousness as a moment in which "to remember" his-tory, as "work" in Jameson's account of commodity fetishism, makes her feel guilt about a recent time in America when the affect of racial dis-course was hostile toward Asians because white people perceived them as threats both to America's economic order and to the dominant position of whites at the top of this order. Emi's assertion that "being multicul-tural" makes her invisible figuratively rips apart a commodity-fetishist fabric that covers and conceals America's ugly history of racism against Japanese Americans, when they were imprisoned in concentration camps during World War II. Her cynical remarks are, like Jameson's, a shaming provocation against forgetting history.

But why is the diversity-adoring woman not able to recall history? Does her naïveté have anything to do with her claim that Los Angeles is a "true celebration of an international world" and that there is "something so positive" about Japanese culture, in particular, which figures prominently in this diversity? As the woman suggests through her optimism for a multicultural Los Angeles, because she "can find anything in the world to eat" right there, the only way that Japanese culture can signify "something so positive" in an international city such as L.A. is if it exists as a fetishized commodity. When she says that she adores Japanese culture, she implies an expectation that Asians in America personify the material benefits of consumer multiculturalism, which have become something positive because they are now apparently available to everyone in the United States without regard to race, ethnicity, gender, and historical context. As a necessary condition of profit extraction, then, consumer multiculturalism entails forgetting history, if we understand this history as the traces of production that commodity fetishism effaces.

Through her characterization of Emi as a cynical and therefore a "bad" subject in her novel, Yamashita critiques an expectation that Asian Americans conform to their stereotypical representation as figures of economic exemplarity.[8] To be Asian American in multicultural capitalist America means having to accommodate the perception that Asians not only represent a fetishized emotional product but also must *perform* it as agents of finance capital whose job, figuratively speaking, is to carry out the affective labor for the commodity happiness of liberal multiculturalism. As labor that "produces or manipulates affects such as a feeling of ease, well-being, satisfaction, excitement, or passion" (Hardt and Negri, *Multitude* 108), affective labor figures prominently in the operation of the US capitalist system because this system is an economic and emotional organization of production affecting all aspects of modern life and society, especially in the workplace and in the relations of everyday consumerism. A capitalist culture of affective labor generates and maintains the "collective subjectivities" and "sociality" that are not only "directly exploitable by capital" but also "directly *productive* of capital" throughout wide sectors of the global economy (Hardt, "Affective Labor" 96–97).

Hardt and Negri contend that affective labor can be recognized "in the work of legal assistants, flight attendants, and fast food workers (service with a smile)" (108). But it can also be recognized, I would add, in the racialization process of Asian Americans to the extent that they are racially perceived as agents of finance of capital who have historically produced the accumulation of capital for Euro-Americans and have enabled their play between capital's various forms. As economic subjects of happiness for producing and converting capital, Asian Americans thus *embody* a racial form of affective labor that constitutes a large part of the model minority status that they are expected to perform "with a good attitude and social skills" to show that they are adept at this particular labor (108). Because of their model minority status and the racialized perception that they are subjects of happiness for hire, so to speak, Asian Americans must cheerfully characterize *acquisitive* happiness as their affective labor, which also expresses the expectation of aspiring for financial uplift and success in the global economy.

However, performing this affective labor is something that Emi absolutely refuses to do. This makes her a killjoy, an Asian American bad subject who spoils the happiness of multicultural consumers. By vociferously divulging her antimulticultural attitude in the sushi bar's decidedly multicultural-consumer environment, she expresses irritation and cynicism: negative affects whose restraint in the performance of happiness and optimism for multiculturalism are necessary for the global operation and management of American capitalism. Against happiness, Emi fails to uphold the good life's ideals of success and upward mobility that are at the heart of the American Dream. Her negativity transgresses the racialized perception of Asians as economic exemplars. Indeed, here she resembles the anticapitalist cultural critic—like Jameson—with a poor attitude when it comes to keeping invisible the exploitation and abstraction of labor in commodity fetishism. For the shocked woman with chopsticks in her hair, Emi's negativity implicitly reveals the harsh underside of the global economy. Against happiness, furthermore, she performs another kind of labor: the critical work of making others aware of the structure of economic violence in globalization that Pierre Bourdieu has characterized as "a kind of social neo-Darwinism" (*Acts* 42) because it operates through subcontractual, part-time, or temporary labor and thus generates and profits from the insecurity among workers who feel they are expendable, constantly facing the threat of losing their jobs and teetering on the verge of indigence—surviving, that is, under a corporate hegemony that forces workers into compliance, into accepting their own exploitation with resignation and submission.

## Contained by Capital in *The Collective*

In Bourdieu's terms, the American Dream is, I want to suggest, the subjective experience of upward mobility through acquisition of economic capital in the US capitalist system. But this experience attains its utmost status when it includes one's ability to characterize and display not only the acquisition of cultural and symbolic capital but also one's free *movement* between these other forms of capital by virtue of being able to produce them and to demonstrate the ability to convert economic capital into cultural and symbolic forms.

Although the implied premise of the American Dream is that one's worth and well-being are directly proportional to the money, property, and commodities that one acquires, the ultimate aspiration within this dream, as Don Lee implies in his recent novel *The Collective*, is the ability to *take for granted* that one possesses and moves easily throughout all forms of capital. In Lee's novel, three young Asian American friends meet as undergraduates at Macalester College in the 1990s. They pursue majors in the arts and humanities, partly to defy the model minority conformism of other Asian American students who major in the sciences and partly because the friends truly aspire to create art as a passion. One of the friends is Joshua Yoon, a Korean adoptee raised by an elderly Jewish American couple who are professors at Harvard. Joshua has big dreams to become an acclaimed novelist. He inspires his two friends at Macalester, Eric Cho, a would-be writer and the narrator of the story, and Jessica Tsai, an ambitious visual artist, to form the Asian American Artists Collective, the 3AC. After graduation, Joshua's adoptive parents die, but he inherits a fortune from them and their mansion in Cambridge, Massachusetts. He invites Eric and Jessica to live with him in the mansion. They accept his invitation, and together the three friends grow their collective and sustain their idealism as artists and nonconformists. Following Bourdieu, we might understand how the friends attempt to convert economic capital obtained through Joshua's inheritance, as well as cultural capital acquired through their "educational qualifications" ("Forms" 2), into the symbolic form by living with and supporting each other cooperatively to achieve success in their artistic pursuits.

After a series of mishaps and public scandals, however, both their collective and their friendships fall apart. Jessica and Eric dispense with their aspirations to create art. They leave Joshua alone in his mansion. After selling his home and moving into a small cabin in the woods, Joshua finishes and publishes his first novel, which gets "a fair amount of attention" (19). Following this initial success, however, "Each successive book had met a poorer reception, and he felt he had become irrelevant as an author. It bothered him that he wasn't famous, that his books weren't selling more, that he wasn't winning the big prizes and grants, that he wasn't better reviewed, that he wasn't more influential, that he wasn't among the anointed. He was, in other words, a typical writer" (19–20). Failing to achieve his dream to join "the canon, the pantheon, of American writers" (21), Joshua spirals into depression, drug abuse, and self-loathing. He commits suicide by running in front of a speeding car that crashes and kills its two occupants, a father and his four-year old daughter. The accident causes an uproar in the media because of the child's death, which redefines Joshua's suicide "from a tragedy to an atrocity" (16). As Eric explains, "There's an established protocol to this, writers committing suicide" (17), and unlike the famous suicides of canonical Euro-American writers such as Hart Crane, Sylvia Plath, Ernest Hemingway, and John Kennedy Toole, who all received flattering obituaries in the media, Joshua "was being remembered as a murderer" (17). That Joshua becomes "irrelevant," that he is far from being "among the *anointed*" and that in death he gets rebuke instead of tributes from the media, conveys the historical matter of racial containment or the politics of immobility, as Sau-ling Wong would put it, for Asian Americans.

Joshua's failure to succeed as an artist allegorizes the Asian American subject's experience of racial containment within economic capital, a containment registered by the inability to convert finance capital (i.e., money acquired from his inheritance and mansion) into symbolic capital. In other words, the inability of Asian Americans in Lee's novel to play between the forms of capital as *individuals*—as "social agents," in Bourdieu's terms—indicates their containment within economic capital. Yet this containment is a historical condition of the perception that construes Asians through affectively charged economic tropes. This is the perception of the Asiatic racial form that is informed and structured by an emotional culture identifying Asians both as threats—as figures of an impending danger—and as economic exemplars—as a means to acquire happiness in America's liberal democracy.

Joshua's failure to convert finance capital into the symbolic form—his powerlessness to take for granted the ability to move freely between all forms of capital—registers a tension in *The Collective* between the Asian American subject who aspires to obtain symbolic capital by creating art and the racialized perception of Asians as uniformly economic subjects, a perception that construes Asians as agents of finance capital and contains them within a racial form of economic capital. In Lee's novel, this tension is exemplified through the power of the media—a commodifying force in capitalism—to depict Joshua as a "murderer" and render his death dishonorable by indirectly associating him with a stereotypical Asiatic threat traceable to yellow perilism.

Another form of capital needs to be considered in *The Collective* and, I suggest, in other Asian American writings about the experience of aspiring to live and succeed as an artist. This is the form of political capital, and as Mark Chiang argues, it "entails not the transmission of any particular politics, so much as the transmission of political capital—specifically, the political capital of representation" (41). In founding their collective, Joshua, Eric, and Jessica attempt to politicize both their identity and their art as Asian Americans. In doing this, they want to represent and acquire public recognition as Asian American artists who *rebel against* naturalized assumptions of Asian Americans as a monolithic model minority. They aim to contribute to Asian American culture its own specificity through art and literature that are separate and distinct from Euro-American cultural works. And they desire success as individual artists on their own terms. Here we can interpret the politicization of their racial identity, individualism, and work as the attempt to transmit and gain political capital. Together, the friends create the 3AC as a way to acquire and institutionalize Asian American political capital on the Macalester campus and later in Cambridge, where they expand the collective in Joshua's mansion and seek recognition as an Asian American cultural institution and political force.

As I noted earlier, Asian Americans run counter to the political and symbolic forms of capital that signify Euro-American individualism. And we can see how this individualism functions in the context of political and symbolic capital for the Euro-American artist in the modernist cultural movement. The modern American artists of the early twentieth century defined and expressed individualism by producing cultural works considered "avant-garde" because they upended traditional modes of representation and expressed new sensibilities of their time. The "great" writers, musicians, and thinkers of this period acquired fame and symbolic capital by creating innovative or experimental art aligned with the avant-garde movement's mantra to "make it new."[9] But as we can see in Joshua's abject failure and the demise of the 3AC, this artistic individualism born from Western modernism and its attendant forms of political and symbolic capital are achievable for Euro-American artists, not for the Asian Americans in *The Collective*.

In Lee's novel, the failure of Asian Americans to produce art indicates that the very idea of vanguard cultural production continues to be "coded as white" (Wang 190). The 3AC's failure is a historical consequence of Asian American exclusion from modernism's "great art"—a racialized failure that allegorizes the Asian American experience of containment in America's modern capitalist society. For this reason, happiness must be denied. *The Collective* ends with Eric and Jessica meeting to discuss Joshua's suicide. They talk about the meaning of happiness now that they have abandoned their dreams to live and attain success as artists. Eric admits that he squanders his talent by working for a marketing firm, and Jessica explains that she operates a private business "making custom dildos and novelty porn clothes for celebrities" (308). Both succeed in commerce, but their failure to make a living by creating art consigns them to the realm of ethnic abjection. When Eric asks Jessica if she is happy, she replies, "Happiness is sometimes the greatest hiding place for despair" (308). In this sense, the meaning of failure for aspiring Asian American artists in the novel is clear: it is a form of ethnic abjection in consequence of racial containment as an economic subject, which further implies the inability to move freely into the realm of artistic individuality because this realm is traditionally the affective possession and preserve of Euro-Americans.

## The Anger of Critical Consciousness in *Fixer Chao*

In *Fixer Chao*, Han Ong articulates a critical consciousness that brings into focus the way capitalist forces of objectification exploit an underclass of racialized minorities and immigrants. Here I want to suggest that Ong depicts the articulation of "critical consciousness," Paolo Freire's social concept grounded in Marxian critical theory. As we have seen for Bulosan in chapter 2, critical consciousness focuses on the way oppressed subjects come to understand social contradictions that are created by exploitative economic and political systems. It is the cognitive awakening of oppressed subjects that affirms their becoming aware of totality by questioning the nature of their own historical and social situation. By developing an in-depth understanding of their own objectification and dehumanization in processes of alienated labor, for instance, oppressed subjects can transcend capitalist alienation and "be owners of their own labor" (Freire 164). Articulating a critical consciousness in his novel, Ong depicts anger to call into question dehumanizing effects of commodification. The exploited, subjugated, and abjected Filipino immigrants in *Fixer Chao* live in a modern society replete with social and economic inequalities that have resulted from global economic liberalism.

In the beginning of *Fixer Chao*, William Paulinha feels disoriented while walking the streets of his East Village neighborhood; his disorientation suggests his alienation and displacement amid the dizzying swirl of commercialism and financial transactions so aggressively at the surface of daily life in New York near the end of the twentieth century. Younger generations of Wall Street investment bankers, trust-fund kids, salespeople, and twenty-somethings armed with Ivy League degrees and eager for their slice of the dot-com pie have taken over William's neighborhood. These "younger people were everywhere around us," William explains, "spilling outside the open doors of . . . refurbished cafes . . . all the while talking and shrieking in party tones whose meanings eluded us and made us feel like tourists from a depressed country" (29). Estranged amid this flood of prosperity in New York, William takes a close look at his downwardly mobile status; he has spent years doing minimum-wage temp work and laboring as a small-time prostitute. The global economy transforming New York with the swift arrival of wealthy hipsters has marginalized him; he laments, "So many things emphasized a sense of being at a remove, of being in America and not in America at the same time, that I could have sworn I was dreaming and that this was the same place I visited every night—not-Manila and not-New York, not-past and not-present. Stuck in limbo. Between departure and arrival. A place like the future, thought of and imagined in ways that barely touched the circumference of its incomprehensibility" (32). Seething beneath the surface of Williams's estrangement and dislocation is his rage against an upper-class society that effortlessly benefits from a neoliberal economy taking over all of the city.

In *Fixer Chao*, Ong excoriates New York's class society through critical feelings of anger. Rage in his novel expresses the subjection of alienated Asian migrants like William. Yet William's exclusion from the system that benefits upper-class New Yorkers is not permanent. With Shem C, he concocts a revenge scheme to pose as the Feng Shui master William Chao. Together, William and Shem deceive wealthy New Yorkers who are anxious to keep up appearances by displaying the most fashionable multicultural trends. In this scheme, William's desire for vengeance conveys an anticapitalist consciousness that critiques the alienation of Filipino immigrants. *Fixer Chao* thus underscores injustices of social division in a time of inexorable capitalist globalization. In particular, the rage expressed in the novel registers the harsh underside of America's neoliberal global economy. This rage figuratively gives voice to an immense population of exploited and disregarded migrant laborers in the US global city, an underside of racialized violence and abjection.

As Eleanor Ty argues in her reading of *Fixer Chao*, Ong narrates the experience of "emotional and psychic transnationalism," which structures the rage of Filipino migrants who are stuck in limbo between the values of neoliberalism and the self-reproachful attitudes of other migrants ("Abjection" 121). What resonates so powerfully throughout *Fixer Chao* is, then, a rational outrage against an exploitive economic system under which everybody lives. In the global economy of New York are marginalized people—transmigrant and dislocated people dispossessed because they lack the skills, values, and capital necessary to survive in a city whose structural operative is neoliberal privatization. And their rage, Ong suggests, underscores the dehumanizing effects of objectification—evident in William's struggle to survive under the predations of ceaseless competition consequent to the profit economy, a system thriving on social division.

*Fixer Chao* concludes much as it begins, with an indictment of human life under forces of commodification. William is revealed to be a fake Feng Shui master. His downfall is swift. Nearly everyone abandons him and seeks to profit from their disassociation, including Shem, who has made William his dupe. Back to taking a close hard look at his downwardly mobile life, William cynically observes, "All around the world, there were people like me, rebounders, scrappers, survivors. People who cheated and schemed, and who, having found that the schemes had run their course, retreated" (355). Fallen within a multitude of dispossessed transients in New York, William becomes an invisible man. Before fleeing to Los Angeles, he spends his final days in New York with his sole remaining friend Devo, a "layabout" who, like William, is the human detritus of New York's neoliberal global economy. Devo "stated in a clean, simple way the same thing I hadn't realized I'd always felt until I was in the thick of it: how we shared a common hatred for those who did better than us, for whom New York seemed to have been exclusively built. Immediately, all those forgotten occasions returned to memory: staring at the padlocked facades of houses on the Upper East Side; having been stared at every time we went into a fancy shop to admire the goods" (352). Feeling the force of his alterity and abjection, William prepares to leave New York and the upper-class society that has spurned him, a society that has become rich at the expense of racialized migrants laboring in low-paid, unstable jobs.

In this sense, Ong shares with Yamashita articulations of anger within a critical structure of feeling that expresses a key feature in literary realism as Georg Lukács conceptualized it. According to Lukács, literary realism emerged as a dominant cultural force in Europe during the nineteenth century, when "rapidly growing forces of capitalism" superseded older forms and relations that brought about a sweeping transformation of everyday life by transmuting all things into commodities that could be bought and sold (*Historical Novel* 84). Although realism developed within a specific historical period and location, I want to suggest that it continues to be a dominant cultural force informing the contemporary American art and literature of racial minorities. The cultural works of US racial minorities clearly express the realist project to represent "a process in which the categories of capitalism as forms of human living" have penetrated into all aspects of everyday life in a modern society (Lukács, *Studies* 148). As Ong reveals through the anger expressed in *Fixer Chao*, capitalism has transformed human beings and their social relations into commodities that can be bought and sold. Anger in the contexts of both critical consciousness and realism brings into relief the ways in which capitalism has irrevocably affected everyday life by transforming all societies and cultural expressions into commodities. If realism originates, as Lukács argued, from "the *feeling* first that there is such a thing as history, that it is an uninterrupted process of changes and finally that it has a direct effect upon the life of every individual" (23, italics added), then we might understand that anger in Ong's novel registers the feeling of our present historical moment within capitalism's totality of social relations, an underlying mechanism in the racialized perception that generates a racial form for abjected and impoverished nonwhite people in America. This is the everyday practice of capitalist production and exchange, reflected by a consciousness of racialized perception and evident in the critical structure of feeling articulated by racial minorities in their cultural works.

Anger articulated by racially abjected minorities in the effort to critique capitalism thus carries the potential to actualize collective struggle and remember history. As in Bulosan's writings, anger may contain critical context about which we can learn a great deal when it is expressed publicly and creatively to address oppression and the social remembering of past injustices. It is therefore the case for William Paulinha that between the dialectic of feeling exploited and disenfranchised in commodity capitalism and articulating anger about it, the critical consciousness of the racialized minority subject emerges. In validating the anticapitalist critique embedded in the anger of critical consciousness, the negative emotions through which *Fixer Chao*'s Filipino queer subaltern comes to express himself are accordingly one of capitalism's most poignant contradictions to belonging in the neoliberal global city.

# Conclusion: The Comfort of Belonging

In this book, I have coined the term *racial feelings* to depict and inter-rogate capitalism's production of emotions in the logic of individualism and the formation of Asian America. The term indicates the pivotal role these emotions and, in particular, the pursuit of happiness have played in the racialized perception of Asian Americans. In their cultural works, Asian Americans critically represent and evaluate this perception by showing how Asian American subjects accommodate, rechannel, and resist racial feelings produced by liberal capitalism.

In Jhumpa Lahiri's deeply moving novel *The Namesake*, racial feel-ings of alienation, conflicting loyalties, and divided identity are central thematic concerns. To reinforce the importance of racial feelings in Asian American cultural works, I turn to the Indian American protago-nist Gogol Ganguli in Lahiri's novel to address her critique of the white racial ideal of individuality. Gogol's affects of divided identity—of feel-ing that there is no single place to which he fully belongs—contradict and critique the comfort of belonging that he desires by his identification with Euro-American cultural and symbolic forms of capital. As Lahiri demonstrates in her depiction of Gogol's attempt to feel belonging by changing his name and falling in love with an affluent Euro-American woman, this identification is an aspirational norm of white personhood in America's liberal capitalist society. By examining Gogol's conflicting loyalties to his Indian immigrant parents that trigger within him affects of divided identity, I aim to indicate the stakes of racial feelings produced by the ideology of Euro-American personhood for Asian American cultural works. For Lahiri shows us in her novel that whiteness as a race and culture, as an ideological practice in modern America, is produced and maintained by an emotional life that is consistent with preserving capitalist material interests and social relations.

Beginning in 1968 and ending in 2000, *The Namesake* describes the birth and upbringing of Gogol Ganguli, the American-born son of an Indian immigrant couple, Ashima and Ashoke, who struggle to form a life in a Boston suburb far from the Bengali homeland to which they are accustomed. When their son is born in a Cambridge hospital, they have not yet named him and are told they cannot take him home until they give him a legal name. Bengali cultural tradition calls for a new baby to be named by an elder. Ashoke and Ashima have been waiting to find out the name of their baby in a letter sent by Ashima's grandmother, just before she dies. Unfortunately the letter never arrives. Ashoke suggests their new baby be named Gogol, in honor of his favorite writer, the Russian author Nikolai Gogol, whose story "The Overcoat" he was reading as a young man when he survived a train derailment with many fatalities in Bengal. In the hospital, Ashoke and Ashima agree on two names: Gogol as their son's pet name, which they decide to use on his birth certificate, and Nikhil as his good name to be used in public.

As a child in elementary school Gogol prefers his pet name over his good name. But as a teenager he feels that other students perceive his name as strange. It becomes a source of alienation and shame for him. He feels most ashamed of his name when his English teacher assigns "The Overcoat" and he learns that Nikolai Gogol was one of Russia's most talented but oddest writers. Mr. Lawson, the teacher of the class, explains: "The writer Ivan Turgenev described him as an intelligent, queer, and sickly creature. He was reputed to be a hypochondriac and a deeply paranoid, frustrated man. He was, in addition, by all accounts, morbidly melancholic, given to fits of severe depression. He had trouble making friends. He never married, fathered no children. It's commonly believed he died a virgin" (91). As Gogol listens to this description of his namesake, he experiences intense feelings of discomfort, distress, and humiliation: "Warmth spreads from the back of Gogol's neck to his cheeks and his ears. Each time the name is uttered, he quietly winces. His parents never told him any of this. He looks at his classmates, but they seem indifferent, obediently copying down the information as Mr. Lawson continues to speak. . . . He feels angry at Mr. Lawson suddenly. Somehow he feels betrayed" (91). More than anything, Gogol wants to conform and belong as a typical American teenager. He longs to feel the comfort of belonging as an ordinary person among his school's largely Euro-American classmates. Yet he has become acutely aware of how his immigrant parents and their Bengali traditions display conspicuously, in his mind, a foreignness that utterly contradicts the ideal of American personhood for the white citizen. In this sense, the alienation, distress, and shame that Gogol experiences because of his name may be understood as racial feelings born from his perception of being marked with an excessively conspicuous racial difference that positions him outside the bounds of normativity, relegating him to the abject realm of *queerness*.

That Gogol has his name because of Bengali cultural tradition only serves to intensify his belief that his classmates perceive immigrants of South Asian descent, such as his parents, as incapable of refusing racial difference and, therefore, as unable to claim the individuality that means being an American, which means being white (Song 107). This racial feeling, which registers the discomfort of estrangement and queerness for Gogol, is obvious when he asks his parents why they had to name him after "someone so strange" (100), why they had to give him a pet name in the first place. Ashima replies, "It's our way, Gogol. . . . It's what Bengalis do" (99). For Gogol, his mother's answer inextricably associates his name with a "way" of upholding Bengali custom that culturally displaces his parents in America and maintains ties that inextricably bind them to their Indian homeland. As Gogol sees it, these stubborn ties deny his parents' identification with an American way of belonging by asserting allegiance to citizenship through a white racial ideal of liberal individualism.

Gogol's belief that his parents too-pronouncedly maintain Bengali tradition makes him ashamed of being racially different, which, in turn, causes him to feel conflicting loyalties. He feels a conflict between the marginalized position of his displaced immigrant parents and the dominant white culture that values Euro-American proprietary notions of personal identity. Although Gogol perceives himself as not yet belonging contentedly within the white social world, he believes that he would be capable of fitting into it if he were to exhibit a socially acceptable way of claiming individuality, such as changing his name. By changing his name, Gogol trusts that he can define himself as an individual. In this sense, to change his name is for Gogol to assert the liberal-individualist pursuit of happiness that traditionally has been the premise for belonging as a self-possessing individual in America. Through the characterization of Gogol's conflicting loyalties powerfully signified by the shame he feels for his pet name, Lahiri's novel demonstrates how one's name does indeed manifest and carry particular affects of personal identity and belonging.

This becomes clear in the part of the novel that describes the moment in which it first occurs to Gogol that he can change his legal name. While sitting in the waiting room of his dentist, Gogol flips through an issue of *Reader's Digest* and finds an article that causes him to stop:

> The article was called "Second Baptisms." "Can you identify the following famous people?" was written beneath the headline. A list of names followed and, at the bottom of the page, printed in tiny letters upside down, the famous personalities they corresponded to. . . . They had all renamed themselves, the article said, adding that it was a right *belonging* to every American citizen. He read that tens of thousands of Americans had their names changed each year. All it took was a legal petition, the article had said. And suddenly he envisioned "Gogol" added to the list of names, "Nikhil" printed in tiny letters upside down. (98–99, italics added)

Billed as one of the world's most successful consumer magazines that touts American values of individualism, *Reader's Digest* characteristically features articles that champion the ideology of Euro-American personhood with its objectives of wealth, self-assurance, and freedom of personal choice. The articles reinforce aspirations for an everyday life that is normative in terms of one's desire to prosper and belong in America's liberal capitalist society. What Gogol comes to believe from reading "Second Baptisms" is that changing his legal name is not only "a right belonging to every American citizen" but also his entitlement as a person born in America whose name is affectively charged with belonging as a citizen. By renaming himself, Gogol thinks he will exercise the inalienable rights of life, liberty, and the pursuit of happiness that publicly signal one's claim to personhood as property in America's liberal capitalist society. He believes, furthermore, that replacing "Gogol" with "Nikhil" as his legal name will relieve his feelings of estrangement and queerness with the comfort of belonging as an ordinary citizen. For Gogol to achieve this comfort, it can be deduced from his reading the article, would be for him to realize a primary affect of the proprietary subjectivity that constitutes the American Dream.

To the extent that the American Dream is an affect of proprietorship and consumption in liberal capitalist society, it may be understood in the context of Gogol's name change as his pursuit of happiness through financial transaction. In other words, his dream is a normative aspiration to individualism, actualized through an object-oriented happiness that articulates his freedom to choose his own way over against his parents' Bengali values. Lahiri indicates this in her description of Ashoke when he signs the change-of-name form for Gogol "with the same resignation with which he signed a check or a credit card receipt" (100). That Ashoke reluctantly consents to his son's plans suggests that he understands the commodity psychology intrinsic to the pursuit of happiness in America. Further, his resignation implies that he perceives Gogol's desire to rename himself as his exercise of a citizenship right that avows the American concept of freedom. But such freedom is to be actualized through spending economic capital that would demonstrate Gogol's citizenship right in opposition to his meeting the expectations of his parents. "In America anything is possible," Ashoke tells Gogol cynically. "Do as you wish," he adds, intimating the consumer capitalist logic that conventionally defines the freedom of personal choice in America as something causing his son to put aside the needs and considerations of family.

Upon completing the procedure to change his name in a family courthouse, Gogol boards a train that takes him to Boston, where he strolls onto a high-end shopping street. On this street, he ponders feeling a newfound freedom and "wonders if this is how it feels for an obese person to become thin, for a prisoner to walk free" (102). Tellingly, he "wanders up Newbury Street" to go shopping for things he will take with him to college. "He dashes into Newbury Comics, buys himself *London Calling* and *Talking Heads: 77* with his birthday money, a Che poster for his dorm room. He pockets an application for a student American Express card, grateful that his first credit card will not say Gogol in raised letters at the bottom" (102). To be sure, Lahiri describes Gogol's shopping spree as his exhibiting the freedom of American personhood through buying and accumulating commodities. That he observes how others do not really notice him as they go about their own business, however, is also noteworthy. To be seen and treated as someone who does not conspicuously stand out indicates for Gogol that he is now perceived as an ordinary citizen. When an attractive female cashier "hands him his change and looks past him to the next customer" (102), he interprets her blasé attitude as evidence of his fitting into everyday society.

The affect of belonging afforded by "Nikhil" as his new legal name enables, moreover, his self-assurance in being a heterosexual male; "He thinks of how many more women he can now approach, for the rest of his life, with this same unobjectionable, uninteresting fact" (102–3).

Purchasing items that a typical teenage male would want to have and display in his dorm room actualizes for Gogol the affect of being heteronormative enabled by his new legal name. If he can have a credit card with Nikhil "in raised red letters at the bottom," he can use and affirm his new legal name through financial transactions that are charged with the feeling of relating normatively to other Americans. In this sense, owning a credit card to signify the affect of his heteronormativity—an object he can display for women to register the "unobjectionable, uninteresting fact" of his new name—relieves him of the shame of being attached to queerness.

What is most important for Gogol in being heteronormative is that Euro-American women will find him desirable. He wants these women to want him as they would other men in the white social world. Being heteronormative in this world, Gogol believes, is a way to achieve belonging as a heterosexual *male* individual according to the white racial ideal of manhood, where traditionally a white man has the ability and the privilege to take for granted possessing and moving freely throughout the economic, cultural, and symbolic forms of capital that signify individualism. Living up to this ideal explains why Gogol dates only white women when he is in college at Yale and also after he graduates and moves to New York City, where he works as an architect and where he prefers to live because he does not have to "remain unquestionably" in the world of his parents (126). At a party, Gogol meets Maxine Ratliff, a woman of white Anglo-Saxon Protestant heritage who confidently expresses her desire for him: "Maxine has a way of focusing her attention on him completely, her pale, watchful eyes holding his gaze, making him feel, for those brief minutes, the absolute center of her world" (129). Indeed, from the beginning Maxine holds Gogol in the center of her *privileged* world. She invites him to dinner at her home, a Greek Revival mansion in Manhattan where she lives with her parents, Gerald and Lydia. Maxine, her parents, and their palatial house embody achievement of the good life with its comforts of wealth, security, and well-being. They unassumingly display the consumption habits of elite class status, which avows their ability to convert and move easily between the economic, cultural, and symbolic forms of capital. As Maxine shows Gogol the house, he marvels at the hallways on every floor with shelves ascending to the ceiling, "crammed with all the novels one should read in a lifetime, biographies, massive monographs of every artist, all the architecture books Gogol has coveted" (131). At dinner, he notices the obvious fact of their being entirely accustomed to a life of having, spending, and representing capital. "The Ratliffs are vociferous at the table, opinionated about things his own parents are indifferent to: movies, exhibits at museums, good restaurants, the design of everyday things. They speak of New York, of stores and neighborhoods and buildings they either despise or love, with an intimacy and ease that make Gogol feel as if he barely knows the city" (133).

Personifying the ability to take for granted success and prosperity, the Ratliffs are "assured" that their good life will appeal to Gogol (137). He quickly falls in love with Maxine, "the house, and Gerald and Lydia's manner of living, for to know her and love her is to know and love all of these things" (137). That Gogol in his love for Maxine conflates her with the commodities and consumption habits of her elite status clearly demonstrates his attachment to the ideology of Euro-American personhood. Because he loves the Ratliffs for their capital—for "all of the things" that they unquestionably *know* will always be available to them as high-status Americans of English Protestant ancestry—Gogol's love is a racial feeling. It expresses his desire to know intimately a life of entitlement: his identification with American liberal personhood that logically equates individuality with the absence of racial difference. This is clear in Gogol's admiration for Maxine's unqualified acceptance of her life.

> He realizes that she has never wished she were anyone other than herself, raised in any other place, in any other way. . . . In addition, he is continually amazed by how much Maxine emulates her parents, how much she respects their tastes and their ways. At the dinner table she argues with them about books and paintings and people they know in common the way one might argue with a friend. There is none of the exasperation he feels with his own parents. No sense of obligation. Unlike his parents, they pressure her to do nothing, and yet she lives faithfully, happily, at their side. (138)

Maxine does not wish to be "anyone other than herself" because she knows that her parents' manner of living—"their tastes and their ways"— quintessentially represent the values of dominant white culture, the way to live "happily" in America's liberal capitalist society. She can accept her life absolutely—indeed love being who she is unconditionally—because her family's wealth and prestige exemplify the ideal of whiteness. Maxine's high status affords her the "pressure to do nothing," which implicitly can be understood as her comfort in knowing that her family belongs atop the white social world. This is something safely assumed and given for the Ratliffs because they have nothing in the way or form of negative traits to disqualify them from belonging in America as the epitome of the white racial ideal.

By unfavorably comparing his parents to the Ratliffs, however, Gogol intimates conflicting loyalties to his Indian immigrant background that elicits within him affects of divided identity. When Maxine asks him to move into her family's home, he is "quietly thrilled" to accept (139). But as he becomes more included in her family and partakes in the consumption habits of their affluent lifestyle, he feels the beginning pangs of disloyalty. "At times, as the laughter at Gerald and Lydia's table swells, and another of bottle of wine is opened, and Gogol raises his glass to be filled yet again, he is conscious of the fact that his immersion in Maxine's family is a betrayal of his own" (141). Here Gogol briefly feels that immersing himself in the Ratliffs' world entails denying his own parents and disavowing identification with their cultural values. He will understand eventually that accommodating and internalizing the ideal of American personhood comes with the great cost of disparaging his family's ethnic heritage, in effect reproaching his Bengali origins and his own self.

Lahiri has discussed her concept of "divided identity" as an affect that American-born children of Indian immigrant parents often experience (Interview). Growing up in England and America as the daughter of Bengali immigrants, Lahiri in her youth was bothered by the feeling that there was no single place to which she fully belonged. "It was always a question of allegiance, of choice. I wanted to please my parents and meet their expectations. I also wanted to meet the expectations of my American peers, and the expectations I put on myself to fit into American society. It's a classic case of divided identity. . . . As a young child, I felt that the Indian part of me was unacknowledged, and therefore somehow negated, by my American environment, and vice versa. I felt that I led two very separate lives" (Interview). As Gogol becomes increasingly attached to Maxine and her life of privilege, his feeling of wanting distance from his parents and of leading two very separate lives intensifies. While vacationing with Maxine at Gerald and Lydia's lake house in New Hampshire, for example, Gogol becomes enraptured with their summer home and the bountiful landscape in their possession: "The family seems to possess every piece of landscape, not only the house itself but every tree and blade of grass. Nothing is locked, not the main house, or the cabin that he and Maxine sleep in. . . . The Ratliffs own the moon that floats over the lake, and the sun and the clouds. It is a place that has been good to them, as much a part of them as a member of the family. The idea of returning year after year to a single place appeals to Gogol deeply" (155). In contrast to the romance of the Ratliffs' lake house, Gogol ponders, is the dislocation he has experienced on vacations with his family and their Bengali friends: "Some summers there had been road trips with one or two Bengali families in rented vans. . . . They had stayed in motels, slept whole families to a single room, swum in pools that could be seen from the road" (155). Within the confines of his parents' purview and their suburban residence Gogol considers himself constricted. But nestled with Maxine in the pastoral beauty of her parents' summer home, he concludes, "he is free" from the environs of his parents' way of life (158).

The split that Gogol creates between his parents—whose way of life he understands is of "no relevance, no interest, to Maxine" (146)—and the Ratliffs—whose manner of living is freedom for him—manifests dualistic thinking wrought by his feelings of divided identity. These affects are not painful for Gogol until he is given the news at the Ratliffs' home that his father has died suddenly from a heart attack. Gogol travels to Ohio to identify his father's body and to pack up his belongings in the apartment where he lived while working temporarily for a corporation. In the apartment, Gogol becomes upset upon realizing that his father lived "alone here these past three months" (174). After discarding Ashoke's things as his mother instructed—"'Don't bring anything back,' his mother had told him on the phone. 'It's not our way'" (175)—Gogol thinks of his father and regrets the distance he's sought from him. He decides to stay overnight in the empty apartment, even though Maxine has implored him to check into a hotel. While falling in and out of sleep, he imagines that some sign of his father might show itself, "putting a stop to the events of the day" (178). In mourning his father's death, Gogol remembers when his parents grieved the deaths of their own parents: "He knows now the guilt that his parents carried inside, at being able to do nothing when their parents had died in India, of arriving weeks, sometimes months later, when there was nothing left to do" (178). In his grief, Gogol now understands the regret his parents felt at not being able to perform the Bengali ritual of mourning with their own families in India. Their guilt becomes, then, his self-reproach as he realizes how his absorption into Maxine's life of privilege is the consequence of his attachment to the white social world, which has caused him to disparage and relinquish ties to his family's diasporic ancestry and heritage.

Yet there is much that Gogol can and must do to uphold the Bengali way of grieving. He willingly and thoroughly follows the Hindu custom of full mourning for eleven days with his mother, sister, and Bengali friends. Maxine comes to pay her respects but also to intervene and persuade Gogol to go with her back to New York. He considers her presence an intrusion and her attempt to convince him to leave his family an indication of her self-interestedness. "'I'm so sorry,' he hears her say to his mother, aware that his father's death does not affect Maxine in the least. 'You guys can't stay with your mother forever,' Maxine says when they are alone for a moment after the ceremony, upstairs in his room. . . . 'It might do you good,' she says, tilting her head to one side. She glances around the room. 'To get away from all this'" (182). Gogol curtly replies that he does not "want to get away" (182), which means he is undergoing a significant change in his feelings about belonging with his own family and affirming his South Asian heritage. That he steps out of Maxine's life for good "a few months after his father's death" (188) is a turning point in the novel in which he will reorient his identification with Bengali culture and tradition.

Even love for Gogol will change. On the recommendation of his mother, he meets Moushumi Mazoomdar, the daughter of Bengali friends of his parents. When they date, she reveals to him her "shameful truth" of criticizing her family and rejecting her heritage during her years in high school and college (213). Her past of disparaging other Bengalis mirrors Gogol's own. He falls in love with Moushumi, and they marry within a year. For both of them, marrying each other is about sharing and implicitly affirming ties to Bengali origins, attempting to remedy their feelings of a bifurcated identity. Although Gogol and Moushumi's marriage does not last, Lahiri exhibits great sensitivity in her depiction of their partnership. She makes it clear that the love they have for one another is based in large part on their shared ethnic heritage, which can be understood as a "powerful announcement of the coming-of-age of the second generation of South Asian Americans" (Srikanth, *World* 147).

As Lahiri's portrayal of divided identity in *The Namesake* reveals, the attempt to belong in America by living up to the ideal of liberal personhood not only produces conflicting loyalties in the second generation of South Asian Americans but also creates feelings of dislocation, displacement, and alienation. These racial feelings, born out of the Asian American subject's attempt to achieve a liberal ideal of the self-made white individual, articulate a material grounding of affects in capitalism that an Asian American cultural work such as *The Namesake* both represents and calls into question. The racial feeling of ambivalence that expresses Gogol's divided identity is historically immanent within America's capitalist culture of emotion. The comfort of belonging in America that is effectively modeled by the white racial ideal of individualism may be seen as an affect that structures and animates Lahiri's novel. It is, moreover, part of an array of other racial feelings generated in modern capitalist societies that can be understood to give rise to all Asian American cultural works.

# Notes

## Introduction

1. By *Asian American*, I refer to people of Asian descent in the United States who are both immigrant and US born. Scholars have argued about the problem of "Asian American" as a panethnic identity that can adequately include the complex demographics of the Asian American population. See Chiang and Chuh.

2. See Wong, *Reading*; David Eng, *Racial Castration* and *Feeling of Kinship*; V. Nguyen; Lowe, *Immigrant Acts*; Robert Lee, *Orientals*; Palumbo-Liu, *Asian/American*; and Koshy, *Sexual Naturalization*.

3. See Lye, *America's Asia*, and So.

4. I use *America* interchangeably with *the United States* in accordance with its usage in the cultural works this book examines. My intention is not to subordinate Canada and the rest of the Americas by equating America with the United States. See Ty and Goellnicht on the problem of equating America with the United States for artists and writers of Asian descent in Canada.

5. See Chiang; also Lye, *America's Asia*, and So.

6. By *Euro-Americans*, I refer to people of European descent in the United States who have historically defined themselves as "white" against non-Europeans. Although this definition of Euro-Americans as white is traceable to the 1790 Naturalization Act, which limited naturalization to immigrants who were "free white persons" from Europe, it was during the labor movements of the mid- to late nineteenth century that European immigrants defined themselves as white against Asian immigrants. As Bonacich has argued, European immigrants in the US labor movement after the Civil War identified as white in order to benefit from laws that excluded non-European immigrants and cultural practices that discriminated against nonwhites (117).

7. *Affect* and *emotion* both refer to the expression of feeling. However, as Sianne Ngai explains, in psychoanalytic discourse they are distinguished by third-person and first-person representations of feeling, "with 'affect' designating feeling described

from an observer's (analyst's) perspective, and 'emotion' designating feeling that 'belongs' to the speaker or analysand's 'I'" (25). Scholars in affect theory have argued for a stronger difference between affect and emotion, claiming that emotion is feeling that has "function and meaning" while affect is feeling that stays "unformed and unstructured" (25). Although it is important to acknowledge difference between affect and emotion, I do not find it necessary to maintain this distinction. In this book, I refer to *affect* and *emotion* interchangeably to designate feelings that are identifiable as either overt or restrained expressions of human subjectivity such as comfort, happiness, optimism, anxiety, fear, alienation, anger, ambivalence, and shame. I refer to *affect* and *emotion* interchangeably in agreement with scholars who argue that emotions and affects are rhetorical constructs and therefore are "irreducibly social" in form and context (Gross 28). See Massumi for a reading of affect that distinguishes it from emotion.

8. See Althusser for his theory of "hailing" individuals "as concrete subjects" through discursive practices of addressing, labeling, and categorizing, which are always a function of the way ideology creates subjects (173).

9. See also Bourdieu in *Distinction, Logic of Practice,* and *Practical Reason.*

10. In Bourdieu's words, social capital is "the sum of the resources, actual or virtual, that accrue to an individual or a group by virtue of possessing a durable network of more or less institutionalized relationships of mutual acquaintance and recognition" (Bourdieu and Wacquant 119).

11. According to Sklair, the transnational capitalist class "sees its mission as organizing the conditions under which its interests of the system can be furthered in the global and local contexts" (299).

12. The Declaration's other drafters were John Adams, Thomas Jefferson, Robert R. Livingston, and Roger Sherman.

13. See Yun.

14. Okihiro explains that the term *yellow peril* was likely coined by Kaiser Wilhelm II of Germany in 1895. The Kaiser had a painting made to illustrate it. "Austria, England, France, Germany, Italy, Russia, and 'the smaller civilised States' are represented in the painting as women in martial garb, all looking, with varying degrees of interest and resolve, toward an approaching 'calamity [Asiatic invasion] which menaces them'" (*Margins* 118).

15. The transformation of anxieties about US imperialism in Asia into fears of Oriental immigration describes the anti-immigrant racism of Stoddard's *Rising Tide of Color.* Stoddard's eugenicist argument about the collapse of white-world empire because of Asiatic migration to Europe and North America demonstrates a pervasive climate of yellow peril fears in the early twentieth century.

16. Williams elaborates on structure of feeling in *Long Revolution.* See also an interview with Williams in which he discusses structure of feeling as "an articulation of an area of experience" in literature and art for a plurality of classes and social groups ("On Structure" 47).

17. See Chua, who controversially deploys this discourse in her work.

18. By *neoliberalism,* I refer to the political economic model of free markets in the late twentieth century to the present that calls for reducing state spending on education, health care, and social services in order to increase corporate profits and guarantee the sanctity of private property (Harvey, *Brief History* 2–3). The neoliberal agenda

includes "shrinking public institutions, expanding private profit-making prerogatives, and undercutting democratic practices and noncommercial cultures" (Duggan xv). The privatization of state-owned enterprises and the ideological emphasis on personal responsibility are cultural imperatives in neoliberalism aimed at redistributing material resources upward, concentrating wealth in the hands of an economic elite, and creating, as well as exacerbating, inequalities along lines of class, race, sexuality, and gender.

19. See also Santa Ana, "Emotions as Landscapes," in which I read Tan's work in a transnationalist context to show that he figuratively illustrates how Australia and the United States have been slow to acknowledge their past discriminations against Chinese immigrants and indigenous people prior to and under the anti-Chinese exclusion acts.

20. For a reading of Chang-rae Lee's *Native Speaker* through a materialist framework of the emotions, see also Santa Ana, "Affect-Identity."

## 1 / Feeling in Historical Memory

1. The White Australia Policy was legislatively instituted in 1901 as a statement of the country's white supremacist ideologies. Racially discriminatory practices and hostility against the Chinese, however, had been happening in Australia since the 1850s.

2. Sara Ahmed argues that Australia has recognized and remembered its history of subjugating and dispossessing Aboriginal people through a "collective politics of shame" (*Cultural Politics* 102). Australia's expressions of "national shame" for its oppression of Aboriginal people are a form of nation building. But her argument suggests that a nation's lack of shame or shamelessness would also be important to nation building. It would seem that Australia's forgetting and not recognizing its history of anti-Chinese racism would be a form of nation building in a neoliberal capitalist regime.

3. For more on the politics of "post-race," see the scholarship of Cho, Winant, and Goldberg.

4. See Fukuyama.

5. See Honneth for his account of reification as a "forgetting of our antecedent recognition" whereby "we develop a tendency to perceive other persons as mere insensate objects," and we see our social surroundings "as a totality of merely observable objects lacking all psychic impulse or emotion" (57–58).

6. Mandel argues that one of the characteristic features of post–World War II economic growth in America was the expansion of the capitalist mode of production and private accumulation by the United States through the production of weapons and military expenditure. The growth of the permanent arms economy after World War II "performed, among other things, the very concrete function of protecting the vast foreign capital investments of the US, of safe-guarding the 'free world' for 'free capital investments' and 'free repatriation of profits,' and of guaranteeing US monopoly capital 'free' access to a series of vital raw materials" (308).

7. The act enforced the deportation of undocumented immigrants. It also prohibited various classes of nonwhite immigrants from entering Australia by making them take a dictation test. The test required an immigrant who wanted to enter Australia to write out a passage of fifty words dictated to them in any European language,

not necessarily English, at the discretion of an immigration officer. The test allowed immigration officers to evaluate applicants on the basis of European language skills (London 11).

8. See also Welch; Minnerup and Solberg.

9. The Page Act of 1875 and the Chinese Exclusion Act of 1882 passed by Congress were discriminatory laws that targeted the Chinese in an anti-Asian movement pervasive in California and the western United States.

10. Chinese workers finally won civil rights protections in 1886 in *Yick Wo v. Hopkins*, a case brought by Chinese laundrymen. In a breakthrough civil rights decision, the US Supreme Court ruled in favor of the Chinese launderers who sought protection from laws that discriminated against them. According to Okihiro, these "laws, however neutral their language, that discriminate in their application violate the equal protection clause of the Fourteenth Amendment. By subjecting to scrutiny the intent and application of the law in determining discrimination, *Yick Wo* became one of the most cited decisions in cases involving equal protection under the Constitution" (*Columbia Guide* 19).

## 2 / Happiness for Hire

1. Augusto Espiritu notes that Bulosan, "the son of semi-literate peasants," migrated to the United States with the support of his family after they lost their land in the 1920s (47). Because they were US colonial subjects, Filipinos came to America as "nationals" with some rights of immigration. Although permitted unrestricted entry as nationals until the mid-1930s, Filipinos could not become citizens. They could travel freely within the territorial domain of the United States, but they had to live under laws that discriminated against them on the basis of race.

2. *Benevolent assimilation* refers to the proclamation of American sovereignty throughout the Philippines issued by President William McKinley on December 21, 1899. McKinley justified colonial annexation of the Philippines and assimilation of Filipinos, whom Americans believed to be a backward and alien race, into Western civilization. McKinley said in his proclamation: "'We come not as invaders or conquerors . . . but as friends, to protect natives in their homes, in their employments, and in their personal and religious rights. . . . The mission of the United States is one of benevolent assimilation'" (qtd. in M. Ngai 99).

3. See Volpp, Koshy, and Kim.

4. In her reading of white fear and its effect of subjection on black people, Sara Ahmed explains that "fear works through and on the bodies of those who are transformed into its subjects, as well as its object" (*Cultural Politics* 62). Ahmed notes that "fear works by establishing others as fearsome insofar as they *threaten to take the self in*. Such fantasies construct the other as a danger not only to one's self, but to one's very life . . . [and] hence work to justify violence against others" (64, italics in original).

5. Hochschild uses the term *emotional labor* to "mean the management of feeling to create a publicly observable facial and bodily display; emotional labor is sold for a wage and therefore has *exchange value*" (7, italics in original).

6. According to Harvey, modern capitalism generates anxiety because it is a system in which money must constantly be "in motion" (*Limits* 194), turning into more and more money. New avenues must constantly be found for investment until the profit

accumulation reaches its limit and becomes "overaccumulation" (*Limits* 195). Capitalist attempts to overcome the limits of investment have generated a pervasive anxiety felt nearly everywhere in the world. In his reformulation of reification to describe the power of late capitalism on consciousness, Bewes equates the term with a "deep anxiety" that results from the loss of spiritual truths and religious experiences at the end of the twentieth century (247).

7. See Giddens for a study of how forces of capitalist production and accumulation produce mass anxiety and alienation in modern Western societies.

8. In *America*, Carlos explains that he has to stop writing because his right hand, "the one smashed by the police patrol in Klamath Falls, was rapidly becoming paralyzed" (320).

9. Fear is a person's emotional response to an approaching and identifiable danger. According to Fisher, "It is this model of a single person facing a threat to his life—a snake, a soldier about to fire, a ship about to sink—that generated the root idea of the salient elements of an experience of fear" (117).

10. Koshy reads two "primal scenes" in *America* as examples of white perceptions about Filipino "hypercorporeality": first, when an American tourist pays a young Carlos to pose nude before her camera, and second, when a young white woman recoils in horror at the sight of Bulosan and other Filipinos lying on the deck of a ship that transports them to the United States. Koshy argues that these two scenes demonstrate "Bulosan's awareness of the centrality of sexuality and embodiment to the racial subjection of Filipino/Americans" (*Sexual Naturalization* 102).

11. Chong argues that the racialized Asian subject incorporates ideologies of racial difference and inferiority. In this negotiation process, all racialized subjects understand and see themselves through discourses that predominate in the US media and public sphere. Chong contends that the Asian subject is racially constructed through racial interpellation in which ideology structures the subjectivity of the Asian subject by his negotiation with mediated discourses of race, gender, and sexuality (34).

12. Other early Asian American writings similar to Bulosan's in their critique of anti-Asian racism are Tsiang's *And China Has Hands* and Kang's *East Goes West*.

## 3 / Feeling Asian/American

1. Chan points out that the model minority thesis originated in the 1960s, "when journalists began publicizing the high educational attainment levels, high median family income, low crime rates, and absence of juvenile delinquency and mental health problems among Asian Americans" (167). A 1966 article in the *U.S. News and World Report* praised the accomplishments of Chinese Americans and Japanese Americans and contrasted these accomplishments with the widespread poverty of African Americans. The article was, in effect, telling African Americans and Latinos to follow the example of Asian Americans and discontinue "using militant protests to obtain their rights" (167).

2. The former University of California regent and affirmative action foe Ward Connerly has relied on neoliberal rhetoric to legislatively enforce a color-blind society, most notoriously in 2003 through his Proposition 54, the so-called Racial Privacy Initiative (RPI). Voters defeated the RPI, but if it had passed it would have forced the state of California not to "classify any individual by race, ethnicity, color or national

origin in the operation of public education, public contracting or public employment" ("Proposition 54"). In crafting Proposition 54, Connerly said that because race is "unfixed" and "unreliable" it should not be used in any way to identify specific groups or to collect data in California's public institutions (Connerly, "Public Forum"). He further said that the RPI's passage would signal "America's first step towards a colorblind society. Think how refreshing it would be to throw out the entire system of checking little boxes" (Connerly, "Public Forum").

3. In chapter 5, I examine yellow peril fears in advertisements for the 2012 election campaigns.

## 4 / Feeling Ancestral

1. For a reading of the emotions and mixed racial ancestry in *The Gangster of Love*, see Santa Ana, "Feeling Ancestral."

2. The concept of feeling ancestral is an expressed identification with the Asian homeland. Yet this emotional condition of an ethnic identity grounded in history is never an absolute or a teleological process. Nor should it be understood in totalizing terms that privilege an ethnic subject's identification with history and ancestry as a representative feature for an entire subgroup. I want to suggest that we articulate feeling ancestral in *discursive* terms from a perspective that underscores its specificity in material history and in multiple (and contradictory) experiences.

## 5 / Happiness, Optimism, Anxiety, and Fear

1. "By highlighting the success of high achieving Asian immigrants," the AAPIPRC claimed, the report "shifts the immigration policy debates away from the concerns and contributions of Latino immigrants, especially the large numbers who are undocumented. This 'model minority' framing can have a damaging impact on intergroup collaborations."

2. In its Overview, the report claims that "Asian Americans sometimes go overboard in stressing hard work" (Pew Research Center 4), particularly in the pressures that Asian American parents put on their children to succeed in education. That Asian American parents "put too much pressure on their children to do well in school" is evidenced by the "publication last year of 'Battle Hymn of the Tiger Mother,' a comic memoir about strict parenting by Yale Law Professor Amy Chua, the daughter of immigrants, [which] triggered a spirited debate about cultural differences in parenting norms" (4).

3. Political analysts criticized Romney's "Stand Up to China" ad for distorting facts. Factcheck.org, for example, criticized the Romney ad for stretching "the facts when it suggests the Obama administration's refusal to 'stand up to China' and label it a currency manipulator has cost the U.S. 2 million jobs. The jobs figure is unrelated to currency manipulation" (Kiely).

4. In an interview on National Public Radio, Jeff Yang condemned the "Chinese Professor" ad for exploiting anti-Asian sentiment and inciting anti-Chinese xenophobia.

5. Chan publicly apologized for offending Asian Americans by performing as the "yellow girl" in the ad ("Lisa Chan"). "I am deeply sorry for any pain that the character I portrayed brought to my communities," Chan posted on Facebook. "As a recent college grad who has spent time working to improve communities and empower those

without a voice, this role is not in any way representative of who I am. It was absolutely a mistake on my part and one that, over time, I hope can be forgiven. I feel horrible about my participation and I am determined to resolve my actions."

6. In the script, Choi's van is called "the Chinaman's panel van."

7. In *Homo Sacer*, Agamben writes, "The protagonist . . . is bare life, that is, the life of homo sacer (sacred man), *who may be killed and yet not sacrificed*, and whose essential function in modern politics we intend to assert. An obscure figure of archaic Roman law, in which human life is included in the juridical order . . . solely in the form of its exclusion (that is, of its capacity to be killed), has thus offered the key by which not only the sacred texts of sovereignty but also the very codes of political power will unveil their mysteries" (12, italics in original).

8. By *bad subject*, I refer to Althusser's concept of the subject who does not "work" according to the dominant and ruling ideology of the state and thus "provokes the intervention of the detachments of the (repressive) State apparatus" (181).

9. The phrase "make it new" is from Ezra Pound.

# WORKS CITED

Adams, James Truslow. *The Epic of America.* 1931. New York: Simon, 2001.
Adams, Jeff. *Documentary Graphic Novels and Social Realism.* New York: Peter Lang, 2008.
Adorno, Theodor. *Negative Dialectics.* New York: Seabury Press, 1973.
Agamben, Giorgio. *Homo Sacer: Sovereign Power and Bare Life.* Ed. Daniel Heller-Roazan. Stanford: Stanford University Press, 1998.
Ahmed, Sara. *The Cultural Politics of Emotion.* New York: Routledge, 2004.
———. *The Promise of Happiness.* Durham: Duke University Press, 2010.
Althusser, Louis. *Lenin and Philosophy and Other Essays.* Trans. Ben Brewster. New York: Monthly Review Press, 1971.
Ambrose, Stephen E. *Nothing Like It in the World: The Men Who Built the Transcontinental Railroad, 1863–1869.* New York: Simon and Schuster, 2000.
Ang, Ien. *On Not Speaking Chinese: Living between Asia and the West.* New York: Routledge, 2001.
Appadurai, Arjun. *Fear of Small Numbers: An Essay on the Geography of Anger.* Durham: Duke University Press, 2006.
Asian American and Pacific Islander Policy Research Consortium. "Letter to Pew Research Center." Asian American and Pacific Islander Policy Research Consortium. Press release. 22 June 2012. www.aapiprc.com/home-1/pressreleases/pewopenletter.
Association for Asian American Studies. "Association for Asian American Studies Response to the Pew Research Center Report: 'The Rise of Asian Americans.'" Association for Asian American Studies. 16 July 2012. aaastudies.org/content/index.php/77-home/117-whats-new.

Bascara, Victor. *Model-Minority Imperialism*. Minneapolis: University of Minnesota Press, 2006.

Bauman, Zygmunt. *Globalization: The Human Consequences*. New York: Columbia University Press, 1998.

Berlant, Lauren. *Cruel Optimism*. Durham: Duke University Press, 2011.

Bewes, Timothy. *Reification, or, The Anxiety of Late Capitalism*. London: Verso, 2002.

Bhabha, Homi. *The Location of Culture*. New York: Routledge, 1994.

Bonacich, Edna. "U.S. Capitalist Development: A Background to Asian Immigration." *Labor Immigration under Capitalism: Asian Workers in the United States before World War II*. Ed. Lucie Cheng and Edna Bonacich. Berkeley: University of California Press, 1984. 79–129.

Bourdieu, Pierre. *Acts of Resistance: Against the Tyranny of the Market*. Trans. Richard Nice. New York: Free Press, 1998.

———. *Distinction: A Social Critique of the Judgement of Taste*. Cambridge, MA: Harvard University Press, 1984.

———. "The Forms of Capital." *Handbook for Theory and Research for the Sociology of Education*. Ed. John G. Richardson. Westport, CT: Greenwood Press, 1985. 241–58.

———. *The Logic of Practice*. Stanford: Stanford University Press, 1990.

———. *Practical Reason: On the Theory of Action*. Stanford: Stanford University Press, 1998.

Bourdieu, Pierre, and Loïc Wacquant. *An Invitation to Reflexive Sociology*. Chicago: University of Chicago Press, 1992.

Brenner, Neil, and Roger Keil. "Global City Theory in Retrospect and Prospect." *The Global Cities Reader*. Ed. Neil Brenner and Roger Keil. New York: Routledge, 2006. 3–22.

Bulosan, Carlos. *America Is in the Heart*. 1946. Seattle: University of Washington Press, 1973.

———. *On Becoming Filipino: Selected Writings of Carlos Bulosan*. Ed. E. San Juan Jr. Philadelphia: Temple University Press, 1995.

Butler, Judith. *Bodies That Matter: On the Discursive Limits of Sex*. New York: Routledge, 1993.

Carbado, Devon W. "Racial Naturalization." *American Quarterly* 57.3 (2005): 633–58.

Catanese, David. "Hoekstra Team: 'Yellow Girl' a Web Typo." *Politico.com*. 7 Feb. 2012. www.politico.com/blogs/david-catanese/2012/02/hoekstra-team-yellow-girl-a-web-typo-113745.html.

Chan, Sucheng. *Asian Americans: An Interpretive History*. New York: Twayne, 1991.

Cheng, Anne Anlin. *The Melancholy of Race: Psychoanalysis, Assimilation, and Hidden Grief*. New York: Oxford University Press, 2001.

Chiang, Mark. *The Cultural Capital of Asian American Studies: Autonomy and Representation in the University*. New York: New York University Press, 2009.

Chiu, Monica. "Postnational Globalization and (En)gendered Meat Production in Ruth L. Ozeki's *My Year of Meats.*" *LIT* 12 (2001): 99–128.

Cho, Sumi. "Post-racialism." *Iowa Law Review* 94 (2009): 1589–1649.

Chong, Sylvia. "'Look an Asian!' The Politics of Racial Interpellation in the Wake of the Virginia Tech Shootings." *Journal of Asian American Studies* 11.1 (2008): 27–60.

Chow, Rey. *The Protestant Ethnic and the Spirit of Capitalism.* New York: Columbia University Press, 2002.

Chua, Amy. *Battle Hymn of the Tiger Mother.* New York: Penguin, 2011.

Chuh, Kandice. *Imagine Otherwise: On Asian Americanist Critique.* Durham: Duke University Press, 2003.

Connerly, Ward. "A Public Forum on Proposition 54: The Racial Privacy Initiative." Debate with Eva Paterson. Booth Auditorium, University of California, Berkeley, School of Law. 16 Sept. 2003.

Connerton, Paul. *How Modernity Forgets.* Cambridge: Cambridge University Press, 2009.

Connolly, C. N. "Miners' Rights: Explaining the 'Lambing Flat' Riots of 1860–61." *Who Are Our Enemies? Racism and the Australian Working Class.* Ed. Anne Curthoys and Andrew Markus. Sydney, NSW: Hale and Iremonger, 1978. 35–47.

*Contagion.* Dir. Stephen Soderbergh. Warner Brothers, 2011. Film.

*Crash.* Dir. Paul Haggis. Lionsgate, 2004. Film.

Derrida, Jacques. 1993. *Specters of Marx: The State of the Debt, the Work of Mourning and the New International.* Trans. Peggy Kamuf. New York: Routledge, 2006.

Didi-Huberman, Georges. *Images in Spite of All: Four Photographs from Auschwitz.* Trans. Shane B. Lillis. Chicago: University of Chicago Press, 2008.

Douglass, Frederick. *Narrative of the Life of Frederick Douglass, an American Slave.* 1845. New York: Oxford University Press, 1999.

Duggan, Lisa. *The Twilight of Equality? Neoliberalism, Cultural Politics, and the Attack on Democracy.* Boston: Beacon, 2003.

Eng, David. *The Feeling of Kinship: Queer Liberalism and the Racialization of Intimacy.* Durham: Duke University Press, 2010.

———. "Melancholia in the Late Twentieth Century." *Signs* 25.4 (2000): 1275–81.

———. *Racial Castration: Managing Masculinity in Asian America.* Durham: Duke University Press, 2001.

España-Maram, Linda. *Creating Masculinity in Los Angeles's Little Manila: Working-Class Filipinos and Popular Culture, 1920s–1950s.* New York: Columbia University Press, 2006.

Espiritu, Augusto Fauni. *Five Faces of Exile: The Nation and Filipino American Intellectuals.* Stanford: Stanford University Press, 2005.

Fenkl, Heinz Insu. *Memories of My Ghost Brother.* New York: Plume, 1997.

Fisher, Philip. *The Vehement Passions.* Princeton: Princeton University Press, 2002.

Fitzgerald, John. *Big White Lie: Chinese Australians in White Australia.* Kensington, NSW: University of New South Wales Press, 2007.

Freire, Paolo. *Pedagogy of the Oppressed.* 1970. New York: Continuum Press, 1996.

Fukuyama, Francis. *The End of History and The Last Man.* New York: Free Press, 1992.

Fulbeck, Kip. *Paper Bullets: A Fictional Autobiography.* Seattle: University of Washington Press, 2001.

———. *Part Asian, 100 Percent Hapa.* San Francisco: Chronicle Books, 2006.

Giddens, Anthony. *Modernity and Self-Identity: Self and Society in the Late Modern Age.* Stanford: Stanford University Press, 1991.

Giroux, Henry A. "The Politics of Disimagination and the Pathologies of Power." *Truthout.* 27 Feb. 2013. http://truth-out.org/news/item/14814-the-politics-of-disimagination-and-the-pathologies-of-power.

Goldberg, David Theo. *The Threat of Race: Reflections on Racial Neoliberalism.* Malden, MA: Wiley-Blackwell, 2008.

Greeson, Jennifer Rae. "The Prehistory of Possessive Individualism." *PMLA* 127.4 (2012): 918–24.

Gregg, Melissa, and Gregory J. Seigworth, eds. *The Affect Theory Reader.* Durham: Duke University Press, 2010.

Gross, Daniel M. *The Secret History of Emotion: From Aristotle's Rhetoric to Modern Brain Science.* Chicago: University of Chicago Press, 2006.

Hagedorn, Jessica. *Dogeaters.* New York: Penguin, 1990.

———. *The Gangster of Love.* New York: Houghton Mifflin, 1996.

Haggis, Paul, and Bobby Moresco. "*Crash* Screenplay." Blackfriar's Bridge and Harris, 2004. www.awesomefilm.com/script/Crash.pdf.

Hardt, Michael. "Affective Labor." *boundary 2* 26.2 (1999): 89–100.

Hardt, Michael, and Antonio Negri. *Empire.* Cambridge, MA: Harvard University Press, 2000.

———. *Multitude: War and Democracy in the Age of Empire.* New York: Penguin, 2004.

Harvey, David. *A Brief History of Neoliberalism.* New York: Oxford University Press, 2005.

———. *The Limits to Capital.* London: Verso, 1996.

Hedges, Chris, and Joe Sacco. *Days of Destruction, Days of Revolt.* New York: Nation, 2012.

Hennessy, Rosemary. *Profit and Pleasure: Sexual Identities in Late Capitalism.* New York: Routledge, 2000.

Highmore, Ben. *Everyday Life and Cultural Theory: An Introduction.* 2002. New York: Routledge, 2010.

Hirschman, Albert O. *The Passions and the Interests: Political Arguments for Capitalism before Its Triumph.* 1977. Princeton: Princeton University Press, 1997.

Hoban, Benjamin. "Anti-Chinese Riots and Rorts—SBS." *SBS Gold.* Victorian Cultural Collaboration, n.d. www.sbs.com.au/gold/story.php?storyid=56.

Hochschild, Arlie. *The Managed Heart: Commercialization of Human Feeling.* Berkeley: University of California Press, 1983.

Hong, Grace Kyungwon. *The Ruptures of American Capital: Women of Color Feminism and the Culture of Immigrant Labor.* Minneapolis: University of Minnesota Press, 2006.

Honneth, Axel. *Reification: A New Look at an Old Idea.* New York: Oxford University Press, 2008.

Illouz, Eva. *Cold Intimacies: The Making of Emotional Capitalism.* Malden, MA: Polity, 2007.

Isaac, Allan Punzalan. *American Tropics: Articulating Filipino America.* Minneapolis: University of Minnesota Press, 2006.

Jameson, Fredric. *The Geopolitical Aesthetic: Cinema and Space in the World System.* Bloomington: Indiana University Press, 1992.

———. *Late Marxism: Adorno, or, the Persistence of the Dialectic.* London: Verso, 1990.

———. *The Political Unconscious: Narrative as a Socially Symbolic Act.* Ithaca: Cornell University Press, 1981.

———. *Postmodernism, or, The Cultural Logic of Late Capitalism.* Durham: Duke University Press, 1991.

———. *Signatures of the Visible.* New York: Routledge, 1992.

JanMohamed, Abdul R. "The Economy of Manichean Allegory: The Function of Racial Differences in Colonialist Literature." *Critical Inquiry* 12 (1985): 59–87.

Jay, Martin. Introduction. *Reification: A New Look at an Old Idea*, by Axel Honneth. New York: Oxford University Press, 2008. 3–16.

Jin, Ha. *A Free Life.* New York: Vintage International, 2007.

Kang, Younghill. *East Goes West.* 1937. New York: Kaya, 1997.

Keller, Nora Okja. *Comfort Woman.* New York: Penguin, 1998.

———. *Fox Girl.* New York: Penguin, 2003.

Kennedy, Liam. *Race and Urban Space in Contemporary American Culture.* Edinburgh: Edinburgh University Press, 2000.

Kiely, Eugene. "Romney Ad on China Mangles Facts." *factcheck.org.* 25 Sept. 2012. www.factcheck.org/2012/09/romney-ad-on-china-mangles-facts/.

Kim, James. "Petting Asian America." *MELUS: Multi-Ethnic Literature of the U.S.* 36.1 (2011): 135–55.

Kingston, Maxine Hong. *China Men.* New York: Vintage International, 1989.

———. Lecture on *China Men.* University of California, Berkeley, 7 April 1992.

Kong, Belinda. *Tiananmen Fictions outside the Square: The Chinese Literary Diaspora and the Politics of Global Culture.* Philadelphia: Temple University Press, 2012.

Koshy, Susan. "Minority Cosmopolitanism." *PMLA* 126.3 (2011): 592–609.

———. *Sexual Naturalization: Asian Americans and Miscegenation.* Stanford: Stanford University Press, 2004.

Kuo, Karen. *East Is West and West Is East: Gender, Culture, and Interwar Encounters between Asia and America.* Philadelphia: Temple University Press, 2013.

Lack, John, and Jacqueline Templeton. *Bold Experiment: A Documentary History of Australian Immigration since 1945.* New York: Oxford University Press, 1995.

Lahiri, Jhumpa. Interview with Jhumpa Lahiri. *ReadersRead.com,* Nov. 2003. www.readersread.com/features/jhumpalahiri.htm.

———. *The Namesake.* New York: Houghton Mifflin, 2003.

Lee, Chang-rae. *Native Speaker.* New York: Riverhead, 1995.

Lee, Don. *The Collective.* New York; London: Norton, 2012.

———. *Country of Origin.* New York: Norton, 2004.

———. "An Interview with Don Lee." Interview by Terry Hong. *Bookslut,* July 2012. www.bookslut.com/features/2012_07_019143.php.

Lee, Rachel. *The Americas of Asian American Literature: Gendered Fictions of Nation and Transnation.* Princeton: Princeton University Press, 1999.

Lee, Robert G. Foreword. *East Main Street: Asian American Popular Culture.* Ed. Shilpa Davé et al. New York: New York University Press, 2005. xi–xv.

———. *Orientals: Asian Americans in Popular Culture.* Philadelphia: Temple University Press, 1999.

Leys, Ruth. "The Turn to Affect: A Critique." *Critical Inquiry* 37 (2011): 434–72.

Lipsitz, George. "Noises in the Blood: Culture, Conflict, and Mixed Race Identities." *Crossing Lines: Race and Mixed Race across the Geohistorical Divide.* Edited by Marc Coronado et al. Santa Barbara: Multiethnic Student Outreach, University of California, Santa Barbara, 2003. 19–44.

"Lisa Chan: Lisa Chan, Actress in Pete Hoekstra China Ad, Apologizes: 'It Was Absolutely a Mistake.'" *Huffington Post,* 15 Feb. 2012. www.huffingtonpost.com/2012/02/15/lisa-chan-pete-hoekstra-apologizes_n_1280271.html.

Locke, John. *Second Treatise of Government.* Ed. C. B. MacPherson. 1962. Indianapolis: Hackett, 1980.

———. *Two Treatises of Government.* 3rd ed. Ed. Peter Laslett. Cambridge: Cambridge University Press, 1988.

London, H. I. *Non-white Immigration and the "White Australia" Policy.* New York: New York University Press, 1970.

Lorde, Audre. *Sister Outsider: Essays and Speeches by Audre Lorde.* Freedom, CA: Crossing, 1984.

Lott, Eric. "White Like Me: Racial Cross Dressing." *Cultures of United States Imperialism.* Ed. Amy Kaplan and Donald E. Pease. Durham: Duke University Press, 1994). 474–95.

Lowe, Lisa. *Immigrant Acts: On Asian American Cultural Politics.* Durham: Duke University Press, 1996.

———. "The International within the National: American Studies and Asian American Critique." *The Futures of American Studies*. Ed. Donald E. Pease and Robyn Weigman. Durham: Duke University Press, 2002. 76–92.

———. "The Intimacies of Four Continents." *Haunted by Empire: Geographies of Intimacy in North American History*. Ed. Ann Laura Stoler. Durham: Duke University Press, 2006. 191–212.

Lukács, Georg. *The Historical Novel*. Trans. Hannah Mitchell and Stanley Mitchell. 1962. Lincoln: University of Nebraska Press, 1983.

———. *History and Class Consciousness*. Trans. Rodney Livingstone. Cambridge, MA: MIT Press, 1971.

———. *Studies in European Realism: A Sociological Survey of the Writings of Balzac, Stendhal, Zola, Tolstoy, Gorki and Others*. Trans. Edith Bone. London: Hillway, 1950.

Lye, Colleen. *America's Asia: Racial Form and American Literature, 1893–1945*. Princeton: Princeton University Press, 2005.

———. "The Literary Case of Wen Ho Lee." *Journal of Asian American Studies* 14.2 (2011): 249–82.

———. "Racial Form." *Representations* 104.1 (2008): 92–101.

MacPherson, C. B. *The Political Theory of Possessive Individualism: From Hobbes to Locke*. Oxford: Oxford University Press, 1962.

Mandel, Ernest. *Late Capitalism*. Trans. Joris De Bres. New York: Verso, 1978.

Marx, Karl. *Capital*. Vol. 1. *A Critique of Political Economy*. Trans. Ben Fowkes. New York: Penguin, 1992.

Marx, Karl, and Frederick Engels. *Manifesto of the Communist Party*. *The Marx-Engels Reader*. 2nd ed. Edited by Robert C. Tucker. 1888. New York: Norton, 1978.

———. *On Literature and Art*. Moscow: Progress, 1976.

Massumi, Brian. *Parables for the Virtual: Movement, Affect, Sensation*. Durham: Duke University Press, 2002.

McCloud, Scott. *Understanding Comics: The Invisible Art*. New York: Harper Perennial, 1993.

Melamed, Jodi. "The Spirit of Neoliberalism: From Racial Liberalism to Neoliberal Multiculturalism." *Social Text* 24.4 (2006): 1–24.

Mills, Charles W. "Racial Liberalism." *PMLA* 123.5 (2008): 1380–97.

Minnerup, Gunter, and Pia Solberg, eds. *First World, First Nations: Internal Colonialism and Indigenous Self-Determination in Northern Europe and Australia*. East Sussex: Sussex Academic Press, 2011.

Misztal, Barbara. *Theories of Social Remembering*. Maidenhead: Open University Press, 2003.

Miyoshi, Masao. "A Borderless World? From Colonialism to Transnationalism and the Decline of the Nation-State." *Global/Local: Cultural Production and the Transnational Imaginary*. Ed. Rob Wilson and Wilmal Dissanayake. Durham: Duke University Press, 1996. 78–106.

Moïsi, Dominique. *The Geopolitics of Emotion: How Cultures of Fear, Humilia-tion, and Hope Are Reshaping the World.* New York: Anchor, 2009.

Ngai, Mae M. *Impossible Subjects: Illegal Aliens and the Making of Modern America.* Princeton: Princeton University Press, 2004.

Ngai, Sianne. *Ugly Feelings.* Cambridge, MA: Harvard University Press, 2005.

Nguyen, Kien. *The Unwanted: A Memoir.* Boston: Little, Brown, 2001.

Nguyen, Viet. *Race and Resistance: Literature and Politics in Asian America.* New York: Oxford University Press, 2002.

Ninh, Erin Khuê. *Ingratitude: The Debt-Bound Daughter in Asian American Lit-erature.* New York: New York University Press, 2011.

Nora, Pierre. "Reasons for the Current Upsurge in Memory." *The Collective Memory Reader.* Ed. Jeffrey K. Olick et al. New York: Oxford University Press, 2011. 437–41.

Okihiro, Gary. *The Columbia Guide to Asian American History.* New York: Co-lumbia University Press, 2001.

——. *Margins and Mainstreams: Asians in American History and Culture.* Se-attle: University of Washington Press, 1994.

Omi, Michael, and Howard Winant. *Racial Formation in the United States.* 2nd ed. New York: Routledge, 1994.

Ong, Han. *Fixer Chao.* New York: Picador, 2002.

Ozeki, Ruth L. *All over Creation.* New York: Viking, 2003.

——. *My Year of Meats.* New York: Viking, 1998.

Palumbo-Liu, David. *Asian/American: Historical Crossings of a Racial Frontier* Stanford: Stanford University Press, 1999.

——. "Assumed Identities." *New Literary History* 31.4 (2000): 765–80.

——. *The Deliverance of Others: Reading Literature in a Global Age.* Durham: Duke University Press, 2012.

——. "Rational and Irrational Choices: Form, Affect, and Ethics." *Minor Transnationalism.* Ed. François Lionnet and Shu-mei Shih. Durham: Duke University Press, 2005. 41–72.

——. "Universalisms and Minority Culture." *Differences: A Journal of Femi-nist Cultural Studies* 7.1 (1995): 188–208.

Pelaud, Isabelle Thuy. "*Catfish and Mandala*: Triple Vision." *Amerasia Journal* 29.1 (2003): 221–35.

Pew Research Center. "The Rise of Asian Americans." *Pew Research Center*, 19 June 2012. www.pewsocialtrends.org/2012/06/19/the-rise-of-asian-americans/.

Pfister, Joel. "Getting Personal and Getting Personnel: U.S. Capitalism as a Sys-tem of Emotional Reproduction." *American Quarterly* 60.4 (2008): 1135–42.

Pham, Andrew X. *Catfish and Mandala: A Two-Wheeled Voyage through the Landscape and Memory of Vietnam.* New York: Picador, 1999.

Postone, Moishe. *Time, Labor, and Social Domination: A Reinterpretation of Marx's Critical Theory.* Cambridge: Cambridge University Press, 1993.

Pound, Ezra. *Make It New.* New Haven: Yale University Press, 1935.

"Proposition 54." California Statewide Special Election. 31 Aug. 2003. http://vote2003.sos.ca.gov/propositions/2-3-4-text.html.

Rekdal, Paisley. *The Night My Mother Met Bruce Lee: Observations on Not Fitting In.* New York: Pantheon, 2000.

Roberts, Adam. *Fredric Jameson.* London: Routledge, 2000.

Rodriguez, Dylan. *Suspended Apocalypse: White Supremacy, Genocide, and the Filipino Condition.* Minneapolis: University of Minnesota Press, 2010.

Roediger, David. "Gook: The Short History of an Americanism." *Monthly Review* 43.10 (March 1992): 50–54.

Roley, Brian Ascalon. *American Son.* New York: Norton, 2001.

Rothberg, Michael. *Multidirectional Memory: Remembering the Holocaust in the Age of Decolonization.* Stanford: Stanford University Press, 2009.

Said, Edward. *Orientalism.* New York: Vintage, 1979.

San Juan, Jr., E. Introduction. *On Becoming Filipino: Selected Writings of Carlos Bulosan.* Ed. E. San Juan Jr. Seattle: University of Washington Press, 1995.

Santa Ana, Jeffrey. "Affect-Identity: The Emotions of Assimilation, Multiraciality, and Asian American Subjectivity." *Asian North American Identities: Beyond the Hyphen.* Ed. Eleanor Ty and Donald Goellnicht. Bloomington: Indiana University Press, 2004. 15–42.

———. "Emotions as Landscapes: Specters of Asian American Racialization in Shaun Tan's Graphic Narratives." *Drawing New Color Lines: Transnational Asian American Graphic Narratives.* Ed. Monica Chiu. Hong Kong: Hong Kong University Press, 2014. 145–64.

———. "Feeling Ancestral: The Emotions of Mixed Race and Memory in Asian American Cultural Productions." *positions: east asia cultures critique* 16.2 (2008): 457–83.

Sassen, Saskia. "Cities and Communities in the Global Economy." *The Global Cities Reader.* Ed. Neil Brenner and Roger Keil. New York: Routledge, 2006. 82–88.

Sklair, Leslie. "Social Movements and Global Capitalism." *The Cultures of Globalization.* Ed. Fredric Jameson and Masao Miyoshi. Durham: Duke University Press, 1998. 291–311.

So, Christine. *Economic Citizens: A Narrative of Asian American Visibility.* Philadelphia: Temple University Press, 2008.

Song, Min. *The Children of 1965: On Writing, and Not Writing, as an Asian American.* Durham: Duke University Press, 2013.

Srikanth, Rajini. *Constructing the Enemy: Empathy/Antipathy in U.S. Literature and Law.* Philadelphia: Temple University Press, 2012.

———. *The World Next Door: South Asian American Literature and the Idea of America.* Philadelphia: Temple University Press, 2004.

Stoddard, Lothrop. *The Rising Tide of Color against White-World Supremacy.* New York: Scribner's Sons, 1920.

Stone, Michael. "'Yellow Girl? Asian Bashing Hoekstra Super Bowl Ad Con-

demned as Racist." *Examiner.com*, 7 Feb. 2012. www.examiner.com/article/
yellow-girl-asian-bashing-hoekstra-super-bowl-ad-condemned-as-racist.

Takaki, Ronald. *Strangers from a Different Shore: A History of Asian Americans.*
New York: Little, Brown, 1989.

Tamony, Peter. "Chinaman's Chance." *Western Folklore* 24.3 (1965): 202–5.

Tan, Shaun. *The Arrival.* New York: Arthur A. Levine, 2006.

———. "Comments on *Tales from Outer Suburbia.*" *shauntan.net*, n.d. www.
shauntan.net/books/suburbia%20more%20comment.html.

———. "Comments on *The Arrival.*" *shauntan.net*, n.d. www.shauntan.net/
books/the-arrival.html.

———. "Comments on *The Lost Thing.*" *shauntan.net*, n.d. www.shauntan.net/
books/lost-thing.html.

———. "A Conversation with Illustrator Shaun Tan." Interview with Chuan-Yao
Ling. *World Literature Today* 82.5 (2008): 44–47.

———. *Lost and Found: Three by Shaun Tan.* New York: Arthur A. Levine, 2008.

———. *Tales from Outer Suburbia.* New York: Arthur A. Levine, 2008.

Tsiang, H. T. *And China Has Hands.* 1937. New York: Ironweed, 2003.

Ty, Eleanor. "Abjection, Masculinity, and Violence in Brian Roley's *American
Son* and Han Ong's *Fixer Chao.*" *MELUS: The Journal of the Society for the
Study of Multi-Ethnic Literature of the United States* 29.1 (2004): 119–36.

Ty, Eleanor, and Donald Goellnicht. Introduction. *Asian North American Identities: Beyond the Hyphen.* Ed. Eleanor Ty and Donald Goellnicht. Bloomington: Indiana University Press, 2004. 1–14.

Tyson, Lois. *Psychological Politics of the American Dream: The Commodification
of Subjectivity in Twentieth-Century American Literature.* Columbus: Ohio
State University Press, 1994.

Virno, Paolo. "The Ambivalence of Disenchantment." *Radical Thought in Italy: A Potential Politics.* Ed. Paolo Virno and Michael Hardt. Trans. Mauriza
Boscagli et al. Minneapolis: University of Minnesota Press, 1996. 17–18.

Volpp, Leti. "American Mestizo: Filipinos and Antimiscegenation Laws in California." *U.C. Davis Law Review* 33.4 (2000): 795–835.

Wang, Dorothy J. *Thinking Its Presence: Form, Race, and Subjectivity in Contemporary Asian American Poetry.* Stanford: Stanford University Press, 2014.

Weber, Max. *The Protestant Ethic and the Spirit of Capitalism.* New York:
Charles Scribner's Sons, 1958.

Welch, A. R. "Aboriginal Education as Internal Colonialism: The Schooling of
an Indigenous Minority in Colonial Australia." *Comparative Education* 24.2
(1988): 203–15.

Willard, Myra. *History of the White Australia Policy to 1920.* Melbourne: Melbourne University Press, 1978.

Williams, Raymond. "Advertising: The Magic System." *The Cultural Studies
Reader.* Ed. Simon During. New York: Routledge, 1993. 320–26.

———. *The Long Revolution.* New York: Columbia University Press, 1961.

———. *Marxism and Literature*. New York: Oxford University Press, 1977.

———. "On Structure of Feeling." *Emotions: A Cultural Studies Reader*. Ed. Jennifer Harding and E. Deidre Pribram. New York: Routledge, 2009. 35–49.

Winant, Howard. *The New Politics of Race: Globalism, Difference, Justice*. Minneapolis: University of Minnesota Press, 2004.

Wise, Amanda. "Sensuous Multiculturalism: Emotional Landscapes of Interethnic Living in Australian Suburbia." *Journal of Ethnic and Migration Studies* 36.6 (2010): 917–37.

Wong, Sau-ling Cynthia. "Denationalization Reconsidered: Asian American Cultural Criticism at a Theoretical Crossroads." *Amerasia Journal* 21, nos. 1 and 2 (1995): 1–27.

———. *Reading Asian American Literature: From Necessity to Extravagance*. Princeton: Princeton University Press, 1993.

Yamashita, Karen Tei. *Tropic of Orange*. Minneapolis: Coffee House Press, 1997.

Yang, Caroline H. "Indispensable Labor: The Worker as a Category of Critique in *China Men*." *Modern Fiction Studies* 56.1 (2010): 63–89.

Yang, Jeff. "Critics Say Political Ads Hint of Xenophobia." *npr.org*, 27 Oct. 2010. www.npr.org/templates/story/story.php?storyId=130860571.

Yu, Phil. "An Extra in the Chinese Professor Ad Speaks Out." *Angry Asian Man*. Phil Yu, 26 Oct. 2010. http://blog.angryasianman.com/2010/10/extra-in-chinese-professor-ad-speaks.html.

Yun, Lisa. *The Coolie Speaks: Chinese Indentured Laborers and African Slaves in Cuba*. Philadelphia: Temple University Press, 2008.

Zizek, Slavoj. "Multiculturalism, or, The Cultural Logic of Multinational Capitalism." *New Left Review* 225 (1997): 28–51.

# Index

Page numbers in italics refer to illustrations.

# About the Author

Jeffrey Santa Ana is Associate Professor of English at Stony Brook University.

Also in the series **Asian American History and Culture:**

Lisa Yun, *The Coolie Speaks: Chinese Indentured Laborers and African Slaves in Cuba*

Estella Habal, *San Francisco's International Hotel: Mobilizing the Filipino American Community in the Anti-Eviction Movement*

Thomas P. Kim, *The Racial Logic of Politics: Asian Americans and Party Competition*

Sucheng Chan, ed., *The Vietnamese American 1.5 Generation: Stories of War, Revolution, Flight, and New Beginnings*

Antonio T. Tiongson Jr., Edgardo V. Gutierrez, and Ricardo V. Gutierrez, eds., *Positively No Filipinos Allowed: Building Communities and Discourse*

Sucheng Chan, ed., *Chinese American Transnationalism: The Flow of People, Resources, and Ideas between China and America during the Exclusion Era*

Rajini Srikanth, *The World Next Door: South Asian American Literature and the Idea of America*

Keith Lawrence and Floyd Cheung, eds., *Recovered Legacies: Authority and Identity in Early Asian American Literature*

Linda Trinh Võ, *Mobilizing an Asian American Community*

Franklin S. Odo, *No Sword to Bury: Japanese Americans in Hawai'i during World War II*

Josephine Lee, Imogene L. Lim, and Yuko Matsukawa, eds., *Re/collecting Early Asian America: Essays in Cultural History*

Linda Trinh Võ and Rick Bonus, eds., *Contemporary Asian American Communities: Intersections and Divergences*

Sunaina Marr Maira, *Desis in the House: Indian American Youth Culture in New York City*

Teresa Williams-León and Cynthia Nakashima, eds., *The Sum of Our Parts: Mixed-Heritage Asian Americans*

Tung Pok Chin with Winifred C. Chin, *Paper Son: One Man's Story*

Amy Ling, ed., *Yellow Light: The Flowering of Asian American Arts*

Rick Bonus, *Locating Filipino Americans: Ethnicity and the Cultural Politics of Space*

Darrell Y. Hamamoto and Sandra Liu, eds., *Countervisions: Asian American Film Criticism*

Martin F. Manalansan IV, ed., *Cultural Compass: Ethnographic Explorations of Asian America*

Ko-lin Chin, *Smuggled Chinese: Clandestine Immigration to the United States*

Evelyn Hu-DeHart, ed., *Across the Pacific: Asian Americans and Globalization*

Soo-Young Chin, *Doing What Had to Be Done: The Life Narrative of Dora Yum Kim*

Robert G. Lee, *Orientals: Asian Americans in Popular Culture*

David L. Eng and Alice Y. Hom, eds., *Q & A: Queer in Asian America*

K. Scott Wong and Sucheng Chan, eds., *Claiming America: Constructing Chinese American Identities during the Exclusion Era*

Lavina Dhingra Shankar and Rajini Srikanth, eds., *A Part, Yet Apart: South Asians in Asian America*

Jere Takahashi, *Nisei/Sansei: Shifting Japanese American Identities and Politics*

Velina Hasu Houston, ed., *But Still, Like Air, I'll Rise: New Asian American Plays*

Josephine Lee, *Performing Asian America: Race and Ethnicity on the Contemporary Stage*

Deepika Bahri and Mary Vasudeva, eds., *Between the Lines: South Asians and Postcoloniality*

E. San Juan Jr., *The Philippine Temptation: Dialectics of Philippines–U.S. Literary Relations*

Carlos Bulosan and E. San Juan Jr., eds., *The Cry and the Dedication*

Carlos Bulosan and E. San Juan Jr., eds., *On Becoming Filipino: Selected Writings of Carlos Bulosan*

Vicente L. Rafael, ed., *Discrepant Histories: Translocal Essays on Filipino Cultures*

Yen Le Espiritu, *Filipino American Lives*

Paul Ong, Edna Bonacich, and Lucie Cheng, eds., *The New Asian Immigration in Los Angeles and Global Restructuring*

Chris Friday, *Organizing Asian American Labor: The Pacific Coast Canned-Salmon Industry, 1870–1942*

Sucheng Chan, ed., *Hmong Means Free: Life in Laos and America*

Timothy P. Fong, *The First Suburban Chinatown: The Remaking of Monterey Park, California*

William Wei, *The Asian American Movement*

Yen Le Espiritu, *Asian American Panethnicity*

Velina Hasu Houston, ed., *The Politics of Life*

Renqiu Yu, *To Save China, To Save Ourselves: The Chinese Hand Laundry Alliance of New York*

Shirley Geok-lin Lim and Amy Ling, eds., *Reading the Literatures of Asian America*

Karen Isaksen Leonard, *Making Ethnic Choices: California's Punjabi Mexican Americans*

Gary Y. Okihiro, *Cane Fires: The Anti-Japanese Movement in Hawaii, 1865–1945*

Sucheng Chan, *Entry Denied: Exclusion and the Chinese Community in America, 1882–1943*